Thinking in Jewish

RELIGION AND POSTMODERNISM
A SERIES EDITED BY MARK C. TAYLOR

JONATHAN BOYARIN

✌ *Thinking in Jewish* ✌

THE UNIVERSITY OF CHICAGO PRESS

Chicago & London

Jonathan Boyarin has written several books, including *Palestine and Jewish History* and *Storm from Paradise: The Politics of Jewish Memory*, and is the editor of *Remapping Memory: The Politics of TimeSpace* and *The Ethnography of Reading*.

The University of Chicago Press, Chicago 60637
The University of Chicago Press, Ltd., London
© 1996 by The University of Chicago
All rights reserved. Published 1996
Printed in the United States of America
05 04 03 02 01 00 99 98 97 96   1 2 3 4 5
ISBN: 0-226-06926-5 (cloth)
0-226-06927-3 (paper)

Library of Congress Cataloging-in-Publication Data

Boyarin, Jonathan.
  Thinking in Jewish / Jonathan Boyarin.
    p.   cm.
  Includes bibliographical references and index.
  1. Jews—Identity.   2. Jews—Intellectual life.
3. Judaism—20th century.   I. Title.
DS143.B8   1996
305.892′4—dc20   95-43357
                                                         CIP

For Daniel, who got me thinking

∿CONTENTS∿

Acknowledgments   *ix*

Introduction   *1*

1   Waiting for a Jew: Marginal Redemption
at the Eighth Street Shul   *8*

2   Self-Exposure as Theory:
The Double Mark of the Male Jew   *34*

3   Death and the Minyan   *63*

4   Before the Law There Stands a Woman: In Re *Taylor v. Butler*
(with Court-Appointed Yiddish Translator)   *87*

5   From Derrida to Fichte? The New Europe, the Same Europe,
and the Place of the Jews   *108*

6   At Last, All the *Goyim:*
Notes on a Greek Word Applied to Jews   *140*

7   Jews in Space; or, The Jewish People in
the Twenty-first Century   *160*

Appendix: *Yidishe visnshaft un di postmodern*   *183*
Yiddish Science and the Postmodern   *191*
translated by Naomi Seidman

References   *201*

Index   *213*

∽ ACKNOWLEDGMENTS ∽

Portions of this book have appeared in earlier form. Chapter 1, "Waiting for a Jew," was published in *Between Two Worlds*, ed. J. Kugelmass (Ithaca: Cornell University Press, 1986, pp. 57–76). © Jonathan Boyarin. Used by permission of the publisher, Cornell University Press. Chapter 2, "Self-Exposure as Theory," was written with Daniel Boyarin and published in *Rhetorics of Self-Making*, ed. Debbora Battaglia (University of California Press, 1994, pp. 16–42). Copyright © 1994 The Regents of The University of California. Chapter 3, "Death and the Minyan," is reprinted by permission of the American Anthropological Association from *Cultural Anthropology* 9:1 (February 1994). Not for further reproduction. Chapter 4, "Before the Law There Stands a Woman," originally appeared in 15 *Cardozo Law Review* 1303 (1995). And chapter 6, "At Last, All the *Goyim*," appeared in *Postmodern Apocalypse*, ed. Richard Dellamora (Philadelphia: University of Pennsylvania Press, 1995, pp. 410–58). Grateful acknowledgment is made to the above grantors for permission to reprint.

Introduction

Besides the spirit of fornication which is in their midst—that is, in their hearts—of whom ought it more appropriately be said than of the devil Bentamalyon, that he restored to them circumcision, the Sabbath, and the other rituals which God removed through the agency of the Romans? The devil undoubtedly . . . misled them and deprived them of a sense of understanding the truth, so that they are less intelligent than asses as regards divine scriptures.

> —Raymond Martini, *Pugio Fidei*
> (quoted in Cohen 1982:147)

[T]he destruction of the Temple by the Romans . . . was a stroke of great fortune, for it is questionable whether Christianity would have succeeded in completely detaching itself from the Temple if the Temple had persisted. (Renan 1943)

What do I mean, *Thinking in Jewish?* Several things, or any one of them at a time.

Above all (since I am a Jewish ethnographer of the grandchildren's generation, living on the Lower East Side), the phrase alludes to the use of the term "Jewish" to designate the language otherwise known as Yiddish. This usage is peculiar to a certain intermediary generation, child immigrants and children of immigrants from Jewish Eastern Europe. It is a partial translation, a failed translation, evidence of a barely possible attempt to display attachment and competence in an ancestral idiom on one hand, while demonstrating an educated, responsible awareness of the new idiom on the other: to claim an identity without being claimed by it. What's ironic is how strongly this neutralized gloss on Yiddish marks one who uses it today, now that its use is nearly extinct. It's not hip to call Yiddish Jewish anymore. As a transitional marker, the phenomenon of speaking *in* English *of* Yiddish   *1 as* Jewish fascinates me, and I want to record it before it disappears altogether.

More likely, however, the phrase first came to me by analogy to the title of Jane Gallop's work in feminist theory, *Thinking Through the Body* (Gallop 1988). This suggests a reading of my title as "thinking in a Jewish body"—not, of course, *the* Jewish body, which can only be a construct of the Jew as other (Gilman 1992). The pronoun "through" in Gallop's title does double duty, making the title indicate on one hand a discourse of thought that is grounded in embodiment and (as the cover photograph on her book makes unmistakably clear) in reproduction, but also a critical thinking through the sign "body" against the illusion that when we talk about the body we enjoy direct access to material reality. This particular link to feminist theory allows me to state (as others have stated in recent years) that Jewish self-making is done through processes of embodiment, not only in communal ritual and textuality; and that since thinking is never separate from embodying, assuming this link problematizes in turn the process by which the body remains or becomes conceived as a separate object of discourse (see Marin 1993; Taylor 1989, chapter on Descartes). Indeed, while the chapter titled "Self-Exposure as Theory" [1] may be conventionally read as a further investigation of circumcision understood as the key moment in making a male human body Jewish, the connection to feminist theory should also help emphasize its point that Jewish males are never autonomous or self-made.

Thinking in Jewish could also mean thinking in a Jewish milieu, a Jewish social context, allowing me to explore further the constraints or demands on academic theory that are occasioned by my participation in a Jewish world, and the resources that such participation affords theory. This work of situating thought in a Jewish place is most evident here in "Death and the Minyan," where I attempt the difficult task of shaping a highly localized and anecdotal *shul* ethnography into a critique of Jean-Luc Nancy's recent attempt to rethink the impossible desire for universal community. Yet this is not a Hegelian critique that intends to transcend the limitations of its subject, and hence supplant it. Rather

---

1. An essay in which the rhetoric of "doubling" indicates my collaboration with Daniel Boyarin in its writing.

it is one that aims to set up a necessary and contentious dialogue about the situation of theory.

Not only is thinking situated, but contrary to our common assumptions, theory itself is a topos, a kind of place. To say that this is a volume of critical theory—or at least a set of engagements with recent theoretical writing—hardly means that it is about everything, or that it is written in some master language which allows one to discuss anything one wishes to. Much of the discussion might seem so heady and rarefied (or so normative, so filled with the impulse to think of things as they should be rather than as they are) as to open me to a charge of indulging in critical privilege. When lecturing and when writing, I always welcome the interjection that indicates communication, so I don't want to defend myself too tightly in advance. Yet I *can* plead that this text is intended to reflect much of the interruptions, transitory passions, and frustrations that pushed me to complete it; without them, as I state in "Before the Law There Stands a Woman" (chapter 4), the claim that thinking is always situated and interested loses its own critical force.

Yiddish has the intransitive verb *zikh arayntrakhtn*, literally to think oneself into something, meaning to consider a matter in depth. Programmatically, and most ambitiously as far as any kind of "autonomous" Jewish group identity might be concerned, thinking in Jewish could also be a transitive, indicating an ushering in of a different Jewish identity through thought. It would be then a critical recognition, a welcoming in (by analogy here to the welcoming of the Sabbath Bride late every Friday afternoon) and a fiction, an invention of another "Jewish" idiom, which would be a different one since the immigrant Yiddish language is so neutralized that it can safely be called by its own ethnonym.[2] Not only the identity but the language in which to think it are in this sense before us, on the other side of a gate that we must struggle to keep open. I have no desire to be the *one* that ushers in Jewish; yet some of the odd moves in this text, such as the suggestion of curious affinities between melancholy Benjaminian critics and enthusiastic Lubavitch Hasidim, might be taken as possible starting points by those interested in sharing the project.

2. The persistence of Yiddish in Hasidic and Yeshiva communities is a powerful exception to this neutralization.

In all of these potential meanings of "thinking in Jewish," there is the same insistence that thinking *is not free.* It is grounded and constrained, though the grounds and constraints will never "be" what we state them to be. In any case, the ground referred to here is not a nation-state. And if one's idiom is *not* the language of any nation-state, this implies an important qualification of Iain Chambers's suggestion that we inculcate in ourselves a "weakened" sense of our own idiom (Chambers 1994:31). What if "one's own," *contra* the liberal individualist tradition of Lockean obsession with land ownership as the guarantee of freedom, need not be exclusive, need not even be fixed? What of the problem of "identity" then? Two of the chapters here directly employ the particular grounded yet nonexclusive place that Yiddish affords. "Before the Law" assumes the standpoint of one who would translate into Yiddish, in order to interrogate two highly suggestive, mutually incompatible accounts of identity written in English. The appendix, *Yidishe visnshaft un di postmodern,* is an experiment in writing thought in Yiddish, not just in Jewish.[3]

For whatever reasons, the keyword "identity" seems to be highly suspect in some recent advanced theory (e.g. Michaels 1992). Evidently, the various ways of linking "identity" with "politics" appear to some critics to have resulted in a debilitating combination of narcissism and fragmentation, rather than an advance beyond an older, overly abstract and dehistoricized notion of politics. I think it will be helpful to maintain a certain distinction here between "identity politics" (as explicitly and consciously organized writing, discourse, or action) and the "politics of identity" (as a constitutive problematic of everyday life as well as high criticism). The distinction might be observed, to some extent, in the gap between the narrative *Bildungsethnographie* of "Waiting for a Jew" (chapter 1) and the interrogative, anecdotal, and opportunistic style of the other essays in the book. That gap itself was partially filled by my earlier book *Storm from Paradise.* There the keyword was "memory," and there (just a few years ago) I held out, much more as it seems to me than I do here, for memory as key

3. I am grateful to Alan Thomas, my editor, for his eager willingness to include the Yiddish, and to Naomi Seidman for intelligently carrying out a translation that would only have been a betrayal had I tried to do it myself.

to some possible vision of ultimate liberation. By now, my vision tends to flicker between the political-economic screen, which shows us living or dying within a reshaped, highly mobile, and contingent capitalism, and the ideological-narrative screen, where scenes of eco-extinction increasingly crowd out scenes of a rational and more just organization of our species' life.

"Waiting for a Jew" reaches back still earlier, to a time before children, when my own individual future seemed much more important than it does now, to the beginning of the time where I began to see my writing as both the record of a life and directing signs for a life, to the years when I was, as they say, looking for my voice. The closing anecdote of that chapter overtly introduces the theme of the *minyan*, which preoccupies me elsewhere in the book as well. But as I read it retrospectively, it also seems to announce the arrival of myself as a Jew, as a Jew who *can*, yes, and will speak. I will never write a piece like "Waiting for a Jew" again; its categories seem too preformed, its denouement too nearly determined in advance. I contend nevertheless that without that moment of arrival, an enriching and complicating awareness of the possibility that identity can be *released* or at least rethought is much more difficult to sustain. Partly for that reason, I am not nearly as ready to abandon identity politics as some people seem to be. Social action that has the articulation of group identities and differences as both aim and strategy (identity politics) need not assume an identity that is either triumphant or fixed, which appears to be the main complaint against identity politics. Yet my concern, now that I can speak (and hence question) in Jewish, is more with the broader politics of identity. Generally, this book raises issues both of Jewish identity and of the very notion of "identity," in theory and in ethnography, and at its most ambitious moments, *as* a critical ethnography of European high theory.

Tant pis that some readers, including friends, will complain that I seem fixated on a notion from the eighties when the millennium demands "something new" in criticism (cf. the conclusion to Lambropoulos 1992). My contention, to some extent as a peculiar interpretation of an argument by Derrida (1992), is that the very problem of identity is precisely constitutive of "Europe." As yet, whether we would or no, we certainly haven't rid ourselves of "Europe," and as Etienne Balibar (1990, quoted in this volume) has observed, Jewish difference is a central term in the persistent discussion of what Europe *is,* of European identity. Hence the relevance of the epigraphs above. Both Raymond Martini in his medieval anti-Jewish tract, *Dagger of the Faith,* and the nineteenth-century historian Ernest Renan believed that the shedding of particularities relating to practice and place was all to the good. Martini, in a move instructively "reminiscent" of modern European colonial rhetoric, assumes that only demonic coercion could lead a people who had once been released from their backward ritual limitations back into error and away from the freedom offered by empire. At the same time he asserts that when empire works to remove difference it is indeed doing God's work. Renan focuses rather on the insurance policy granted to the universalizing moment in Christianity by the imperial destruction of the Jewish ritual center. In the ancient Roman empire, in the Middle Ages of a Europe enunciating its own identity, in a West European nineteenth century confident of progress, in a United States academy battling to preserve liberal faith against both criticism and reaction at the end of the second Christian millennium, Jewishness remains an inspiring or irritating exemplum.

The question of identity, the politics of identity, will not go away, even if we declare it boring or sterile. On the contrary, it may very likely become an increasingly murderous politics whatever theoretical interventions we do or do not make; but I continue to insist that it need not be so. Of course, insisting that thinking is not only "intimately related to" practice but *is* human practice does nothing whatsoever to guarantee an effective relation between critical arguments and the possibilities of the world. As this book goes to press, representative, elected politics in the United States and elsewhere seems to move further and further away from any need to seek legitimation from the secular academy. Yet we hardly hear anyone asking plainly what implications this has for the persistent grounding of criticism in enlightenment. How can we talk and think with any effect now, for the next five years, for the next decade? Or, as the deliberately catachristic subtitle of the last chapter, "The Jewish People in the Twenty-First Century" (chapter 7), is meant to imply: How could we possibly imagine Walter Benjamin's angel of history turning around? How can an identity based in an image of the past and in the imperative of genealogical continuity (hence, *pace* Benjamin, necessarily in the images of *both* liberated grandchildren and enslaved ancestors) begin to imagine a future without hope—that is, to do that imagining without reliance on the illusory resource of "hope?" The question cannot be adequately "thought." But how can we not think it?

Waiting for a Jew
Marginal Redemption
at the Eighth Street Shul

My story begins in a community, with an illusion of wholeness. I am between the age when consciousness begins and the age of ten, when my family leaves the community and my illusion is shattered. Our family lives on the edge of the Pine Barrens in Farmingdale, New Jersey, along with hundreds of other families of Jewish chicken farmers who have come from Europe and New York City in several waves, beginning just after World War I.

Among the farmers are present and former Communists, Bundists, Labor Zionists, German refugees who arrived in the 1930s, and Polish survivors of concentration camps. These, however, are not the distinctions I make among them as a child. Johannes Fabian has shown us that when we write ethnography we inevitably trap those about whom we write into a hypostatic, categorical, grammatical "present" (Fabian 1983). An autobiographer has the same power over the memory of himself and those he knew in prior times as the fieldworker who later obliterates the narrative aspect of his encounter with his subjects—the power to deny their autonomy in hindsight.[1] Those of the farming com-

---

1. Compare Pierre Bourdieu's critique of the structuralist theory of "reciprocal" gift exchange: "Even if reversibility [i.e., the assumption that gifts entail counter-gifts of equivalent value] is the objective truth of the discrete acts which ordinary experience knows in discrete form and calls gift exchanges, it is not the whole truth of a practice which could not exist if it were consciously perceived in accordance with the model. The temporal structure of gift exchange, which objectivism ignores, is what makes possible the coexistence of two opposing truths, which defines the full truth of the gift" (1977:6).

Similarly, in a narrative such as this one, because I, as author, already know the ending, it may seem as though each successive element fits into those that precede and follow it in such a way that their necessity is perfectly known. Actually my aim

munity whom I will later remember, I know therefore by their own names and places: my grandparents closer to Farmingdale proper; the Silbers off on Yellowbrook Road, with a tree nursery now instead of chickens; the Lindauers, stubbornly maintaining an egg-packing and -distribution business, while others find different ways to earn a living.

My child's world is not exclusively Jewish, nor am I brought up to regard it as such. Across our road and down a few hundred yards is a tiny house built by Jewish farmers when they first came to settle here. It is now, incredibly, occupied by a black family of ten. Next to them lives an equally poor and large white family. Shortly before we leave Farmingdale, the old Jew in the farm next to ours passes away, and the property passes to a Japanese businessman. The young men he hires live in the farmhouse, growing oriental vegetables on the open field and bonsai in a converted chicken coop, and they introduce me to the game of Go. The nearest Jewish household is that of my great-uncle Yisroel and his wife Helen, the third house to the right of ours.

Yet we are near the heart of Jewish life in Farmingdale. Half a mile—but no, it must be less—down Peskin's Lane (the name my grandfather Israel Boyarin gave to what was a dirt road in the 1930s) is the Farmingdale Jewish Community Center, on the next plot of land after Uncle Yisroel's house. Just past the community center is the farm that once belonged to my father's uncle Peskin, the first Jew in Farmingdale. Fifteen years after Peskin's death, the bodies of two gangsters were found buried on the farm. The local papers noted: "Mr. Peskin was not available for comment."

Our own farm consists of eleven acres. Facing the road is the house my grandfather built, with a large front lawn and an apple tree in back. Farther back, four large chicken coops mark the slope of a hill ending in our field, behind which woods conceal the tiny Manasquan River. The field, well fertilized by chickens allowed to scratch freely on it during the day, is leased each summer by a dirt farmer who grows corn. My father has joined the insurance agency begun by my mother, and they have gotten rid

---

is to show how the background that nurtured me shaped in part my unpredictable responses to situations that in themselves were historically rather than culturally determined. See my conclusion, where I refer to one of the communities I now participate in as "haphazard but intentional."

of the birds. The coops stand empty by my fourth birthday. One day, though, while a friend and I chase each other through the coops in play, we are startled by a pair of chickens. Their presence in the stillness and the faint smell of ancient manure is inexplicable and unforgettable. Thus, on the abandoned farm, my first memories are tinged with a sense of traces, of mystery, of loss. Do all who eventually become anthropologists have this experience in some form, at some time in their early lives?

My mother's turn to business is wise: chicken farming as the basis for the community's livelihood is quickly becoming untenable. Nor is it surprising, as she had given up a career as a chemist to come live with my father on the farm—thus taking part in the process of Jewish dispersal from the immigrants' urban centers, which in the last quarter of the century would be mirrored by a shrinking of Jewish communities in small towns and a reconsolidation of the Orthodox centers. My mother's father, an Orthodox Jew from a leading Lithuanian rabbinical family, has struggled to learn English well and has gone into the insurance business himself. After his death, my mother tells me that he had originally resisted her desire to marry the son of a Jewish socialist, but he consented when he met my father's father's father, a Lubavitcher Hasid named Mordechai.

My grandfather's concern for his daughter's future as an observant Jew was well founded. The Sabbath is marked in our family only on Friday nights: by my mother's candle-lighting, and her chicken soup in winter; by the challah; by the presence of my grandfather. We do not keep kosher, nor do we go to shul on *shabbes*.

The Jewish Community Center—with its various functions as social and meeting hall, synagogue, and school—is nevertheless a focus of our family's life. Most of the ten or so other children in these classes I see at other times during the week as well, either in public school or playing at one another's homes. I am there three times each week, first for Sunday school, and then for Hebrew school on Tuesday and Thursday afternoons. This odd distinction is no doubt a practical one, since some parents do not choose to send their children three times a week. But since Sunday school was first a Christian institution, it also reflects an accommodation to Christian church patterns, as evidenced by the fact that Sundays are devoted to teaching stories of the Bible. One Sunday school teacher we have in our kindergarten year captivates me with his skill in making these stories come to life, as when he imitates the distress of an Egyptian waking up to find his bed covered with frogs.

Another teacher, a young woman with a severe manner and a heavy black wig, the wife of a member of the Orthodox yeshiva in Lakewood, later causes general misery because of her inability to understand children, although I will eventually appreciate the prayers she teaches us to read. One time I come in to Hebrew school immediately after yet another in a series of martyred family dogs has been run over in front of our house. Her attempt to comfort me is like some malicious parody of Talmudic reasoning: "You shouldn't be so upset about an animal. If a chicken and a person both fell down a well, which one would you save first?"

In addition to this somewhat haphazard religious training, there is the local chapter of Habonim, the Labor Zionist Youth Organization, to which my older brother and sister belong. I tag along and am tolerated by their peers. Once I am given a minor role in a stage performance by the chapter. Though I am too young to remember quite what it is about, the phrase *komets-aleph:aw* stands in my memory.

Later I will learn that this phrase occurs in a famous and sentimental Yiddish folksong. It is the first letter of the Hebrew alphabet, the first thing countless generations of Jewish children have been taught. Here is an unusual case in which a traditional lesson—how to pronounce the alphabet—is successfully inculcated in the secularized framework of a dramatic performance about the traditional setting. Perhaps this is because of the necessary rehearsals, in which I must have heard, as the song puts it, "once more, over and over again, *komets-aleph:aw.*" The memory reinforces my later preference for this older, European pronunciation of the Hebrew vowels, my sense of the Israeli *kamets-aleph:ah* as inauthentic.

Also memorable at the Jewish Community Center is the annual barbecue run by the Young Couples' Club. Though my father will assure me in an interview years later that its association with the Fourth of July was purely a matter of convenience, the atmosphere is certainly one of festival, even including "sacrifices" and "altars": My father and his friends set up huge charcoal pits with cement blocks, and broil vast amounts of chicken; corn is boiled in aluminum garbage cans to go with it.[2] For the children, a Purim-like element of riotous excess is added: This one time each year, we are allowed to drink as much soda as we want. One year "wild," blond-haired Richie L., whose parents have a luncheonette booth for a kitchen table and an attic filled with antiques, claims to drink fourteen bottles, thus adding to the mystique he holds for me.

But it is the days when the Community Center becomes a synagogue that leave the strongest impression on my memory. There must be services every Saturday morning, but I am completely unaware of them. What I will remember are the holidays: Purim, Rosh Hashanah, Yom Kippur, Simchas Torah, and a crowd of people who just a few years later will never be there again. On the fall holidays, the shul is full of movement, impatience, noise, and warmth. Except for a few moments such as the shofar blowing, we children are free to come and go: By the steps in front, tossing the juicy, poisonous red berries of a yew that was planted, I am told, in memory of my brother Aaron, whom I never knew; inside the main doors, to look left at Walter Tenenbaum wrapped in a *tallis* that covers his head, standing at a lectern by the Ark of the Torah as he leads the service, or to look right, along the first long row of folding chairs for our fathers; thence a few rows back to where our mothers sit separately from the men, although unlike most synagogues that look and sound as traditional as this one, there is no *mekhitse*, no barrier between women and men; and finally out through the side door and down a flight of wooden steps to the monkey bars, into the ditch where one miraculous day we found and drank an intact bottle of orange soda, or into the kitchen, social room, and classroom in the basement. Once each year we children are the center of attention, as we huddle under a huge tallis in front of the Ark on Simchas Torah to be blessed.

In classic ethnographies of hunting-and-gathering groups, landscapes are described as personalized, integral elements of culture. This was true of the landscape of my childhood friendships, which today is as obliterated as any *shtetl* in Eastern Europe.

2. Even if it was no more than a matter of convenience, this annual event demonstrates Jonathan Woocher's point that American Jewish "civil religion expects Jews to take advantage of the opportunities which America provides, and to use them to help fulfill their Jewish responsibilities" (1985:161).

Any marginal group in mass society may be subject without warning to the loss of its cultural landscape, and therefore those who are able to create portable landscapes for themselves are the most likely to endure.

The Jews have been doing so for thousands of years; the Simchas Torah tallis can stand in front of any Ark, and the original Ark, in the biblical account, was itself transported from station to station in the desert. Yet the members of a community are orphaned when the naive intimacy of a living environment is torn away from them. Such a break appears often in Jewish literature— significantly with the emphasis not forward on the beginning of adulthood, as in the European *Bildungsroman,* but rather on the end of childhood.[3]

I suddenly discover the distance between the world and myself at the end of August in 1966. When my parents pick me up from camp, they take me to a new house. For the last time, we attend high holiday services in Farmingdale. It is the only time we will ever drive there, and our family's friends no longer join us during the afternoon break on Yom Kippur for a surreptitious glass of tea and a slice of challah. Farmingdale is no longer home, and though our new house is only ten miles away, it is another world.

We live now in an almost exclusively white, middle-class suburb

3. This may seem an outrageously loose claim, and I am quite willing to be proven wrong by literary scholars. But compare the conclusion of James Joyce's *Portrait of the Artist as a Young Man:*

> Mother is putting my new secondhand clothes in order. She prays now, she says, that I may learn in my own life and away from home and friends what the heart is and what it feels. Amen. So be it. Welcome, O life! I go to encounter for the millionth time the reality of experience and to forge in the smithy of my soul the uncreated conscience of my race. (1968:252–53)

with the end of Moshe Szulsztein's memoir of a Polish Jewish childhood:

> When the truck was already fairly far along Warsaw Street and Kurow was barely visible, two more relatives appeared in a great rush, wanting to take their leave. These were my grandfather's pair of pigeons. The pigeons knew me, and I knew them. I loved them, and perhaps they loved me as well. . . . But the truck is stronger than they are, it drives and drives further and further away from Kurow. My poor pigeons can't keep up, they remain behind. . . . Before they disappear altogether from my view I still discern them within the distant evening cloud, two small flying silver dots, one a bit behind the other. That, I know, is the male, and the second, a bit in front, is the female. (1982:352)

with many Jews, but our older, brick house is isolated on a block of working-class cubes. While neighbors my age play football in our yard, I often retreat to my room and console myself with sports books for preadolescents. My new and bewildering sense of marginality leads me to develop an exquisite self-consciousness. It is manifested in an almost constant internal dialogue, which keeps me company and will interfere with my adolescent sexuality.

Ostracism is often the fate of a new kid on the block, and it may last longer when his family is Jewish and his home better than those on either side. There is a custom in this part of New Jersey of tolerating petty vandalism on "mischief night," the night before Halloween. Pumpkins are smashed, and we, along with other unpopular families on the block, have the windows of our cars and house smeared with soap. One Halloween I wake up to see graffiti chalked in bold letters on the sidewalk in front of our house: "Jon the Jew, a real one too." My father summons the kids next door—whom we suspect of being the authors—to scrape the words off the sidewalk, as I burn with shame.

He and I never discuss the incident, but later I will compare it with a memory of Freud's: As a child, he was walking with his father, when a gentile knocked his father's hat off. Rather than confronting the man, Freud's father meekly bent over to pick up the hat, and his son's humiliation persisted into adulthood (Bakan 1958; D. Boyarin 1997). The moral is that a victim is likely to view any response as adding insult to injury. In my case, as my father asserts the American principle of equality and "teaches a lesson" to my occasional and vindictive playmates by forcing them to erase what they have written, I feel as though he is inviting them to write the words again, this time making me watch my own degradation.

The new synagogue my parents join is only a partial refuge. It exemplifies the difference between a shul and a temple. Everything in Farmingdale had faced inward: little concern was paid for praying in unison, and though the *shammes* would bang his hand on the table for silence, he was seldom heeded; even the cantor was alone with God, facing away from everyone else, rather than performing for the congregation. Calling a synagogue a temple, by contrast, is doubly revealing. On the one hand, it indicates a striving for the majesty of the ancient House in Jerusalem. On the other hand, just like the English term used to designate it, its trap-

pings are borrowed from the Christian world, down to the black
robes worn by the rabbi and cantor.

These robes lack the warm mystery of Walter Tenenbaum's
tallis. The responsive readings of Psalms in English seem ridicu-
lously artificial to me from the first. And my mother, who still
comes only on the holidays though I sometimes drag my father to
temple on Friday nights, complains of the rabbi's long-winded ser-
mons and yearns aloud for the intimate conversations along the
back wall of the Farmingdale Jewish Community Center.

Unlike some, I do not leave the synagogue immediately after
my bar mitzvah. I teach the blessings of the Haftorah to two reluctant boys a year younger than me. I briefly experience religious
inspiration, and for perhaps two weeks put on *tefillin* every morning. But the atmosphere is hollow, and the emptiness breeds cyni-
cism in me in my teens.

The coldness of the building itself is symptomatic of the lack
of sustenance I sense there. The pretense and bad taste of modern American synagogues are well-known yet puzzling phenomena that deserve a sociological explanation of their own. Even the
walls of the temple are dead concrete blocks, in contrast to the
wood of the Farmingdale Jewish Community Center. Services are
held in a "sanctuary," unlike the room at the Community Center
where activities as varied as dances and political meetings were
conducted when services were not being held. Aside from any
question of Jewish law, there is a loss of community marked by the
fact that everyone drives to the temple rather than walking. It is a
place separated from the home, without the strong and patient
webs spun by leisurely strolling conversations to and from a shul.

Most generally, the temple is victim to the general alienation
of the suburbs. What happens or fails to happen there is dependent on what the people who come there expect from each other.
Those who belong (there are vastly more "members" than regular attendees) seem bound primarily by a vague desire to have
Jewish grandchildren. The poor rabbi, typical of Conservative
congregations, seems hired to be a stand-in Jew, to observe all the
laws and contain all the knowledge they don't have the time for.
They are not bound to each other by Jewish religious ways, nor do
they share the common interests of everyday life—the same livelihood or language—that helped to make a complete community
in Farmingdale.

I go off to college and slowly discover that my dismissal of Judaism leaves me isolated, with few resources. I had realized my individual difference on leaving Farmingdale. Now, much more removed from a Jewish environment than ever before, I become aware of my inescapable Jewishness. In the small northwestern college of my dreams, everyone around me seems "American" and different, though I have never thought of myself as anything but American. Even in the humanities curriculum on which the school prides itself, Jewish civilization is absent. It is as though Western cultural history were just a triumphant straight line from the Greeks to Augustine and Michelangelo (with his horned Moses and uncircumcised David), confusion setting in at last only with Marx and Freud.

Five years too late to benefit me, a Jewish Studies position will in fact be established at the college. Such positions are usually funded by Jewish individuals or organizations, and hence they represent the growing acculturation (not assimilation) of Jews into American academic life. The fact that they are regarded as legitimate by the academic community, however, is part of a reintegration of Jewish thought into the concept of Western humanities. Jewish ethnographers can contribute to this movement—for example, by elucidating the dialectic of tradition and change as worked out in communities facing vastly different historical challenges. We may then move beyond efforts to explain the explosive presence of Jews in post-Enlightenment intellectual life as a result of their "primitive" encounter with "civility" (Cuddihy 1974) to explore how the Jewish belief that "Creation as the (active) speech or writing of God posits first of all that the Universe is essentially intelligible" (Faur 1986:7) provided a pathway from Torah to a restless, unifying modern impulse in the natural and social sciences.

Such notions are far beyond me as an undergraduate. At my college in the 1970s, the social scientists in their separate departments strive to separate themselves from their "objects of study"; the humanists treasure the peace of their cloisters; the artists, knowing they are intellectually suspect, cultivate a cliquish sense of superiority; and there is none of the give-and-take between learning and everyday experience that I have come to associate with the best of Jewish scholarship.

I find a friend, a Jew from Long Island, and we begin to teach

each other that we need to cultivate our Jewishness. We discuss the "Jewish mentality" of modern thinkers, and paraphrasing Lenny Bruce's category of the *goyish,* sarcastically reject all that is "white." "I am not 'white,' " my friend Martin proudly postures, "I am a Semite." Meanwhile, reflecting on my own dismissal of suburban Judaism, I decide not to end willingly an almost endless chain of Jewish cultural transmission. I stake my future on the assumption that a tradition so old and varied must contain the seeds of a worthwhile life for me, and decide to begin to acquire them through study.

Besides, my reading as a student of anthropology leads me to reason that if I concentrate on Jewish culture, no one will accuse me of cultural imperialism (see Gough 1968). No doubt others in my generation who choose to do fieldwork with Jews are motivated by similar considerations. Jewish anthropologists as a class are privileged to belong to the world of academic discourse, and to have an entrée into a variety of unique communities that maintain cultural frameworks in opposition to mass society.

Something deeper than Marxist critiques of anthropology draws me to Yiddish in particular. Before leaving Farmingdale, my best friend had been a child of survivors from Lemberg. I remember being at his house once, and asking with a sense of wonder: "Ralph, do you really know Yiddish?"

Ralph told me that although he understood the language— which his parents still spoke to him—he had never learned to speak it. Still, I was impressed that he knew this secret code. And now that I am finished with college and looking to find my own way home, Yiddish seems to be the nearest link to which I can attach myself. It is the key to a sense of the life of the shtetl, that Jewish dreamtime that I inevitably associate with my lost Farmingdale.

The Farmingdale community has, by this point, completely disintegrated: Virtually no Jews in that part of New Jersey earn their living as chicken farmers anymore. Many of those who have gone into business have moved to nearby towns like Lakewood. The Torah scrolls of the Community Center have been ceremoniously transferred to a new synagogue near housing developments on the highway between Farmingdale and Lakewood. I have never considered becoming a chicken farmer myself.

So, when I finish my college courses, without waiting for graduation, I flee back to New York. "Flee": No one chases me out of Portland, Oregon, God forbid! "Back": The city, though a magnet and a refuge, has never been my home before. Yet for three years I have shaped my identity in opposition to the "American" world around me, and I have reverted, along with my close friends, to what we imagine is an authentic New York accent—the "deses" and "doses" that were drilled out of my parents' repertoire in the days when New York public school teachers had to pass elocution exams.

Rejecting suburban Judaism, belatedly pursuing the image of the sixties' counterculture to the Pacific Northwest, and self-consciously affecting a "New York Jew" style were all successive attempts to shape a personal identity. In each case, the identity strategy was in opposition to the prevailing conventions of the immediate social order. Similarly, opposition to their parents' perceived bourgeois complacency may underlie the involvement of young people with Judaism. Yet as Dominique Schnapper has noted (1983), for young, intellectual Jews becoming involved in Jewish religion, politics, or culture, there can be no question of canceling out prior experience and "becoming traditional." In fact, this is true even of the most seemingly Orthodox and insular Jewish communities. There is a difference between learning about great rabbis of the past through meetings with Jewish graybeards who knew them, and through reading about their merits in the Williamsburg newspaper *Der Yid.*

Of course, not only Jews are in the position of reconstituting interrupted tradition (cf. Clifford 1986:116 ff.). But since they have been in the business of reshaping tradition in a dialogue with written texts for thousands of years, Jews may benefit more directly than others from learning about what other Jews are doing with their common tradition. It is conceivable that individuals may choose to adopt traits from other communities or even join those communities based on what they read in ethnographies. Whether such cultural borrowings and recombinations are effected in an "authentic" manner will depend less on precedent than on the degree of self-confident cultural generosity that results.

Arriving in New York, I adopt a knitted yarmulke, although my hair still falls below my shoulders. I immediately begin a nine-week summer course in Yiddish at Columbia, and it seems as though the language were being brought out from deep inside me. When I go to visit my parents on weekends, my father remembers words he'd never noticed forgetting. When I take the IRT after class back down to the Village, it seems as if everybody on the train is speaking Yiddish. Most important for my sense of identity, phrases here and there in my own internal dialogue are now in Yiddish, and I find I can reflect on myself with a gentle irony that was never available to me in English.

Then, after my first year in graduate school, I am off to Europe the following summer, courtesy of my parents. I arrive at the Gare du Nord in Paris with the address of a friend and without a word of French. I am spotted wearing my yarmulke by a young North African Jew who makes me understand, in broken English, that he studies at the Lubavitch yeshiva in Paris. He buys me a Paris guidebook and sets me on my way in the Metro. At the end of the summer, this meeting will stand as the first in a set of Parisian reactions to my yarmulke which crystallize in my memory:

—The reaction of the generous young Trotskyist with whom my friend had grown close and with whom I stayed for two weeks: She could see the yarmulke only as a symbol of Jewish nationalism and argued bitterly that it was inherently reactionary;

—Of a young North African Jew, selling carpets at the flea market at Clignoncourt, who grabbed my arm and cried, "*Haver! Haver!* Brother Jew!";

—Of another young man, minding a booth outside one of the great department stores, who asked me if I were Orthodox, and interrupted my complicated response to explain that, although he was Orthodox himself, he was afraid to wear a yarmulke in the street;

—Of an old man at the American Express office who spoke to me in Yiddish and complained that the recent North African migrants dominated the Jewish communal organizations, and that there was no place for a Polish Jew to go.

Those first, fragmentary encounters are my fieldwork juvenilia. In assuming the yarmulke, I perhaps do not stop to consider that neither my actions nor my knowledge match the standards that it symbolically represents. But it works effectively, almost dangerously, as a two-way sensor, inducing Jews to present themselves to me and forcing me to try to understand how I am reflected in their eyes.

Externally, I learn many things about the situation of French

Jewry. From the patent discomfort my non-Jewish Trotskyist friend feels at my display of Jewish specificity, I gain some sense of the conflicts young French Jews—coming out of the universalist, antihistorical revolutionary apogee of May 1968—must have felt years later when they first began to distinguish themselves from their comrades and view the world from the vantage point of their specific history. From the young street peddlers, I learn about how much riskier public proclamation of oneself as a Jew is perceived as being in Paris than in New York, and a concomitant depth of instant identification of one Jew with another. My meeting with the old Polish Jew at the American Express office hints at the dynamics of dominant and declining ethnic groups within the Jewish community, so vastly different from those dynamics in the United States.

Internally, I begin to understand that an identifiably Jewish headcovering places its own claims on the one who wears it. The longer it stays put, the more its power to keep him out of non-kosher restaurants grows. More important, people want to know who he is as a Jew. And if he does not know, the desire for peace of mind will spur further his effort to shape an identity.

Returning from Paris, I find an apartment at Second Avenue and Fifth Street in Manhattan. I tell people, "After three generations, my family has finally made it back to the Lower East Side." In fact, none of my grandparents lived on the East Side for a long time after immigrating, even though my mother tells me she regrets having missed the Yiddish theater on Second Avenue during her girlhood. By the time I move in, there is no Yiddish theater left. The former Ratner's dairy restaurant on Second Avenue, where, I'm told, Trotsky was a lousy tipper, is now a supermarket. Though sometimes one still sees a white newspaper truck with the word *Forverts* in lovely blue Hebrew letters on its side drive by late at night, this neighborhood has been the East Village since the sixties, and I think of it as such.

A new friend, who devotes his time to a frustrating effort to rescue Lower East Side synagogues, tells me of a shul still in use on an otherwise abandoned block east of Tompkins Square Park. Though my friend has never been inside, he is sure that I will be welcomed, since such an isolated congregation must be looking for new blood.

The place is called the Eighth Street Shul, but its full name is Kehilas Bnei Moshe Yakov Anshei Zavichost veZosmer—Congregation Children of Moses and Jacob, People of Zavichost and Zosmer. It is owned by a *landsmanshaft* (hometown society) founded by émigrés and refugees from two towns in south central Poland. No one born in either town prays regularly at the shul now, and only one or two of the congregants are actually members of the society.

The shul is located in the center of what New York Latinos call "Loisaida"—an area bounded by Avenue A on the east, Avenue D on the west, Houston Street on the south, and Fourteenth Street on the north. Once the blocks up to Tenth Street were almost exclusively Jewish, and on nearly every one stood a synagogue or a religious school. Now two of those former synagogues stand abandoned, several more have become churches, and the rest have disappeared.

Eighth Street is a typical and not especially distinguished example of turn-of-the-century Lower East Side synagogue architecture.[4] It consists of five levels. The lowest contains a cranky and inadequate boiler. The second is the *besmedresh* or study room, which was destroyed by a suspicious fire in August 1982. The third level is the main sanctuary, long and narrow like the tenements among which it was tucked when it was built. Two rows of simple pews are separated by an aisle, which is interrupted in the center of the room by the raised table from which the weekly Torah portion is read. At the very front is the Ark, surrounded by partially destroyed wooden carvings that are the most artistic aspect of the shul. The walls are decorated with representations of the traditional Jewish signs for the zodiac; the two in front on the left have been obliterated by water damage from the leaky roof. Covering most of this level, with roughly an eight-foot opening extending toward the back, is the women's gallery. The gallery is constructed in such a way that it is easier for women sitting on opposite sides of the opening to converse with one another than to see what the men are doing downstairs. Finally, upstairs from the women's gallery is an unused and cramped apartment that was once occupied

4. For photographs of Eighth Street and other Lower East Side shuls, both surviving and abandoned, see Fine and Wolfe (1978).

by the shul's caretaker. In the roof behind it, an opening that was a skylight until there was a break-in is now covered with a solid wooden framework, allowing neither light nor vandals to enter.

Avenues B and C, which mark off the block, were once lively commercial streets with mostly Jewish storekeepers. There were also several smaller streets lined with tenements, right up to the edge of the East River. When the FDR Drive was built along the river, all the streets east of Avenue D disappeared, the tenements on the remaining available land were replaced by municipal housing, and the stores declined rapidly. During the same years, a massive middle-class housing cooperative, funded by a government mortgage, was built along Grand Street one mile to the south. Many of the remaining Jewish families moved into those houses, leaving virtually no Jews in the immediate area of the Eighth Street Shul.

Yet a minyan has continued to meet there every Saturday morning, with virtually no interruptions, throughout the years of the neighborhood's decline, while the block served as the Lower East Side's heaviest "shopping street" for hard drugs. It has lasted into the present, when buildings all around it are being speculated upon and renovated by both squatters and powerful real estate interests. It appears that until recently the main reason for this continuity was a felicitous rivalry between two men who were unwilling to abandon the synagogue because their fathers had both been presidents of it at one time. Perhaps if there had been only one, he would have given up and made peace with his conscience. Perhaps if the two men had naturally been friends they could have agreed to sell the building and officially merge their society with another still functioning further south in the neighborhood. If they had been able to agree on anything besides continuing to come to the shul, the shul might not have survived this long.

The first time I walk in, a clean-shaven, compact man in his sixties—younger than several of the congregants, who number perhaps seventeen in all—hurries forward to greet me. What's my name? Where do I live? Where am I from originally? And where do I usually go to pray on shabbes? His name is Moshe Fogel, and he sees to it that I am called to the Torah, the honor accorded any guest who comes for the first time, without asking any questions as to his level of religious observance. Later, an older member explains to me: "Once upon a time, you wouldn't get called to the Torah unless you kept kosher and observed shabbes." Now, Moish prefers simply to leave those matters undiscussed.

The history of the East Side as a place where all types of Jews have lived together reinforces his discretion. Externalities such as proper or improper clothing are not essential criteria for participation. This is true of the entire Orthodox community on the East Side and has even become part of its mystique. Rabbi Reuven Feinstein, head of the Staten Island branch of the East Broadway–based yeshiva, Tifereth Jerusalem, noted in a recent speech the common reaction in Boro Park and other thriving Orthodox centers to the nonconformist dress of East Side visitors: "It's okay, you're from the East Side." The president at Eighth Street still wears a traditional *gartl* when he prays, a belt worn over his jacket to separate the pure from the base parts of his body, and no one has suggested that such old customs are out of place today. But partly because the older members at the Eighth Street Shul walked through the East Village in the 1960s and knew there were many young Jews among the longhairs—even if they were horrified at the thought—they were willing to include in the minyan a young man in the neighborhood who, when he first came, wore dreadlocks under a Rastafarian-style knitted cap. It is also doubtless true that at that time there was no other Orthodox synagogue anywhere that he would have contemplated entering.

By contrast, it is impossible for any Jew raised in the middle of secular society (including a Jewish anthropologist) to join a traditionalist community without giving up major parts of his or her identity. The ways in which a researcher of contemporary Hasidic life "becomes a Hasid" are much more dramatic than the way in which one becomes a regular at Eighth Street—but they are probably more transient as well. In order to gain the confidence of the traditionalist communities, the fieldworker has to give the impression, whether implicitly or explicitly, that he or she is likely eventually to accept their standards in all areas of life (Belcove-Shalin 1988). All one has to do at Eighth Street is agree to come back— "a little earlier next time, if possible."

Two things will draw me back to join this congregation, occasionally referred to as "those holy souls who *daven* in the middle of the jungle." The first pull is the memory of Farmingdale: the Ashkenazic accents and melodies (though here they are Polish, whereas Walter Tenenbaum had prayed in his native Lithuanian accent); the smell of herring on the old men's breath and hands; the burning sensation of whiskey, which I must have tasted surreptitiously at the conclusion of Yom Kippur one year in Farmingdale.

The second thing that draws me, though I do not come every week, is a feeling that I am needed and missed when I am absent. It's hard for me to get up early on Saturday mornings, after being out late Friday nights. It still seems like a sacrifice, as though I were stealing part of my weekend from myself. If I arrive in time for the *Shema*, about half an hour into the service, I congratulate myself on my devotion. The summer before I marry, in 1981, I hardly come at all. When I go with my brother to meet Moshe Fogel at the shul and give him the provisions for the kiddush I am giving to celebrate my upcoming wedding, I tell Dan that I usually arrive "around nine-thirty," to which Moish retorts: "Even when you used to come, you didn't show up at nine-thirty!" Though he says it with a smile, a message comes through clearly: If I want to claim to belong, I should attend regularly and arrive on time. Although I am always welcome, only if I can be counted on am I part of the minyan. The dependence of Jews on each other—a theme running through biblical and rabbinic literature—is pressingly literal at Eighth Street.

Meanwhile, my feelings about Paris coalesce into a plan. I know I want to live there for a time, but only if I will be among Jews. Since I am at the point in my graduate school career when I must find a dissertation topic, I decide to look for fieldwork situations with Jews in Paris. I make an exploratory visit with my fiancée, Elissa. Will she agree to a pause in her own career to follow me on this project? Will the organizations of Polish Jewish immigrants whom I have chosen to study be willing to have me study them?

The answer is yes to both questions. Speaking Yiddish and appearing as a nice young Jewish couple seem to be the critical elements in our success. We are invited to sit in on board meetings, negotiations aimed at the reunification of societies split by political differences for over half a century. I am struck by the fact that these immigrants seem so much more marked by their political identification than the East European Jews I've met in New York. Also, I am impressed at the number of societies remaining in a country that has suffered Nazi occupation and that historically has shown little tolerance for immigrant cultural identifications.

But I am drawn not so much by the differences between these Yiddish speakers and those I know in New York as by encountering them in an environment that is otherwise so foreign. Speaking Yiddish to people with whom I have no other common language confirms its legitimacy and reinforces the sense of a distinctive Jewish identity that is shared between generations. I go for a trial interview of one activist, who is disappointed that I didn't bring "the girl," Elissa, along with me. When he discovers to my embarrassment that I have been secretly taping the interview, he is flattered.

Just before leaving Paris, Elissa and I climb the steps of Sacré Coeur. The cathedral itself is an ungracious mass, and the city looks gray and undifferentiated below us. I experience a moment of vertigo, as if I could tumble off Montmartre and drown. Part of my dream of Paris, "capital of the nineteenth century," is an infantile fantasy of becoming a universal intellectual—to be free both of the special knowledge and of the limitations of my knowledge that follow on my personal history. Yet I know I cannot come to Paris and immediately move among its confident, cliquish intellectual elite. Even less will I ever have contact with that "quintessentially French" petite bourgeoisie typified by the stolid Inspector Maigret. My first place will be with the immigrants, whose appearance, strange language, and crowded quarters provided material for unkind portraits by Maigret's creator, Simenon, in the 1930s.[5] If I am unable to come to see Paris as they have seen it, if I cannot make out of a shared marginality a niche in the city for myself, I will be lost, as much as the "lost generation," and in a most unromantic way.

During the two years between our decision to spend a year in Paris and the beginning of that year, I attend the Eighth Street Shul more and more regularly, and Elissa occasionally joins me. Gradually, my feelings when I miss a week shift from guilt to regret. One shabbes, waking up late but not wanting to miss attend-

5. "In every corner, in every little patch of darkness, up the blind alleys and the corridors, one could sense the presence of a swarming mass of humanity, a sly, shameful life. Shadows slunk along the walls. The stores were selling goods unknown to French people even by name" (Simenon 1963:45).

ing altogether, I arrive just in time for the kiddush, to the general
amusement of the entire minyan. One February morning I wake
up to see snow falling and force myself to go outside against my
will, knowing that on a day like this I am truly needed.

Other incidents illustrate the gap in assumptions between myself and the other congregants. I try to bring friends into the shul,
partly because it makes me more comfortable, and partly to build
up the congregation. A friend whose hair and demeanor reflect
his love of reggae music and his connections with Jamaican Ras-
tafarians comes along one Yom Kippur. We reach the point in the
service when pious men, remembering the priests in the days of
the Temple, descend to their knees and touch their foreheads to
the floor. Since no one wants to soil his good pants on the dirty
floor, sheets of newspaper are provided as protection. Reb Simcha
Taubenfeld, the senior member of the congregation, approaches
my friend with newspaper in hand and asks in his heavy Yiddish
accent: "Do you fall down?" The look of bewilderment on my
friend's face graphically illustrates the term "frame of reference."

Another week, the same friend, failing to observe the discretion with regard to the expression of political opinions that I have
learned to adopt at shul, gets into a bitter argument over the Palestinian question. Fishel Mandel, a social worker and one of the
younger members of the congregation, calls me during the week
to convey the message that "despite our political differences, your
friend is still welcome."

After our wedding, I attend virtually every week. When Elissa
comes, she is doubly welcome, since the only other woman who
attends regularly is Goldie Brown, Moish Fogel's sister. Though
Goldie doesn't complain about being isolated in the women's gallery one flight above the men, she seconds Elissa's suggestion that
a mekhitse be set up downstairs. The suggestion gets nowhere,
however: It would entail displacing one of the regular members
of the congregation from his usual seat, and though there is no
lack of available places (I myself usually wander from front to
back during the course of the service), he refuses to consider
moving.

I reason that I will have more of a voice concerning questions
such as the seating of women if I formalize my relationship to the
shul by becoming a member. My timid announcement that I
would like to do so meets with initial confusion on the part of the

older members of the society present. Then Fishel, ever the mediator and interpreter, explains to me that the shul is not organized like a suburban synagogue: "There's a *chevra*, a society, that owns the shul. In order to join, you have to be *shomer mitzves*, you have to keep kosher and strictly observe the Sabbath."

I drop my request. Shiye the president reassures me with a speech in his usual roundabout style to the effect that belonging to the chevra is a separate question from being a member of the minyan: "They send their money in from New Jersey and Long Island, but the shul couldn't exist without the people that actually come to pray here."

Meanwhile, our plans to go to Paris proceed. Our travel plans become a topic for discussion over kiddush at shul. One of the older, Polish-born members tells us for the first time that he lived in Paris for nine years after the war. We ask him why he came to America, and he answers, "*Vern a frantsoyz iz shver* [It's hard to become a Frenchman]," both to obtain citizenship and to be accepted by neighbors.

At the end of the summer, we expect to give a farewell kiddush at the shul. A few days before shabbes, I get a phone call from Moish Fogel: "Don't get things for kiddush. We won't be able to daven at Eighth Street for a while. There's been a fire. Thank God, the Torah scrolls were rescued, but it's going to take a while to repair the damage." It is two weeks after Tisha B'Av, the fast commemorating the destruction of the Temple in Jerusalem.

Leaving New York without saying goodbye to the shul and its congregation, we fly overnight to Brussels and immediately *shlep* (the word "drag" would not do the burden justice) our seven heavy suitcases onto a Paris train. Arriving again at the Gare du Nord, I think of the thousands of Polish Jews who were greeted at the station in the twenties and thirties by fellow immigrants eager to hire workers. As soon as we get off the train, Elissa immediately "gets involved," demanding the credentials of two men who claim to be policemen and attempt to "confiscate" a carpet two Moroccan immigrants are carrying. Upon Elissa's challenge, the "policemen" demur.

We practice our French on the cab driver: I explain to him why we've come to Paris. He warns us that we shouldn't tell strangers we're Jewish. It is only a few weeks since the terrorist attack on Goldenberg's restaurant, and no one knows when the next anti-

Semitic attack may come. I reply that if I hadn't said we were Jewish, we wouldn't have found out he was a Jew as well, adding that in New York the names of taxi drivers are posted inside the cabs. He says he wouldn't like that at all.

So we receive an early warning that ethnicity in Paris is not celebrated publicly as it is in New York, nor are ethnic mannerisms and phrases so prevalent as a deliberate element of personal style. This is the repressive underside of marginality. It appears wherever the individual or community think it is better not to flaunt their distinctiveness, even if they cannot fully participate in the host culture. It leads to suspicion and silence, to the taxi driver's desire for anonymity.

Arriving at our rented apartment, we meet our neighbor Isabel, who will be our only non-Jewish friend during the year in Paris, and who later explains that meeting us has helped dispel her prejudices about Jews. Over the next few days, we introduce ourselves to Jewish storekeepers in the neighborhood: Guy, the Tunisian kosher butcher; Chanah, the Polish baker's wife; Leon, the deli man from Lublin, who insists he didn't learn Yiddish until he came to Paris.

We have a harder time finding a synagogue where we feel at home. For Rosh Hashanah and Yom Kippur, we have purchased tickets at one of the "official" synagogues run by the Consistoire, the recognized religious body of French Jewry set up under Napoleon. Most synagogues run by the Consistoire are named after the streets on which they're located. Meeting a Hasid on the street, I ask him whether he happens to know when Rosh Hashanah services begin at "Notre Dame de Nazareth." He grimaces and makes as if spitting: "Don't say that name, *ptu ptu ptu!*"

The synagogue is strange to us as well. Most of the crowd seems if anything more secular than most American Jews, who go to the synagogue only on the high holidays. Many teenagers wear jeans or miniskirts. Because of the fear of terrorism, everyone is frisked on entering. Inside, the synagogue is picturesque with its nineteenth-century pseudo-Moorish motifs; when it was built, Offenbach was the choirmaster. Yet it is as religiously dissatisfying as the suburban American temple I used to attend. The services seem to be conducted in a traditional manner, but it is hard to tell from among the noisy throng in back. The shammes, as a representative of the government, wears a Napoleonic hat, and the rabbi delivers his sermon from a high pulpit.

After Yom Kippur, I think idly about the need to find a more comfortable shul, and when I hear about an East European–style minyan within walking distance, I consider going on Simchas Torah. Watching television reports of terrorist attacks on Simchas Torah in other European capitals, I am consumed with shame at my own apathy, and thus I walk a kilometer or two to find the synagogue on the rue Basfroi the following shabbes.

Going in, I am first shown into a side room, where men are reciting incomprehensible prayers with strange and beautiful melodies. Eventually I realize that they are North African Jews, and I venture into the main room to ask, "Is there an Ashkenazic minyan here?"

The man I ask replies in French, "We're not racists here! We're all Jews!" at which his friend points out:

"The young man spoke to you in Yiddish!" Continuing in Yiddish, he explains that while everyone is welcome in the main synagogue, the services there are in fact Ashkenazic, and so some of the North African men prefer to pray in their own style in the smaller room.

Gradually I settle in, though I have trouble following the prayers in the beginning. Remembering a particular turn in the melody for the reader's repetition of the Amidah that the president at Eighth Street uses, I listen for it from the cantor here at the rue Basfroi, and hear a satisfying similarity in his voice. I feel like a new immigrant coming to his landsmanshaft's shul to hear the melodies from his town.

Throughout our year in Paris, I attend this synagogue about as frequently as I had gone to Eighth Street at first. Although the congregation is not unfriendly, no one invites me home for lunch, partly out of French reserve, and perhaps also because it is clear that I'm not very observant. I feel "unobservant" here in another sense: I do not register the vast store of information obviously available here about the interaction of religious Jews from different ethnic backgrounds. It escapes me, as though I were "off duty." In contrast to my feelings at Eighth Street, I am not motivated by the desire to make myself a regular here. And this is not my fieldwork situation: Nothing external moves me to push my way through socially, to find out who these people really are and let them see me as well.

The Jews I encounter in the course of my research belong to an entirely different crowd. The landsmanshaftn to which they belong are secular organizations. If I wanted to observe the Sabbath closely, it would be difficult for me to do my fieldwork. The immigrants hold many meetings on Saturdays, including a series of *shabbes-shmuesn,* afternoon discussions at which the main focus this year is the war in Lebanon.

I mention to one of my informants that I sometimes go to the synagogue. "I admire that," he responds. "I can't go back to the synagogue now. I've been away too long; it's too late for me." Toward the end of the year, we invite an autodidact historian of the immigrant community to dinner on Friday night and ask him to say the blessing over the challah. "I can't," he refuses, and will not explain further. Though his intellectual curiosity has led him to become friendly with us, and he is considering doing research on the resurgence of Orthodoxy among young French Jews, his critical stance vis-à-vis his own secularist movement is insufficient to allow him to accept this religious honor. Enjoying the possibilities offered by marginality is sometimes impossible for those who are neither young nor well educated and who have often been deceived in their wholehearted commitments.

Throughout the year, Elissa has been growing stricter regarding *kashres.* She refuses to eat nonkosher meat and will order only fish in restaurants. She articulates our shared impression that Jewish secularism has failed to create everyday lifeways that can be transmitted from generation to generation, and that any lasting Judaism must be grounded in Jewish law and learning. Before parting for the summer—she to study Yiddish at Oxford, I to Jerusalem, to acquire the Hebrew that I will need to learn about Jewish law—we discuss the level of observance we want to adopt on our return to New York, but we come to no decision.

Elissa and I meet at the end of the summer in Los Angeles, for the bar mitzvah of her twin cousins. I am uncomfortable riding on shabbes; after spending an entire summer in Jerusalem, for the first time, it seems like a violation of myself. The roast beef sandwich I eat at the reception is the first nonkosher food I've eaten since leaving Paris.

Thus, without having made a formal declaration, I join Elissa in observing kashres (save for occasional lapses that I call my "*treyf* of the month club" and that become less and less frequent), and she joins me in keeping shabbes, albeit with some reluctance. Preparing to fulfill a promise made in a dream I had while in Paris, I take a further step: At the beginning of November, I begin attending daily services at another East Side shul and thus putting on tefillin again. One of my mother's cousins at the Telshe Yeshiva in Cleveland—whom I have never met—told me in the dream that I would always be welcome there, and I responded that if I got there, I would put on tefillin every day from then on. Later in November, Elissa and I fly to Cleveland for the weekend. Though we are welcomed warmly, it is clear that the rabbis and *rebetsins* at the yeshiva hoped for something more Jewish from me, the great-grandson of the Rosh Yeshiva's second wife, Miriam.

We return to the Eighth Street Shul as well, which has been secured and repaired sufficiently to make it usable once again. There are changes. Old Mr. Klapholz, with whom I hardly had exchanged a word, has passed away. Fishel's uncle Mr. Hochbaum, a congregant for half a century, no longer attends, since he is unable to walk all the way from Grand Street. On the other hand, my long-haired friend has moved into the neighborhood and attends regularly. Two of the younger members of the congregation have small children now, and they must go to a shul where there are other children for their son and daughter to play with. In February, our oldest member passes away, and after Shavuot, another member moves to Jerusalem. Two more young men eventually begin coming regularly and bring along their infant children. Now, in June 1986, the shul has thirteen regular male attendees. I am no longer free to sleep late on Saturday mornings, and fortunately I no longer want to.

All of this, to the extent it is of my own making, is the result of a search to realize that fragile illusion of wholeness which was destroyed when my family and almost all the others left Farmingdale. I will hazard a guess that Jewish anthropologists—perhaps anthropologists in general—are motivated by a sense of loss. Yet the seamless image of community is inevitably a child's image. We cannot regain what is lost, if only because it never existed as we remember it. Nothing in society is quite as harmonious as it seemed to me then, and I later learned about bitter political struggles that had taken place in Farmingdale, just as they had among the immigrants in Paris.

Our strategy, rather, should be to attempt to understand what it is we miss and need, which is available in still-living communities in another form. The image of wholeness which we share is foreshadowed by communities all of us stem from, however many generations back, and it can serve as a guide in the search for the reciprocal relationships of autonomous adulthood.

Anthropology is a tool for mediating between the self and the community. It has helped me to come to belong at the Eighth Street Shul: to withhold my opinions when it seems necessary, without feeling the guilt of self-compromise; to accept instruction and gentle reprimands with good humor; to believe it is worthwhile preserving something that might otherwise disappear. But belonging at Eighth Street does not mean that I have dissolved myself into an ideal Orthodox Jew. If I attempted to do so, I would be unable to continue being an anthropologist. If I fit into any category, it may be what my friend Kugelmass calls the "funky Orthodox": that is, those who participate in the community but whose interests and values are not confined to the Orthodox world. In fact, there are no ideal Orthodox Jews at Eighth Street; it is our respective quirks that provide the *raison d'être* of this haphazard but now intentional once-a-week community.

The fact that I have found a religious community that needs me because of its marginality and will tolerate me because of a generosity born of tradition is what I mean by the marginal redemption of one Jew. Likewise, if the shul survives, it will be because of its very marginality, because of the many individuals who have recognized the creative possibilities of a situation that demands that they create a new unity, while allowing each of them to retain their otherness. Isn't this the dream of anthropologists? Whether attempting to communicate knowledge between different Jewish communities, or between communities much more distant in tradition and empathy, we are messengers. We spend our own lives in moving back and forth among the worlds of others. As we do so, in order to avoid getting lost along the way we must become cultural pioneers, learning to "get hold of our *trans*cultural selves" (Wolff 1970:40). Communities on the edge of mass society, or even on the fringes of ethnic enclaves, seem to be among the most congenial fields in which to do so.

Let me finish with a parable:

Two Jews can afford to be fastidious about the dress, comportment, and erudition of a third. It gives them something to gossip about and identify against. Ten healthy Jews can have a similar luxury; an eleventh means competition for the ritual honors. It's nine Jews who are the most tolerant, as I learned one forlorn shabbes at Eighth Street. It was almost ten o'clock, and there was no minyan. Since everyone seemed content to wait patiently, I assumed that someone else had promised to come, and asked, "Who are we waiting for?"

"A *yid,*" our oldest member replied without hesitation.

Eventually a Jew came along.

TWO

Self-Exposure as Theory
The Double Mark of the Male Jew

> On the stand Chief Flying Eagle often sounds like a social studies teacher; his speech is loaded with pat anecdotes and homilies.
>   Only once, toward the end of his testimony, does he do something unexpected. Asked whether he often wears Indian regalia, Mills answers no, only at powwows. Then he suddenly tugs at his necktie, pulling two thin strings of beads from under his shirt. One, he says, is turquoise, from the Southwest. The other small strand was a gift from his father.
>   Many people in the courtroom are surprised by this apparently spontaneous revelation—surprised and, as Mills stuffs the beads back into his shirt and fumbles to readjust his tie, a little embarrassed.
>
> —James Clifford, "Identity in Mashpee" (1988)

This essay is a semi-legendary narrative told by two native brothers to each other. Our purpose is to inquire into the formation of strong ethnic self-identification in a culture in which totality is already displaced—or, to put it another way, how cultural relativists can have culture. Moreover, we wish to raise seriously the issue of how ethnic cultural identity can be constructed without the pernicious moral and political effects of "othering." We will be using ourselves and each other as participant informants. The central metaphor for our analysis is the "double sign" of Jewish male ethnic identity: one inscribed on our genitals before we were ever able to exercise will, the other placed upon our heads in a free-willed if ambivalent act of self-identification with ethnicity that we carry with us into such social spaces as anthropology conventions.[1] We will of course address the androcentric na-

1. In revising this paper for publication, we have chosen to retain the marks of
34   its original venue, including our joint appearance as brothers—an affinity both

ture of both of these "signs" and the troubling questions that it raises.

There are two parts to the essay as well. The first tends to focus on circumcision and the historical context of early Judaism, hence to the "given" in personal identity. The second, structured in response to a concise and cogent statement about pluralism and "strong identity" by a leading political theorist, draws largely on contemporary personal vignettes and has more to say about the headcovering. Yet our choice of anecdotes and contexts within a broad sweep of Jewish textuality and experience is largely intended to subvert the common assumption that the given in identity is linked to domination, while the chosen necessarily implies free choice noncoercive of others.

Perhaps an appropriate departure is the word "natives," which we used in our first sentence. It could be objected that we are cloaking ourselves in the rhetoric of authentic knowledge of a bounded and *sui generis* culture. The term bears the traces of the imperial, territorializing context in which it became part of anthropology. Its history is that of the effort to create a unique mapping of human groups onto the globe, to separate and order them and keep them in their places (see, e.g., Fabian 1983, Ratzel 1898). What would it mean to imply, as we do here, either that some of us are indeed natives (and some are not), or that one can choose consciously to be a native? In this case the answer has to do with a more specific return to the connections with birth implied by nativity. We understand ourselves as more profoundly born to, native to, an anamnestic generational tradition than to any national state or territory. The mark on our bodies, it seems to us, works harder than our birth certificates. Partly for that reason, we have chosen to affirm this mark in its detachable double, the headcovering that signals us as observant Jews.

If we stopped here, however, we would never get to the American Anthropological Association, which is hardly a forum for the shoring up of totalizing identities, whether "illusory" or "essential." Seeing ourselves as pre-placed and placing ourselves within the tradition, we are also cognizant of the demands expressed by Walter Benjamin's dictum that "in every era the at-

---

given and chosen—on the convention podium at the American Anthropological Association.

tempt must be made anew to wrest tradition away from a conform-
ism that is about to overpower it" (Benjamin 1969:255). This
threatening conformity within Jewish discourse is to be found
outside us—for example, in the decidedly nontraditional Gush
Emunim idolatry of the Land of Israel, which applies biblical
rhetoric toward a thoroughly modernized version of territorialist
nationalism (Schwartz 1992; Lustick 1988). More subtly we hope,
but certainly more significantly for this discussion, the threat of
conformity is also within us. There is a measure of imposition, a
kind of symbolic violence or at least cognitive dissonance induced
by our exhibitionist or tricksterlike appearance as "Orthodox"
Jews in such unorthodox settings. More systematically, the marks
we ground our selfhood in are only imposed on and available to
male Jews—and hence inescapably inscriptions of hierarchizing
and reifying difference.

The exigency of our times lays out the general agenda for our
tradition of rescue work. We work at creating, "within" the tradition (for at some point we cannot escape spatializing metaphor),
space for the autonomous existence of the sexual and ethnic
Other. But it is inherent precisely in our public identification with
a specific, rather than generically humanist tradition, that the creative outcomes of this rescue work are always contingent, rather
than functionally predictable—hence the episodic and even de-
contextualized character of some of the ethnography herein. Nor
do we necessarily suppose that we are pioneering what will become a new, hegemonic mode of Jewish self-imagining. While it
has long been recognized that even in ancient times, "each generation had first to become Israel" (Von Rad 1962:162), it becomes somewhat difficult, given the increasing fragmentations of
our times, to claim that in every time and place, Jews combine
tradition and contemporaneity to produce a sum total that is "Israel." Although Jewish identification remains defined as an identification with other Jews, the fissures in such a corporate ideology
are painfully obvious. Here, in fact, we focus more on corporeal
than on corporate identity.

Recognizing the artifice and power of the specific form of
postmodern self-fashioning that leads us to emphasize Judaism in
our own selves, we see our work as the opening of a nonreified
difference in the space between the circumcision and the yar-

mulke/kippah/skullcap. We seek not to occupy a marginal position purified to a point, along the model of the solitary modern hero, but rather to travel along a marginal trajectory providing a connecting thread among an ever-widening field of articulated differences. In order for such a marginal trajectory to be traversable, it must be moored in the past, oriented toward a future however generally sensed, and given dimension by identifications with others in the present. To put it another way, in order for the margins to exist at all, they must have some content that affords them the possibility to resist pressure to evacuate or implode. Margins therefore produce their own centralizing and conformist pressures. Critical intellectuals with a strong group identification project their identities through a simultaneous testing and reinforcement of these marginal boundaries.

The relevance of our project to this group effort rests on a very specific reading of Debbora Battaglia's phrase "the rhetoric of self-making." We take it to refer not so much to a universal human process of ego development having rhetorical aspects, but rather to the particular ideology summed up in the phrase "the self-made man." Nevertheless we will not analyze that kind of self-making directly. Nor will we employ an older functionalist rhetoric to discuss circumcision and covering the head as techniques that a superorganic ethnic collective imposes in order to maintain external boundaries and internal continuity. Rather we will consider them as techniques that continue to ground a version of selfhood that is an alternative to the privatized and dehistoricized modern notion of "self-making."

The conscious embrace of these alternatives is inseparable from questions of scholarly method. Reflections contained in a recent paper by James Boon (1994) are extremely helpful here. Remarking that the topic of male circumcision (let alone clitoridectomy) arouses immediate and strong unreflective opinions when discussed even in the scholarly community, Boon notes the critical difference between "empathy/distance vis-à-vis other (rather than own) circumcisions or uncircumcisions." Our examination of Jewish circumcision here, of course, concerns our "own" circumcisions. Insofar as we are speaking as Jews, this possessive pronoun implies the authoritative articulation of a common ethnic experience and reflection—something we have already tried to cast into question. Therefore we will leave open the question of whether "own" here refers to the two of us, or to all male Jews.[2]

Consistent with his plea that circumcision be treated with the same respect for cultural context that other kinds of difference enjoy, Boon emphasizes the need for a "diacritic" rather than evaluative view of circumcision. This emphasis is most appropriate, perhaps, in a study like his of "other" circumcisions/uncircumcisions. It should not be taken, however, to mean that the meanings attached to the foreskin or its absence are limited to the separation of one group from its neighbors.

Boon's paper is subtitled "An Essay amidst the History of Difficult Description," and we will similarly integrate references to the so-called past with discussions of the contemporary situation. Moving a step further, we will argue that circumcision especially raises questions about the relation between formations of chronology and those of selfhood. The story of the self-made man, stripped down to its common features, starts from a zero point. It has no prehistory. It continues in linear fashion, step by step, progressively. In this version, the word "success" has lost its connotations of coming after, inheriting, taking the place of; this success, this doing well, is all about finding a high place in a capitalist hierarchy that is constantly evolving and expanding.

We suggest that this American ideal is closely linked to the Christian (and especially Protestant) notion of individual salvation, and through this to the assumption of the discrete self as existing in a uniquely defined time, such that chronology is coterminous and contingent with a sequential and progressive individual biography. The story of the self-made man, that is, begins with his birth (if he is described as having "humble beginnings," this is primarily to show that he owes nothing to anyone) and it ends with his death. The son of the self-made man cannot be self-made.

On the contrary, we will claim that a "male Jewish self"—no

2. Gil Anidjar (1996) criticizes us here for assuming that the circumcision is performed upon what already *is* a "boy," rather than seeing the millah as a process of boy-making, as would be implied by the insight of Judith Butler that "the moment when an infant becomes humanized is when the question, 'is it a boy or girl?' is answered" (1990:111).

matter how vast the differences elided by this rubric may be—
cannot be limited to such a unilinear, bounded, and progressive
conception of time. The incorporation, both literal and figura-
tive, of Jewishness as an aspect of the self implies an experience of
time that is panchronic and empathetically expanded. We do not
want to claim that the marks of male Jewish difference constitute
essential differences from some putative white middle-class male
European norm. Yet they can be articulated as presenting quite
rich contrasts to the rhetoric of the self-made man. The question
of the link between conceptions of time and conceptions of the
self is perhaps the clearest lens for examining such differences.

What we have said so far implies a more radical disjuncture
than actually obtains. It suggests that an acceptance of the mark
of circumcision and all of the involuntary connections that it implies place a Jewish male into a "dreamtime" or (Robert Paine's
term, 1983) "totemic time" and outside the progressive time
of modern self-making. Especially in contemporary middle-class
America, differences in the sense of time and selfhood between
most Jews and, for example, most Protestants may be negligible
or impossible to determine. This attenuation of difference—sym-
bolized, vis-à-vis the techniques of selfhood we examine here, by
the prevalence in the mid-twentieth century of medical circumcision—is attributable largely to a less thoroughgoing significance
of the "Jewishness" of the Jewish self. It should not let us lose sight
of the distinctive modalities of Christian American selfhood.

Furthermore, our goal is not only to describe the present situation, but also to recover and reevaluate earlier tropes of difference and identity. Thus, rather than dismissing the significance
of marks of ethnic difference in favor of a model of voluntaristic
pluralism and an open marketplace of self-invention, it is worthwhile focusing at least briefly on Jewish circumcision as a "tribal
rite"—a scary one, more consequent and disturbing than ethnic
foods, for instance—persisting within the heart of the enlightened, civilized world. Greater attention to specific Jewish practices and the response to them, particularly in Christian European society, will, among other things, help guard us from a
tendency to dismiss circumcision as merely a particular form of
the general human tendency to grant greater ritual attention to
males. It may also suggest surprising links between the exclusion

of Jews and other forms of exclusion, especially the exclusion of women. As suggested in a review of a recent collection of essays on the medieval blood libel,

> the fact that the victims were overwhelmingly male, and that in many places Jews were accused of either circumcising these youths or of needing their blood to recover that lost in circumcision, raises questions about European ideas about ethnicity and difference. The meaning of genital marking in urban Europe and concomitant ideas about male menstruation may give us greater insights into how Christians viewed Jewish genders and biologies than can be glossed by the term anti-Semitism. (White 1992, reviewing Dundes 1991.)[3]

Such continuing and unresolved "questions about ethnicity and difference" were critical to the paroxysm of mid-twentieth-century Europe, the greatest symptom of which was Nazism. Some sense of the history of "circumcision" as a Christian trope, with its consequences for ideologies of embodiment, identity, and redemption, seems crucial to our ability to diagnose with any specificity the nature of that disease. These tensions are older than Christianity, yet they are perhaps most urgently evident in the writings of Paul. Paul was practically obsessed with circumcision. As a diacritic, the practice stood for everything that disturbed him about historical Judaism, namely its insistence on corporeality and particularly corporeal difference as a sign of real human essences. The hierarchy in his work between that which is only "according to the flesh" or "in the flesh" and that which is "ac-

---

3. The contrast between menstruation and the letting of blood in circumcision on the one hand, and the symbolic representation of the Eucharistic wine as the "blood of Christ" on the other, is consistent with a pattern in which allegorical representation is consistently seen as superior and transcendent over literal or material substances. The application of such hierarchies was later applied to newly colonized peoples. The Spanish writer Sepúlveda explained the native practice of cannibalism by arguing that "such sacrifice represented a diabolic category mistake, a substitution of a living organism, the heart, for a metaphysical entity, 'the pious and sane minds of men.' Instead of metaphorically 'sacrificing' the latter [143], the Indian literally immolates the former" (cited in Pagden 1986:143–44). Shades here—as below in an example drawn from *Jewish* discourse—of Paul's claim that the injunction to circumcise the heart supersedes the injunction to circumcise the flesh.

cording to the Spirit" or "in the Spirit" refers primarily to the practice of circumcision (which is in the flesh), as opposed to the spiritual and universal practices of Christianity (notably baptism "in the Spirit"), marked neither by ethnos nor by gender.

There is evidence that for Paul himself, circumcision made no difference one way or another (1 Corinthians 7:19). Yet when faced with opposition from Jewish Christians who believed that all Christians should be circumcised, Paul could write, "Look out for the dogs, look out for the evil workers, look out for those who mutilate the flesh" (Philippians 3:6). Consideration for a moment of the fact that for a long time Europe's Others consisted of Jews, Turks, "Saracens," and "Moors"—all circumcised, of course—yields the surprising implication that uncircumcision becomes ultimately the diacritic of Christianness, while absorption of Paul's affect as in the passage just quoted renders circumcision a highly charged negative sign of un-Christianness. Othello's cry just before his suicide that thus had he done to a circumcised Turkish dog—an allusion to Paul that educated Christian audiences could not miss—makes this claim palpable.

By the Nazi period, the affect once borne by circumcision as the marker of un-Christianness became transformed into a despising of the Jewish body itself, and circumcision retained a diacritical function of exposing the Jewish body as such. While the problem of circumcision and concealment seems to have been muted in most male Jewish survivors' accounts, it is at the center of Agnieszka Holland's film *Europa, Europa,* based on the memories of Salomon Perel. Perel, a child of Polish Jews who lived in Germany before World War II, survived the war first as an enthusiastic refugee recruit of the Young Communists in the Soviet Union, and then in Berlin and in the German army by posing as an orphaned ethnic German.

Boon has also noted Salomon Perel's remarkable claim, contained in an interview with the author that begins the film, to remember his own circumcision—something most people would consider highly unlikely for an eight-day-old infant. This exaggerated claim to remember serves both of the themes that make this film so remarkable: on the one hand the extraordinary personal talents of its protagonist, which enable him both to react promptly and to dissemble effectively; on the other hand his persistent connection to his own "rooted" Jewishness. In a subtle symmetry, the film's closing returns to Perel, and his assertion that when his own sons were born, he had them circumcised without giving it a second thought. The particular horror of the way the Nazis had turned the concealed sign on the body into a betraying mark, which made murderously clear the simultaneous historicity and panchronicity of identity, failed to prevent Perel from playing his part in this cyclical role of father and son.

By having his sons circumcised, at least as much as by his decision to live in Israel, Salomon Perel refused to eradicate the mark of difference that had so nearly cost him his life, to surrender retrospectively to the racialist-exclusive vision of Europe. At the same time, by writing his memoir, by agreeing to have it filmed, and by appearing in that film, he refused to divorce himself from the vision of Europe as open to historically informed difference. His resistance to the dominant European demand of amnesia is most dramatically signaled in his preternatural claim to remember his own circumcision in infancy.

Recently, however, there has appeared a somewhat widespread movement to refuse circumcision itself. While anti-circumcision sentiments are shared by Jews and others, they clearly have a distinctive valence among Jews. We argue that when Jews refuse to have their sons circumcised, it constitutes, at least in part, a refusal to perpetuate the double relation of Jews to the vision of humanity, simultaneously imperial and empathetic, that "Europe" represents. The mark of history and difference, which only in extraordinary circumstances blocks social or sexual intercourse with non-Jews, is replaced by a rhetoric of "wholeness."

Thus a recent article in the English journal *The Jewish Socialist*, written by an anonymous Jewish couple to explain their decision not to circumcise their infant son, refers to the pain of labor and breastfeeding, and continues with the following two sentences:

> After a couple of days of all that pain, I was certain that I could not take any more. I was simply not prepared to submit my miraculously perfect baby to an unnecessary medical intervention. ("Sharon and Stephen" 1992)

Obviously there is a powerful identification between the mother and the child here, so that the contemplation of even momentary, deliberately inflicted pain for the child is seen as a continuation of the mother's pain. And these are not the first Jewish parents to experience conflict at submitting their infant to this procedure; yet most Jewish parents, who identify with their children no less, still decide that internal conflict in favor of circumcision. Nor is there an explicit desire on these parents' parts to free their child of the burden of Jewish identity; both parents in this article express a concern that their child be able to enjoy being Jewish despite being uncircumcised.

This is not simply an argument about assimilation, then, although surely calling this millah a "medical" procedure betrays the profound involvement of these parents in a discursive paradigm that has nearly nothing to do with being Jewish at all. The distinction reminds us once again that rather than making simplistic and unidirectional claims about the weakening of group identities, we need to analyze specific techniques of difference and identity in context. What is most remarkable here is the reference to perfection, the conviction that the child as it has been born is complete and whole. This particular refusal to circumcise a child constitutes a statement of unwillingness to grant/inflict the irrevocable reminder of group identity, which in the Greco-Christian context has been and remains a confusing intermediary step between individual and generically human selfhood. The insistence on the infant's "perfection" and the denial of meaning to circumcision (calling it "an unnecessary medical intervention") may also well represent an impulse back toward a universalism, and a figuration of circumcision as mutilation, which has had radical manifestations for thousands of years. The desire of these parents for an identity that will not be marked in the body, together with a yearning for a Jewish identity that will be only enjoyed, transforms the specificity of Jewish identity into the ahistoricity of an empty three-letter name.

The "natural" as "perfect" is not a human universal, but historically contingent—even vis-à-vis different discussions of circumcision within Judaism. In rabbinic Judaism the body is not born perfect and then "marred" to socialize it; it must in fact be symbolically "corrected." Circumcision is, as it were, an excess of creation. The following text is exemplary:

> All Israelites who are circumcised will come into Paradise, for the
> Holy Blessed One placed His name on Israel, in order that they
> might come into Paradise, and what is the name and the seal which
> He placed upon them? It is ShaDaY. The Shi"n [the first letter of
> the root], he placed in the nose, the Dale"t, He placed in the hand,
> and the Yo"d in the circumcision. (Tanhuma Tsav 14, cited in Wolf-
> son 1987a:78.)

Far from being understood as a mutilation, then, or as the
disturbance of a "perfection" in nature, circumcision is figured as
a perfection of the human body that sanctifies it, indicating that
the rabbis sensed a contingency, a disjuncture in what we are accustomed to calling "nature." This sensibility resonates with the
poststructuralist critique of the modern image of a dematerialized
human subject confronting a detached nature that includes its
own "housing" (the body) and that in itself is finished, perfect,
and complete.

However, not all strands of Judaism are thus consistent at all
times. Maimonides "denies the implication that any natural thing
could be imperfect" (Stern 1991:36), and hence the rabbinic explanation that this could be the reason for circumcision—which
is consistent with Maimonides' radical bifurcation of an idealized,
apersonal Nature from an idealized Intellect. Lewis M. Barth,
in his response to Stern's paper, refers to the two *mashalim* ("parables") in Bereshit Rabbah that present the view of circumcision
as perfecting the imperfect and cite "Walk before me and be perfect" (Genesis 17:1). He claims that "in the context of the parables, the word *tamim* . . . clearly refers to physical and not spiritual
perfection" (Barth 1991:50). But why assume that this bifurcation was operative for the rabbis? Indeed, there is every reason to
assume the opposite, namely that for them there was no concept
of a spiritual perfection that did not involve a perfection of the
body, in the sense that they understood it, nor a physical perfection that would not imply or entail a spiritual perfection.

> It is written, "Thus, after my skin will have been peeled off, but
> from my flesh, I will see God" [Job 19:26]. Abraham said, after I

circumcised myself many converts came to cleave to this sign. "But from my flesh, I will see God," for had I not done this [circumcised myself], on what account would the Holy Blessed One, have appeared to me? "And the Lord appeared to him." [Genesis Rabbah 48:1, 479]

In other texts, the foreskin is explicitly called a blemish and one, moreover, that renders the person in some sense ugly. God would not want to have spiritual contact with a person who does not remove this ugliness (Wolfson 1987a:196–97).

And thus it says, "Moses said: This is the thing which the Lord has commanded that you do, in order that the Glory of the Lord may appear to you" [Lev. 9:6]. What was "this thing?" He told them about circumcision, for it says, "This is the thing which caused Joshua to perform circumcision" [Josh. 5:4].

"Which God commanded Abraham to do" [Lev. 9:6]. It may be compared to a shopkeeper who has a friend who is a priest. He had something unclean in his house, and he wanted to bring the priest into the house. The priest said to him: If you want me to go into your house, listen to me and remove that unclean thing from your house. When the shopkeeper knew that there was no unclean thing there, he went and brought the priest into his house. Similarly, the Holy, Blessed One, when He wanted to appear to Abraham, His beloved, the foreskin was appended to him. When he circumcised himself, immediately, He was revealed, as it says, "On that very day Abraham was circumcised" [Gen. 17:26], and immediately afterward "The Lord appeared to him" [Gen. 18:1].

For the rabbis, as we see here, there is no disjuncture between the physical perfection of being circumcised and that summum bonum of the spiritual life, seeing God. This, then, is the context in which the conclusion of this text must be understood as well:

Therefore, Moses said to them, God commanded Abraham, your father, to perform circumcision when He wished to appear to him. So in your case, whoever is uncircumcised, let him go out and circumcise himself, "that the Glory of the Lord may appear to you" [Lev. 9:6]. Thus Solomon said, "O Daughters of Zion, go forth and gaze upon King Solomon," the King who desires those who are perfect, as it is written, "Walk before Me and be perfect" [Gen. 17: 1], for the foreskin is a blemish upon the body [Numbers Rabbah: 12:10].

The first "perfect" in this quotation is a pun on the name of Solomon, who is taken here to be God himself, while the daughters of Zion are the circumcised males of Israel. The second "perfect" is the word at issue in the Stern-Barth discussion, and it clearly means both physical perfection, in the sense of the removal of the "blemish" of the foreskin, and the spiritual perfection implied by erotic connection with God. It is precisely this lack of a breach between the physical and the spiritual that was misunderstood in post-Pauline Western culture and even in medieval Judaism from the incursion of Platonic philosophizing on. In other words, both contemporary commentators (Stern and Barth, along with virtually all postmedieval commentators on Judaism) are complicit with Maimonides in a dualistic ontology that fails to recognize rabbinic materialist monotheism.[4]

Yet materialist monotheism does not in itself explain why the rabbis chose this particular defense of circumcision. In fact, the very insistence on the foreskin as blemish is historically a response to the charge that Jews mutilate their infants. This is precisely the same sensibility that we find reoccurring today, along with attacks on the very notion of prophylactic circumcision—and a new fashion for piercing various body parts! Ideas of bodily perfection and imperfection, of what is counted as mutilation and what as adornment, are conditioned by the politics of identity. In the case of the rabbis (who apparently represented a *minority* of the Jews of their time), as in so many other cases, the pathos arises from the pressure on the smaller group to surrender its identity to the larger and more powerful one, and from the internal urgency to resist.

In a revealing way, then, the debates over distinctive bodily markings in late antiquity echo in debates going on in the time that some refer to as late modernity. To misappropriate a term from poststructuralist theory, the foreskin may be seen as one kind of "supplement," the removal of which, over generations for thou-

---

4. Stern does recognize the gap between the rabbis and Maimonides that Barth attempts to reduce.

sands of years, makes the male Jewish self. The tradition of covering the head is a historically variable supplement that when added helps make the male Jewish self in a different way.

In different chronotopes, these two kinds of sign have varied considerably in their significance. The headcovering is much more recent as a specifically Jewish practice, although of course Jewish men have in many times and places worn the same kinds of headcoverings others living around them have worn. From the "biblical" age until this century, circumcision has generally been much more effective as a distinguishing mark of the male Jew. A quick census of attendees at an academic convention in America at present, however, will reveal that most males—religious Jews, nonreligious Jews, and non-Jews—are circumcised, while virtually everyone will readily identify a man with a headcovering like ours as an Orthodox Jew.

To some degree, the extent to which these two marks are matters of personal choice also varies historically and socially. One's "own" circumcision can be taken as given,[5] a point we will develop below. The freedom to decide whether or not to have a Jewish child circumcised, as we have just documented, seems at present to be growing. The headcovering, on the other hand, is today virtually mandatory for Jewish males—but only if they want to be accepted as bona fide members of Orthodox Jewish communities. One of us at least understands his headcovering more as a public mark of Jewishness than as conformity to Orthodox custom.

Although the precise history of such shifts is not to the point here, it was necessary to indicate that the two marks are them-

---

5. Although perhaps not irreversible. The Knoxville, Tennessee, *Metro Pulse* for the week of April 27–May 3 1992 picked this up from the San Jose *Mercury-News:* "An organization of several dozen men meets regularly in the San Francisco area to discuss ways to restore their foreskins. . . . RECAP ('Recover a Penis') members are divided as to technique between surgical reconstruction and 'stretching,' described by founder Wayne Griffiths as pulling loose skin over his penis and taping it in place using 'Foreballs,' a device he invented, consisting of two small ball bearings that add weight to pull the skin down. Griffiths said he wore the device for up to 12 hours a day, five days a week, for a year, and that he now has enough skin to cover the head of his penis without taping. 'The [sexual] feelings are sensational,' he said. Said a urologist who supports the group, 'They want to enhance their image whether it's in their pants or on their face. Who am I to say otherwise? No way. No way.' "

selves bound up in history. Thus, for example, any attempt to determine the meanings of Jewish circumcision at present in America cannot be limited to biblical references or rabbinic homiletics, but must take into account a situation where circumcision is quite common among non-Jews, and anti-Semitism, while present, is relatively muted.

Sensitivity to historical variations in the markings of ethnic difference is a necessary resource for an effective debate over their contemporary functions and their fate. A recent prescription for critical thinking about subjecthood by the political theorist William E. Connolly offers a brace of criteria against which to measure the effects of the male Jewish diacritics we are examining:

> [Thought] may also treat historical variations in forms of selfhood, normality, and otherness as signs of the element of contrivance and contingency in each historically hegemonic formation, thereby multiplying sites at which the issues of freedom and unfreedom can be posed in late-modern life: the time of late modernity itself (as a system of interdependencies without a collectively organized agent), the state (as a center of collective agency and social discipline), the normalized self (as the center of individual agency and self-discipline), the external other produced by this standard of normality, and that in the self which resists normalization (the internal other). Each of these becomes a potential site of freedom and constraint. (1991:35)

Connolly's prescription is at once extremely abstract and remarkably inclusive. The balance of this essay will constitute a response to the five considerations Connolly articulates, analyzing particular instances in which circumcision and the headcovering are deployed in contemporary life as sites of assertion, construction, and assault on identity.

1. The "time of late-modernity itself." As many theorists have pointed out, the particular chronological interrogation characteristic of postmodernism logically forbids us to discuss it as simply another "period," analogous to the Renaissance or the Age of Reason. Rather, "time" changes, taking on distinctive characteristics in our world. As suggested in our opening remarks about circumcision as part of an alternative to the ideology of the self-made man, we operate with a concept according to which connec-

tions are not merely "with the past" along a line of time, but rather multidirectional and located inside a chronotopic field. This understanding is consistent with the sense of recursiveness, the "drag" or hold of the past implicit in the usages "late" or "post" modernity.

Even though most Jewish men, unlike Salomon Perel, do not recall their own circumcisions and are not expected to, the communally sanctioned and communally observed ceremony and the mark it leaves nevertheless serve as reminders that the world existed before one was conscious of it, and will continue to exist after one's own consciousness is extinguished. The organism is bounded not only spatially, but chronologically as well; as an isolate, it has no access to its temporal beyond. Such access is in principle unavailable to the self-made man as well, who must frantically endeavor to create monuments to himself.[6] (A well-publicized recent example is the shrine to the career of Ross Perot located at his corporate headquarters.)

Only in a communal relationship (which of course need not be a "traditional" religious or ethnic community) can such access, or temporal extension of the self, become possible, as Jean-Luc Nancy suggests: "Only the community can present me my birth, and along with it the impossibility of my reliving it, as well as the impossibility of my crossing over into my death" (Nancy 1991 : 15). It is worthwhile stressing that the unavailability to the isolated organism of its birth and death calls into question the possessive forms "me" and "mine" here.

The insistence on a form of "selfhood" that is not plotted out on a nonrepeating, unidirectional time line further challenges language that sees ritual as an aspect of static "social structure." Even the more currently fashionable term "mimesis" is inadequate as a description of the painful cut that simultaneously separates and connects.[7] For who is doing the mimesis here, and who

6. That the phrase "self-made man" is not immediately perceived as oxymoronic is another indication of the dualism that pervades hegemonic modern thinking. Of course nobody is self-made. The more obvious link between women's bodies and the making of other human beings might help to explain why we seldom hear the phrase "self-made woman."

7. In biblical Hebrew, the verb used for making a covenant is precisely "cutting," and another famous covenant between God and Abraham is sealed by Abraham's walking between the cut halves of a sacrificed animal (Genesis 15). It may be en-

is being imitated? The father his father? Perhaps: When Jonah Sampson Boyarin was circumcised, the rabbi present asked rhetorically how the acceptance of circumcision upon himself by an eight-day-old infant could be regarded as the voluntary fulfillment of a commandment. His answer was that the voluntary aspect of this ritual is realized later on, when the child, now grown, permits his own child to be circumcised.

What does Rabbi Singer's homily leave then of the claim by Philippe Lacoue-Labarthe that "there is no subject prior to imitation" (in *La Fiction du Politique,* summarized in Kronick 1990: 137–38)? The structure of the homily suggests that the infant is dependent not only on his father to carry out the commandment of circumcision, but on his promised son as someone upon whom he can then consciously perform the commandment (quite evidently another motivation of whatever preference the tradition may show for offspring bearing penises). The subject or self does not simply imitate an elder and thus sequentially take its place; rather, as a bundle of operated bodily signs, intentions, and actions it is distributed across a temporal weave, a textile or text.

Lacoue-Labarthe's point about the link between imitation and subjectivity also serves as a critique of the self-made man: there is no pure originality, for all subjective action has at least a moment of imitation. In the discursive tradition of rabbinic Judaism, this point is embraced. Discovering that something has already been said by someone greater is no diminution, but an enhancement, and there is an explicit redemptive value attached to citation. As the Talmud avers: "One who cites an utterance in the name of its original speaker brings redemption to the world" (*Ethics of the Fathers,* chap. 6).

2. The "state." While the hegemonic nation-state form per se doubtless bears criticism in its relation to the construal of selfhood, the relation of Jews to different kinds of states differs so

---

tirely too convenient to insist that such symbolism reflects the awareness that such covenants always entail a diminution, a sort of violence to what we fondly take to be the autonomous self. On the other hand, the puzzlement this symbolism evokes among contemporary readers of the Bible suggests that, even though we say "cut a deal," we would much prefer not to be cut by the deals we make. See also Schwartz 1992.

greatly as to make the general question almost inapplicable. Suffice it to say, before entering into specific illustrations, that whereas pre-modern "states" often sought to enforce Jewish distinctiveness by the prescription of distinctive clothing, modern, secular states generally remain neutral or militate against such distinctions.[8] On the other hand, the Jewish state under certain regimes has subtly encouraged the headcovering as a religious-nationalist mark. Thus Menachem Begin, certainly not an Orthodox Jew, campaigned beneath a yarmulke to mark his distance from the secularist and socialist Labor Party, and also to reinforce the link between his party's longtime goal of conquering "Greater Israel" on one hand, and biblical injunctions and promises concerning the land on the other.

Not all Jewish men in Israel or elsewhere who wear a kippah or yarmulke are sympathetic to Jewish-nationalist exclusivism. In fact, different styles of headcovering may sometimes be correlated with differing political stances. The *kippah sruga*, or knitted yarmulke, is generally associated with Modern Orthodoxy and religious nationalism. Certain older styles of headcovering—the round felt hat worn by certain Hasidim, the pure white knitted and pom-pommed yarmulke sported by others—mark the *haredim*, who proclaim that their Judaism does not require a state, or is inimical to the idea of a humanly established Jewish state. Though the styles of the headcoverings that Daniel and Jonathan wear are no clue, we are two more who are opposed to Jewish state nationalism.

When religious Jews venture to communicate with Palestinians suffering Israeli occupation, they face a difficult choice. Certainly, as a matter of physical safety, the guest on the West Bank who does not want to be taken for a settler should not cover his head in public. But during the summer of 1991, when the younger of us introduced the elder to a Palestinian physician

8. Thus there has been a series of lawsuits over the issue of Orthodox Jewish men being permitted to wear beards or to cover their heads while serving in the U.S. military. A more spectacular recent example is the case of the two young Muslim girls from North African families who insisted on veiling their faces when they went to public school. The French state strongly resisted, relented in the face of massive Muslim agitation, and ultimately reversed itself once again, refusing to permit the veil. In that case the major French Jewish organizations actively sided with the Muslims.

friend in Ramallah, Daniel chose to put his yarmulke back on
once we were in our friends' house. When Jonathan next visited
the friend, several weeks later, the physician's wife apologized for
failing to introduce herself and her two young daughters to Daniel on the previous visit. "It's the kippah," she explained. "I know
that your brother's a friend, but you have to understand that to us
it's a frightening symbol; it makes us think the person wearing it
is a murderer. My daughter was convinced that your brother had
a gun." Daniel's intention was to reclaim the symbol from the racist connotations it has acquired, but at least momentarily, he was
defeated. The use of the headcovering as an "opening," examples
of which we offer below, doesn't always work—especially not when
the ethnic symbol is confused with a symbol of state power.

The same yarmulke can be an instrument of resistance to
[Jewish!] state power as well and via the same reification. During
the siege of Bet-Sahour, a town near Bethlehem that undertook
a tax revolt and was cut off economically and socially by the occupying forces to punish it, various Israeli peace and solidarity
groups tried to get through to bring greetings. On one occasion
in September of 1989, a convoy of fifty cars set out from Jerusalem. All were stopped at the check-post except for the one carrying Daniel and several other Orthodox leftists. The soldiers assumed, and we did nothing to disabuse them of their assumption,
that we were settlers heading home to our colony just beyond Bet-
Sahour. As a result of this tricksterism, we were able to bring back
an appeal from the people of the embattled town for solidarity
from Israelis of goodwill. The statement was read by Daniel with
yarmulke/kippah before the television cameras of Europe and
broadcast to millions of viewers throughout the Arab world, affording him fifteen minutes of fame. More important, the moment of fame his yarmulke was afforded disrupted in some small
way the obviousness and univocity of its political meanings.

Circumcision remains a much more nearly ubiquitous practice among Jewish males, and it has not been co-opted by the Jewish state in the same way.[9] Indeed, a relatively early Jewish critique
of circumcision suggests that while the state is masculine, cir-

---

9. Given, however, the nature of ideological state apparatuses and the recently
well-publicized circumcisions of adult immigrants from the former Soviet Union,
this claim may require modification.

cumcision represents an alternate ground of continued collective existence, one inimical to statehood. Thus Spinoza:

> The sign of circumcision is, as I think, so important, that I could persuade myself that it alone would preserve the [Jewish] nation for ever. Nay, I would go so far as to believe that if the foundations of their religion have not emasculated their [the Jews'] minds they may even, if occasion offers, so changeable are human affairs, raise up their empire afresh, and that God may a second time elect them. (Geller 1993:59; also Popkin 1990:431, both citing the Tractatus Theologico-Politicus, 1951 ed., chap. 3, p. 56.)

From our perspective—concerned with Jewish continuity, troubled by some Jewish practices in the light of contemporary criticism, and skeptical of the very desire for an ethnic Jewish state—this is an ambiguous and suggestive statement. Spinoza, hardly an apologist for Jewish Orthodoxy, confirms the central role of male circumcision in guaranteeing the continuity of group identity. But this form of sublimation has had a deleterious effect on the Jews' "minds"—presumably, sapping their pride and independence. For Spinoza, the kind of identity that this practice affords is a sort of sick substitute, which feminizes the [male] Jews and prevents them from erecting ("raising up") their state anew.[10] The reacquisition of a Jewish state would occur despite, not because of, the powerful practice that sustains them in exile. The talk of emasculation and erection linked to statehood is yet another example of the ways in which the modern state is typically figured as male, and the association of Jews with the feminine is also a common theme among both ancient rabbis and modern anti-Semites (Olender 1992). What is more interesting here is the specific way in which circumcision, as a ritual that binds the collective, also cripples the capacity for autonomous masculine action (the reacquisition of a state). Yet with all this, Spinoza affirms that group identity need not be vouchsafed in a nation-state.

3. The "normalized self." The sense in which Connolly uses the term "normalized" here relates primarily to an identity that is unproblematized, taken for granted, or given. In America right now, circumcision is virtually negligible as an agent for provoking

---

10. For discussion of the association between circumcision and castration, see Shell 1988:216, fn. 61 and references therein.

reflections on history, identity, and selfhood; Spinoza's claims for its power would seem out of place in a society where a circumcised penis need not be attached to a Jew. In fact, aside from the fact that it is visible rather than hidden, the headcovering—almost always a style that only Jews wear—is much more effective as a "regulator" of behavior and reminder of identity, as a social mark.

This does not yet mean that circumcision, the mark on the body, is unavailable as a ground for further reflection. If indeed we are correct, and Connolly's "normalization" can be glossed as "givenness," then in a sense the normalized self is an anomaly, as Michael Holquist suggests: "The situatedness of the self is a complicated phenomenon: it has been given the task of not being merely given" (Holquist 1989:15). Connolly acknowledges this further on, when he refers to "that in the self which resists normalization"; but whereas his language of "resistance" retains an individualist, "anti-totalitarian" residue, Holquist opts instead for a paradoxical statement of the tension between givenness (this is me) and construction (I am because making makes a "me") in selfhood.

The gap between the two marks of identity—each having its own valence vis-à-vis the tension of givenness and construction—thus becomes in some ways more acute in a period such as the twentieth century, when a large plurality of Jewish males are circumcised and yet do not actively practice Judaism or identify as religious Jews. Where there is this disjuncture between the promise implied by the prehistory of the self on one hand, and the practices (no matter how deliberately or casually settled on) of adulthood on the other, it becomes remarkably unclear what, exactly, constitutes "the normalized self": the circumcision, sign of inclusion within a limited community with its own high expectations; or the bare head, which accedes to the "normal" expectations of the broader social world.

The point here of course is not to resolve this last point in favor of "assimilation" or "Orthodoxy," but rather to insist, following Holquist again, on the complex situation of any "identity."[11] To stereotype and freeze "the Jew" in time collapses the

---

11. This common term is set off in quotation marks here because it bears a prejudicial charge against ambiguity.

particular webs of relation entailed and enabled by a practice like circumcision, and makes it available for the sort of derision indulged in by the Latin author Petronius, who thus noted its ritual/legal centrality:

> "The Jew may worship his pig-god and clamor in the ears of high heaven, but unless he also cuts back his foreskin with the knife, he shall go forth from the people and emigrate to Greek cities and shall not tremble at the fasts of Sabbath imposed by the law" (Frag. 37). (Cited in Collins 1985:163)

What Petronius elides is precisely the moment of kinship, generation, and ethnicity; for a Roman individualist, there is no difference between Jewish parents having their sons circumcised and "the Jew" circumcising himself.[12] The moment of connection and separation is rhetorically degraded into a slavish and barbaric practice through the assumption of a singular "Jew" who is at once an ethnic stereotype and a disconnected individual. Like the modern self-made man, Petronius' Jew is perfectly and seamlessly responsible for himself; the portrait admits no prehistory

4. The "external other." As we suggested above, the head-covering is more significant in America for this desideratum now than circumcision, which ironically enough fails to produce an external other. In our brief discussion of the politics of identity vis-à-vis the state above, we have suggested how the headcovering tends to reinforce a symbolically and physically violent exclusion of the non-Jewish other from the Jewish state. It is not that most Israeli men cover their heads, nor even that a "normative Israeli" public identity requires the headcovering. Yet the very facts that the state is Jewish; that, in this context, certain types of headcovering reliably indicate that their wearer is Jewish; and that only a minority of those who so cover their heads do not share the tenets of Jewish state nationalism, tend to reinforce the suggestion that this place is for Jews only.

Outside of the Jewish state, the headcovering is also enforced

---

12. Compare the detemporalized and radically individualist critique of culture by Walter Benn Michaels (1992), and our response to Michaels, which forms part of our essay "Diaspora: Generation and the Ground of Jewish Identity" (D. Boyarin and J. Boyarin 1993).

as a mark of conformity to standards of belonging to various religious Jewish collectives. Jews' "external others," that is, may also be other Jews, and the headcovering—generally speaking, unlike circumcision—is readily available for the drawing of this kind of distinction.

Yet such distinctions among Jews need not be pernicious. When they are explicitly articulated, they are sometimes contrasted to a more profound unity that transcends such superficial differences.

An example of such expression is contained in an anecdote told years ago to Jonathan Boyarin by Dr. Shlomo Noble. Noble had once served as an official translator in a court proceeding involving a Hasidic *rebbe* who was also a diamond merchant. Noble realized that the rebbe's response to a certain question might incriminate the rebbe, and rather than translating it immediately, he claimed he hadn't understood the response and asked the rebbe to repeat it. The rebbe took the hint and rephrased his response more judiciously. Later he said to Noble, "Even though you go around bareheaded, nevertheless you have a Jewish heart." The metaphor of "heart" may seem trite to us because it seems to echo Paul's rhetoric, which tells his followers that they need only observe the biblical command to circumcise their hearts—that is, to keep the moral spirit of the law, which is "love"—and not the commandment to circumcise their flesh—here, the equivalent of the external symbol, the headcovering.

Outside the Jewish state, and especially where Orthodox Jews are clearly a minority presence, the headcovering can be a mark of openness and vulnerability, rather than defensiveness or exclusion vis-à-vis non-Jews. Three vignettes occasioned by Jonathan's walking around Lower Manhattan wearing a yarmulke in recent months illustrate different aspects of this claim.

—As he walks through a Latino block late one evening, a young man sitting in front of a bodega calls out "Salaam aleikum!" three times, until the anthropologist finally turns to acknowledge the greeting and mutely waves back, too confused to reply appropriately in Arabic, "Wa'aleikum salaam!" No less than three rather surprising ethnographic points may be surmised from this: First, that young Latinos have been influenced by the Islamization of urban African-American culture; second, that at least in this case, hostility toward Jews does not accompany this cultural influence; third, that for certain urban groups exposed to aspects of both Jewish and Arabic culture, the two are interchangeable. The yarmulke on East Houston Street thus serves as a lightning rod for information that confounds stereotypes.

—One Friday evening while Jonathan is walking to the synagogue, a man passing by him says, "L'chaim." He's fairly tall, "looks like an Indian," wears a studded sort of denim motorcycle jacket and two black braids. He announces that he's a Jewish Indian. He responds to a friendly question that he's originally from South Dakota. The anthropologist, who has had little contact with Native Americans, asks him what "people" he belongs to (a phrase learned from Tony Hillerman's books), but has to ask instead "What tribe?" before the man replies that he's a Sioux. But, he explains, as fate turned out, he was adopted by Jews and raised in Englewood Cliffs. You're a long way from home, Jonathan says sympathetically, but the Jewish Indian replies, "I'm the landlord. . . . This whole country belongs to me."

—One Saturday night as Jonathan walks along East Tenth Street toward his office, four white male teenagers pass by. As they approach one says loudly ". . . and there's too many faggots at the club." Passing on, he adds (seeing the yarmulke), "Oh, he's Jewish." Evidently something about Jonathan had clued the bully into the presumption that Jonathan should be branded a faggot. When he gained more information, his verbal assault on this passerby became more precise.[13] Had the yarmulke not been present to draw the scornful designation "he's Jewish," Jonathan would not even have realized that he was being targeted as queer. The yarmulke—often taken as a symbol of conservative "family values"—here thus served as a medium of enforced empathy between different threatened marginal groups.

In other chronotopes, of course—indeed, in most Jewish communities at most times—the particular way in which Jews practice circumcision has been much more significant as a means

13. The gay community in New York City has recently organized self-defense patrols to counter a dramatic increase in anti-gay street violence. Not until I read a street poster for a march against anti-gay violence while writing a draft of this essay did I realize that I had also risked physical violence on the street that night.

of production of self and other; in both Hebrew and Yiddish, *orel,* "uncircumcised one," is a common term for a non-Jewish male. Yet the double function of circumcision as separation and connection does not apply only to the relation between generations. Circumcision, the ultimate site of male Jewish difference, is also available as an opening toward the Other. In Albert Memmi's autobiographical novel *The Pillar of Salt* (Memmi 1992 [1955]), the narrator, a Jew growing up in Tunis in the 1930s, describes being on a streetcar with various characters—a Bedouin, a Frenchwoman, a "Mohammedan" and his two-and-a-half-year-old son, and a Djerban grocer. The grocer begins a socially accepted form of teasing the little boy, asking whether he's been circumcised yet, confirming that it's going to happen soon, and offering successively higher bids for his "little animal," eventually snatching at the child's groin in mock frustration and provoking the boy's real terror.

This brings the narrator back to a remembered scene in his *kouttab* school (the North African counterpart of the East European *heder*) in which, the teacher having briefly gone out and the class exhausting their anarchic impulse, they "felt that we needed one another and discovered that we were a crowd . . . [then] soon returned to ancestral traditions and decided to play, like adults, at circumcision." They chose one of the younger boys as the victim and carried out a mock circumcision, acting the roles of their fathers and their future selves, until the victim burst out crying and they all collapsed into helpless laughter. The scene from the narrator's school, in which he simultaneously identifies with the victim and is thrilled as part of the crowd performing the sacrifice, allows him an imaginative identification with the Muslim child in the trolley car who, unlike a Jewish infant, will in fact be aware of the cut that is about to be made on his body. The sentences that link the two parts of the chapter confirm this: "Can I ever forget the Orient? It is deeply rooted in my flesh and blood, and I need but touch my own body to feel how I have been marked for all time by it. As though it were all a mere matter of cultures and of elective affinities!" (1992:169).

This is a complex statement. Memmi is postulating an Orient from a position outside it, and simultaneously identifying with it. He is asserting as a link to fellow "Orientals" that which is usually taken (in Europe) as exclusively Jewish. Furthermore, he is making a strong claim for "primal" or given identity against modern bourgeois voluntarism. The notion of "cultures" he derides here is one in which a culture is something one affiliates with, entirely separate from genealogy.

The point of each of these stories is that there is no a priori reason to assume that marks of group identity do more to isolate their bearers from members of other groups than to multiply the possible channels of relation between them. Such an a priori assumption is, of course, consistent with a residual Durkheimian notion that in social life solidarity is essential and contingent relations accidental.[14] The possibilities we have pointed to here respond instead to Connolly's call for an interrogation of the link between the production of an external other and issues of freedom and unfreedom.

5. The "internal other." Coming at the end of the list, this desideratum—laudable for its recognition that antagonism "within" the self is to be expected and looked for, rather than regarded as pathological—hardly seems to have its own effective dynamic that would attract certain citations or anecdotes to itself. Rather, through our discussion of the simultaneous separation and connection that is performed by circumcision, and the ways in which the headcovering can serve to open up unexpected empathies within the self, it has become evident that the divide between internal and external others is only rigidly maintainable within a field of distinctions imagined spatially as between two integral and spatially discrete organisms.

Chronologically, this distinction breaks down more and more, particularly as new technologies affect the relationship between experience and consciousness. Where Salomon Perel rhetorically affects "remembering" his own circumcision, and Albert Memmi finds a form of empathetic connection to a Muslim child who is to be circumcised at the age of self-awareness, the by now much more mundane medium of videotaping enables a young Jewish child to re-experience, as it were, his own circumcision ceremony. We hasten to assure the reader that neither of us was so gauche as

14. The strategy of separating the "essential" from the "accidental" is employed in Western thinking from Aristotle to Hegel.

to film our son's circumcision. A distant relative was kind enough to do that for one of us, however, and so we were able to witness the star of that video, by now age three or four, calling out just before the scene of the fateful cut: "Don't do it!" In a sense that is hardly literal yet still more than allegorical, a simulacrum of one's own circumcision now can be experienced. This suggests a potential heightening of reflection as an integral aspect of self-fashioning. But, once again, there seems no point in trying to determine whether the infant depicted on the television screen is the "internal" or "external" other of the watching child.

The suggestion we are making in this section—that "resistance," rather than being concentrated in some "internal other" that is the locus of individualistic reflection, may be dispersed throughout the various other forms of self-effect that Connolly identifies—contrasts with a passage where Connolly makes clear his association of givenness with inauthenticity. There, criticizing Sartre, he refers to "self-generated pressures toward inauthenticity (pressures to treat identity as given or true rather than forged or chosen)" (1991:103). Yet Connolly hasn't really demonstrated that treating identity as given or true is universally "inauthentic," or—more to the point—necessarily repressive, since he fails to consider that certain identities are themselves, roughly speaking, "hegemonic" and others "resistant." Nor does he quite acknowledge how historically specific is the ideal of treating identity as forged or chosen.[15]

Most important for our discussion here is an assumption that remains implicit within Connolly's argument: that an ironic stance toward given identities is a modern consciousness unfamiliar to "traditional" discourses; that it is something we should and can only cultivate afresh from within ourselves. While Connolly explicitly acknowledges the embeddedness of the self and the necessity of a moment of prior givenness in selfhood, he does not see these as sources for a tolerant play of difference. Rather, the

15. Although, to be fair, he is careful not to advance his ideal as an inevitable or necessary one: "Such a counter-doctrine cannot advance itself as a singular truth. It must not, for instance, strive to purge doctrines that rest upon faith in a true identity or a particular god. It seeks, instead, to give voice to a perspective with a reverence of its own and to limit the extent to which the voices of strong identity can define the terms through which alter-identities are recognized and responsibility is distributed. It seeks to politicize identity and responsibility" (118).

compromises he offers recall the reluctant acknowledgment of human corporeality in certain strands of Christian thinking.

These assertions are not made to dismiss Connolly's lucid discussion. They are rather intended to suggest how difficult it is to negotiate in theory the intellectual tightrope between a celebration of what he would call capital-I Identity on the one hand, and a subtle recourse to the ideal of the autonomous subject on the other. Judith Butler warns that to ignore relations (of kin, and other kinds) is to reproduce the alienated modern subject: "The subject is constituted through an exclusion and differentiation, perhaps a repression, that is subsequently concealed, covered over, by the effect of autonomy. In this sense, autonomy is the logical consequence of a disavowed dependency" (1991:157).

We have been arguing throughout this essay that what theory discusses as the negotiation of pulls toward "individual" and "collective" selfhood, toward conscious autonomy and given relatedness, is imperfectly effected in Judaism through the double mark of the male Jew.[16] If we take the avowal of dependency in Jewish ritual as "that in the self which resists ['self-making'] normalization," then circumcision and the headcovering can indeed be conceived (!) as sites for critical posing of freedom and unfreedom.

A last word remains to be written, however, for as it stands we seem to have striven simply to "vindicate" our own Identity against yet another call for reflexive self-awareness. On the contrary, this investigation itself should stand as evidence that we endorse Connolly's program of investigating the way in which our own identity is constructed. Even though we have emphasized the ways in which traditional signs offer the possibility of a dialogic and nonhierarchical construction of identity, we certainly agree that those signs need also to be examined in their overreaching and imperious effects. Yet we cannot agree that such a critical stance need be opposed to "the voices of strong identity," for as we claimed at the outset, such are our voices. "Weak" or poorly informed identities can be shrilly defensive. "Strong" identities can—it seems obvious once stated—be resilient, self-confident,

16. Imperfectly not only since we have already rejected perfection as a criterion, but more specifically because the mark of circumcision is itself "concealed, covered over" in public.

and ironic. Indeed, identities that bear within themselves the marks of their own generation are most likely to tolerate a "generative doubt" that affords the possibility of "non-isomorphic subjects, agents, and territories of stories unimaginable from the vantage point of the cyclopian, self-satiated eye of the master subject" (Haraway 1991 : 192). Such an alternative vantage point is potentially afforded by the double mark of the male Jew.

⌇THREE⌇

Death and the Minyan

> Blanchot . . . writes: "The Jews incarnate . . . the refusal of myths, the abandonment of idols, the recognition of an ethical order that manifests itself in respect for the law. What Hitler wants to annihilate in the Jew, in the 'myth of the Jew,' is precisely man freed from myth." This is another way of showing where and when myth was definitively interrupted. I would add this: "man freed from myth" belongs henceforth to a community that it is incumbent upon us to let come, to let write itself. (Nancy 1991: 162, fn. 40, citing Blanchot 1984.)

> "Nobody is entitled not to belong to my *absence of community*."
> —Georges Bataille[1]

I. INTRODUCTION

The hierarchical and spatially enforced bifurcation between the practice of ethnography and the discourse of social theory has been undermined in recent decades both by intellectual developments and by world events. Attempts to simply "apply" atopic theories to local situations no longer go unquestioned, whether because of a heightened respect for the particularities of experience or because of greater awareness that the theories themselves are irrevocably linked to their own "local situations." This critical awareness does not necessarily attach itself to contemporary philosophy, however, even when the philosophical work deals with questions that are at the core of decades of ethnographic study. All too easily, even the most politically concerned philosophers

---

1. Cited by Maurice Blanchot in *The Unavowable Community* (1982:3–4). Blanchot's text, translated and published in English before the book by Nancy on which I focus here, is an important commentary and articulation of Nancy. The preface by Pierre Joris to the Blanchot book sets Nancy's work in the context of the writings of Bataille.

still proceed as if the remnants of post-Christian European modernism were generalizable as a universal condition of humankind. In this essay, therefore, I intend to juxtapose an important and frustrating recent French philosophical statement on "community" (Nancy 1986, 1991) with shards of ethnographic narrative from a *very* local situation.[2]

It's not particularly old, as Lower East Side synagogues go. It's not large: one of what I call the "tenement shuls," squeezed long and narrow into lots laid out for crowded immigrant housing. It is not yet the only mark of Jewish presence on this mostly Latino block; across the street is a small shop with a sign bearing the name "Moyshe Hans," and then in English: "Tropical worsted suits." Twice a day still, morning and evening, Rabbi Singer manages to cajole or conjure a minyan, a quorum of ten male adult Jews, to satisfy the minimal demands of presence for collective Jewish prayer.

And I am one who be/comes there. Already I have written obstinately, against some putative allegorization of the name "Jew" into a hall of signifying mirrors, about my walking to this synagogue every morning (J. Boyarin 1992b:introduction). The early hour and the rundown, mostly Latino neighborhood in which the synagogue now finds itself both contribute to a sense that I have a secret yet very real world outside of my professional academic context. More intimately, the leather straps I wind tightly around my forearm leave briefly on my skin the marks of male Jewish practice. Having chosen to incorporate this daily binding of *tefillin* into my theoretical writing as an image of intersection with the Jewish world beyond, I left unwritten there the difficult question of whether my putting on tefillin, in the presence of other Jews, should be thought of as participation in a "community."

In fact that very rhetorical invocation of "practice" and earlier writings about the surviving Jewish institutions of the Lower East Side in which I glossed marginality as redemptive are both

2. Although I cite the English translation for convenience, I am in fact considering here only the first three chapters of the English volume, which comprise the whole of the 1986 French volume.

I would like to thank Daniel Boyarin and Shimen Schneebalg for helpful criticisms.

grounded in a professional genre of salvage ethnography and an esthetic of nostalgia whose critical force is, and will here remain, highly problematic.[3] The implicit claim in these writings is that the persistence of such marginal social forms as Orthodox congregations consisting of a bare quorum of elderly or single Jewish men (quite different from the resurgent character of "traditionalistic" religious movements) provides an alternative to elite criticism as a ground for interrupting the numbing corporatism of passive, consumerist culture. In response to an impossible choice between secular "democracies" that attempt to collapse identity into immediate purchasing power and gratification, and militant ethnic nationalisms greedy for state power and murderously exclusive control of space, such marginal social forms can plausibly be presented as resistant communities of memory. Yet it is impossible—for me at least—to articulate that claim without recourse to the terms of elite criticism.

The solution I opt for here is to set Rabbi Singer's minyan in an agonistic written "dialogue" (see Esonwanne 1990–91) with the pretentious yet questioning terms of Nancy's book. It cannot be stressed enough: the point is not to *raise* ethnographic detail to the level of abstract universality at which philosophy rests. Because their actual and potential membership is so severely limited, because of the antagonisms that pervade them, and because their prospects for continuity beyond the present generation seem virtually nonexistent, it would seem that formations like Rabbi Singer's minyan can hardly be packaged as generalizable models for community.

It remains tempting to write nostalgically of (Jewish) community (especially) as a survival. And yet it remains important to guard against the rhetoric of "survivals" today, because the word presumes the existence of the past of authentic community, when such a presumption in our own present is precisely what we are

3. The recourse to "practice" as a stand-in for some reality outside of the critical gaze is analogous to the comparably widespread discussion of "the body." Michel de Certeau years ago moved away from a conception of "practice" as the subcultures of minorities, and of marginality as limited to such subcultural identities: "Marginality is today no longer limited to minority groups, but is rather massive and pervasive. . . . Marginality is becoming universal. A marginal group has now become a silent majority" (1984:xvii). I trust nevertheless that de Certeau would not regard the present investigation as retrogressive.

trying to interrogate. Richard Terdiman acutely describes the ambiguity of our shared sense of a loss of community:

> It would seem that the problem of community has a clearly determined conjunctural pertinence—namely, the disappearance of our sense of the collective. Social solidarity seems an idealization from some prelapsarian world, a world we distinctly appear to have lost. (Terdiman 1991:112)

As Terdiman goes on to suggest, the very words he uses to describe a situation here—"seem"; "disappearance"; "idealization"; "distinctly appear"—contain the paradox of our doubting that what we mourn the loss of ever existed. So many brutalities, so many violations of any notion of humanly responsible community have been carried out in the name of solidary collectives supposed to have obtained in the past, that Nancy, whose ideas in *The Inoperative Community* Terdiman is directly responding to here, seems to have renounced any possible recourse to memory in his attempt to think through the possibility of there ever being community without coercion. Of there ever *being:* the only community that does not betray the hope invested in that word, Nancy argues, is one that resists any kind of stable existence (Nancy 1991:58). According to this reasoning, there can *be* no generalizable models of community. Rabbi Singer's minyan does not fail the test of generalizability, because that test has already been shown to be invalid.

The problem is that Nancy has in fact attempted a generalized model of community as *nonbeing.* Hence any already existing "community" is out of consideration by its very existence, relegated through philosophical necessity to a world we have lost or that never existed. Following Nancy's rhetoric, the only possible residues of that lost world are false community appearing as either a serial, undifferentiated collective in the same analytic category as the Fascist mass, or alternatively an assemblage of unrelated individuals. And "the individual is merely the residue of the experience of the dissolution of community" (3). And if the members of the minyan turn out to be insufficiently individuated, that is, I suppose, not philosophers? Then where do they exist, if at all?

I want to press, in a sense by literalizing, the opening offered by Nancy in the footnote cited as an epigraph to this essay. The quote from Blanchot seems ambiguous if not contradictory: do the Jews literally "incarnate the refusal of myths," or is that one of Hitler's myths? I will first pursue the first reading, which is both the more flattering and the more dangerous. This reading would tell us that community without myth was once the special possession of the Jews. Nancy's "addition" would then explore the consequences of the release of that secret to "us" as a result of the genocide. What else, after all, can "henceforth" mean? I deeply respect the fact that this and other work of Nancy's is explicitly motivated by the desire to understand and "unwork" the complicity between philosophy and twentieth-century violence (see, for example, Lacoue-Labarthe and Nancy 1990). Nancy would doubtless be horrified and/or furious at the suggestion that his rhetoric is complicit in perpetuating the cultural annihilation of the Jew, yet it seems clear that this is one potential accomplishment of his further allegorization of Blanchot. *That which the Jew represented before "he" was annihilated is that which "we" must let come, must let write itself.* The word "henceforth" indeed implies that the secret of freedom from myth has passed from the Jews to a community that does not exist, that is only imaginable in and by theory. The secret becomes potentially available to all who await a second coming of this sacrificed Jew.

I insist that this plausible yet "uncharitable" reading cannot be stretched to an accusation of anti-Judaism. On the contrary, it is clear that Nancy and thinkers like him are committed to a sympathetic philosophical comprehension of the existence and annihilation of the Jews. My claim is rather that within the thought of philosophers such as Nancy lies a blindness to the particularity of Jewish difference that is itself part of a relentless penchant for allegorizing all "difference" into a univocal discourse.[4]

Yet Nancy's gloss on Blanchot preserves, perhaps, a saving ambiguity. It is barely possible to read the last words as an injunction—finally—to let the Jews "write themselves." However inadequate, this essay represents an attempt to do just that. My warnings about nostalgia notwithstanding, I claim thus that a situation like Rabbi Singer's minyan has import for philosophers. And so I will have recourse once again here to the Lower East

---

4. This discussion of the Blanchot quote and Nancy's gloss on it also appears in Boyarin and Boyarin 1993.

Side, the neighborhood where I and other Jews live (J. Boyarin 1990, 1989).

It is difficult to fit my intimate observations of the minyan at Rabbi Singer's synagogue to the universal scale of Nancy's reflections on community. The juxtapositions that inform the rest of this essay may not always seem harmonious or felicitous. A text that is at points disjointed and incommensurate may be one consequence of the attempt to juxtapose a metadiscourse on community as "singularity" with images of a singular community that, itself, does not indulge in discretely philosophical metadiscourse. Yet I would argue once again that anecdotes serve as necessary antidotes even to those totalizing discourses whose sworn mission is to overcome the discourse of totality (Fineman 1989).[5]

The themes of these "dialogues" between theory and ethnography are: What is a minyan?; Positions; Death and singularity; A singular community.

II. WHAT IS A MINYAN?

The institution of the minyan can be considered simultaneously or serially, first as a response to the loss of the Temple center, and second as a response—not a solution—to the question of identity and difference among male Jews. The minyan ("number") designates both the minimum number of ten adult male Jews[6] needed to carry out a complete prayer service, and any particular gathering fulfilling that requirement. As a chronotopic specification of the situation of worship—these people at this time, in this place—it takes the place of the destroyed Temple, a more overtly

5. Nancy will I hope welcome these anecdotes, despite the harsh implications I have just ventured. In my insistence on the importance of anecdotes, I am relying on a posthumous essay by Joel Fineman, who in turn cites a critique by Nancy of Hegel and "Finite History," presented at Berkeley in 1987.

6. Reform and Conservative Jewish congregations have in recent decades accepted women into the minyan, with consequences I will not consider here. The restriction to males is consistent with the institution of the synagogue until the twentieth century and with contemporary Orthodox Judaism. It is of course troubling to me, since I am *also* a kind of "universalist," and there is no justification for it. The only solution I can think of, since I do not find the kind of marginal redemption described here in most Reform or Conservative congregations, is a sustained discussion of the consequences of taking the word "Jew" to mean "woman." See also below.

spatial specification. Thus if the minyan is a kind of provisional Jewish center, it is one founded on the loss of the Temple as foundational center. It is not, then, that the minyan is the essence of Judaism, if Judaism has an essence at all. Twenty years ago I made this mistake, venturing in a conversation with a rabbi the opinion that "Judaism is a minyan." "No," he said; "Judaism is a school": education and continuity are more important than collective prayer. Furthermore, coming together into a minyan every day is not a commandment in itself, a *mitzvah*, but a *hidur mitzvah*, an enhancement of the commandment. Yet for eleven months after a parent's death and on each anniversary of that death thereafter, the male Jew is obligated to recite Kaddish, the memorial prayer, and this can only be done in the presence of a minyan.

Why is the number of the minyan ten? The *Encyclopedia Judaica* tells us that "the Talmud (Berachot 21b; Megillah 23b) derives this number from the term *edah* ('community'), which in the Scriptures is applied to the ten spies (Num. 14:27)." Given the theme of this essay, it is all too tempting to rely on the encyclopedia's gloss, and proceed as if the minyan were ipso facto a community. But the encyclopedia's gloss is itself casual to the point of arbitrariness. The word *edah* in modern Israeli Hebrew means something closer to "ethnic group," and is never translated as "community." Nor would we usually think of the group of ten spies, gathered for that particular purpose, as a community. Furthermore, there is a remarkable irony present in the text from which the derivation is drawn. There were twelve spies sent into the land, ten of whom, lacking faith, reported that it was invincible by the Israelites. For this reason, in the verse from Numbers cited here, the ten spies are referred to as an *edah ra'ah*, a "bad" *edah*. That a holy convocation—a minyan—could be based on the example of the vilified ten spies, at least tells us that a minyan doesn't have to be made up of "good Jews." The qualification for membership in a minyan is first of all genealogical, and virtually never "spiritual."

In extreme occasions the "tenth" member of the minyan, at Rabbi Singer's shul, may not be an adult, or even a person— though so far it cannot be a woman. On occasion my own small male child, holding a Bible or responding "Amen" to the prayer leader, has been counted as the tenth member of the minyan. A number of times I've seen the scroll of the Torah, revealed when the curtain is drawn back and the Ark is opened, standing in for the tenth. It must be said that not every member of the minyan agrees with this latter practice; in a dispute over the issue recently, a man named Baker—normally quiet—heatedly cited authorities as disparate as the Babylonian Talmud and the *Jewish Press* (an Orthodox English-language weekly) against counting a Torah scroll in the minyan, while Rabbi Singer's older brother (a rabbi as well) cited the authority of the medieval commentator Rabeynu Osher in support of the practice. When the situation came up again weeks later a third member of the minyan, abandoning the argument over precedents, insisted on the principle of consensus: if there are people in the minyan who object to it, then it shouldn't be done.

It is commonly agreed that only six of the adult male Jews present need actually be praying. Frequently Rabbi Singer's minyan is completed with a member or two who has already finished praying at the synagogue around the corner, on Clinton Street; indeed, their schedules are synchronized to permit this duplication of presences in the Lower East Side synagogue economy.

On the other hand, there has been some dispute over whether everyone needs to be present in the room to be counted in the minyan. One participant, unable to stand the stuffiness of the narrow, overheated room in the winter, prays outside in the vestibule, behind a door that's closed for the sake of those who complain of the cold. The latter in turn complain that he can't be counted in the minyan then. Despite these complaints, no one has as yet refused to proceed as though the conditions for a minyan had been fulfilled.

Despite these questions at the edge of Rabbi Singer's minyan, these days—in the first half of 1992—the composition of the group is relatively stable. The president of the congregation has mostly retired from his job as a kosher butcher uptown, and hence comes almost every morning. Rabbi Singer's brother, after years of bad relations with the president of the congregation around the corner, has finally quit as the rabbi there, so he too is now a regular at Rabbi Singer's.

The situation some eight years ago, when I first began participating in the minyan, was much more unsettled. One of the regulars was a furious, nonreligious Israeli immigrant. He disrupted the service for months shouting that another member of the minyan had induced him to pay a lawyer to process his immigration application. The application was rejected, and the immigrant wanted his money back. Two of the oldest members loved to argue loudly in the middle of the service; one of them is dead now, and the other too weak to come regularly. One winter Rabbi Singer, rushing out the door to complete the minyan around the corner, slipped on the ice at the entrance and broke his leg, which left him in the hospital for months.

Precisely because the minyan is relatively stable now, certain standard approaches to face-to-face interaction won't be particularly helpful here. A functioning, small-scale social institution is refractory to analysis in terms of role contradiction, à la Erving Goffman, or social conflict, à la Lewis Coser. Even the attempt to describe the maximization of available, countable Jews within the scarcity of what I have called the Lower East Side shul economy has less pertinence since the wall of Rabbi Heftler's synagogue on Attorney Street collapsed, and the third place nearby needing a minyan was thereby eliminated from consideration.

Nevertheless, the relatively containable quirks and disputes described so far should be adequate to suggest that what occurs every morning at Rabbi Singer's shul is not some mystical communion or melding of identities. If the minyan is readily susceptible neither to sociological theorizing nor to idealization as the transcendence of worldly limitations, it is still the case that we would not know these men—they would not know each other— if they did not come together to make the minyan each morning. Nancy has a word for it: compearance, or in his French, *comparution* (1991 : 58). Nancy strives for a formula to explain the possibility of being together without being the same, and this is what he tells us: "Being in common means that singular beings are, present themselves, and appear only to the extent that they compear (*comparaissent*), to the extent that they are exposed, presented, or offered to one another" (58).

So in a different sense then, I was right in my conversation with a different rabbi many years ago. The minyan—not as an ideal form but as a repeatedly instantiated phenomenon—*is* necessary for the Jew: just as the minyan does not exist separately from the Jews, the Jews of this story do not exist separately from the minyan.

"Of this story": of course when they walk out the door and

leave the minyan, they do not suddenly become "individuals"—
they enter into other networks undreamed of within the confines
of this story. Nancy correctly insists on this point. He says that
"the *singular being* . . . is not the individual" (28), and he reminds
us that "the limit marks the advent of singularity, and its with-
drawal." Opening the door to the synagogue and clumping down
the three worn steps to enter the narrow room and compear with
the minyan, I am singular. But I am just as singular—and no more
an isolated individual—when, leaving early, I rush home to wake
my child for school.

Let me not confine myself to auto-ethnography. In their several ways, various members of the minyan illustrate the partialities
of participation and "belonging." Take Max, a sometime member
of the minyan; his presence can't be relied on. When he does
come, he reads silently to himself, apparently from the English
translation of the prayerbook. Only a few words open up, compear with the vocalizations of the other members of the congregation. From the story of Abraham bringing Isaac to Mount
Moriah, recited near the beginning of each morning service, he
enunciates the words *Adonoy yir'e*, "God will show us," which remain untranslated in the English prayerbook. And thus when he
prays out loud, the words are Hebrew. And yet one other day I
heard him say distinctly, "Egypt." God will show us . . . Egypt?

While not quite a "street person," Max is clearly marginal
to even the marginal Jewish community of the Lower East Side,
being unmarried, poorly educated, and without a steady job. He
makes little pretense to an unproblematic belonging. He defies
the notice on the wall citing a decision by a local rabbinical board
banning smoking in synagogues. In his youth he played minor-
league baseball for a couple of seasons, and he freely tells anecdotes about the cities he visited then. He also likes to tell jokes on
himself. One is about when he studied Hebrew at Seward Park
High School. The teacher was frustrated with his smart-aleck students who refused to study, and once admonished them: "Max is
learning much more Hebrew than you guys, and he's not even
Jewish!" There's a double edge here, of course: although Max
fails to conform to outward signs of Jewish ethnicity, he claims
that as a child he embodied the Jewish ideal of diligent study. So
why does Max read the English prayer book now?

One regular and two more sometime members of the minyan

are almost completely deaf. A few weeks before Passover this year the deaf *kohen* (I have never learned his name) must have marked the *yortsayt,* the anniversary of the death of one of his parents. He came in for the morning minyan and recited Kaddish, slowly and not too clearly. Since he took longer than the other mourners, everyone paid attention to his recital, and we all said "Amen" at the end of each verse. After he finished, he glanced over at the president of the congregation. Was he just checking his own unheard performance, or was he perhaps double-checking that someone had been listening?

Kaddish: that's where you'd expect the mystical—the mythical—communion to take place if it's going to take place. That's where we're all in the business of praising God. And there, for once, was the entire minyan listening to one man saying Kaddish, assenting to the theodicy with one voice. And yet—wonderful irony—the reciter couldn't hear his fellows. The call of Kaddish was detached from the response of "Amen," which raises the question of where this theodicy is really sent: to God, to the minyan, to the memory of the parents. . . . Once the question is raised, we are no longer reassured by an implicit homology between the listeners below and a grandiose yet still anthropomorphized Listener above. Can we then still speak of myth—which, Nancy claims, is an irreducible component of community? And if "the interruption of myth is therefore also, necessarily, the interruption of community" (Nancy 1991 : 57), does this mean that it is really impossible to speak of the relation between a deaf mourner and the minyan who respond to his Kaddish as community? Or can there be an interrupted community, as here, which nevertheless somehow *works,* to match the inoperative (*désoeuvrée,* unworked) community Nancy seeks to adumbrate without founding?

III. POSITIONS

Nancy's attempt to provide a solution to the dichotomy between the individual and the community implicitly refuses any hierarchical distinctions among the singular beings that compear as the community that "never disappears," but "resists" (58). Nancy's image of community—here following Bataille and his comrades in the 1930s—is anarchic, acephalous: to have some person at the head of it, it seems, would deny contingency and singularity. It would mean grounding the identity of the community in one unchanging individual, the guarantor of "just immanent Being" (58), which for Nancy is the antithesis of resistant community. Yet here I speak repeatedly of "Rabbi Singer's minyan." In what ways is it "his?" Is he or is he not the center?

It seems clear at least that he is a sine qua non for the continuity of the minyan. It is around him that the minyan, always temporarily, coalesces. He's the one who's always there, so nearly "always" there that when he went to Israel for the first time in his life a few years ago, it was only for a week and only for a wedding. When he was in the hospital after breaking his leg, the minyan sank into chaos and barely managed to continue. He makes the phone calls, makes the coffee, attends the ignored, soothes the offended. When he gives up or gives out, I fear there will be nothing. Meanwhile, while rarely boastful, he is well aware of the services he performs both inside and outside the synagogue. One day several years ago a Russian Jewish family came in to visit the rabbi. After they left, the rabbi explained to me: "When they came here, they didn't have a thing. I got them an apartment, I got them furniture. . . . It's unbelievable what I did for them!" [7]

Whether he can possibly be an adequate center—whatever that might be—is another question. Some people expect more of a rabbi. One member of the congregation was furious at Rabbi Singer; he claimed that the rabbi paid no attention to women in the congregation. When this man's wife was in the hospital with a broken ankle, Rabbi Singer hadn't gone to visit her; nor had he notified the congregation about the death of an old woman who attended the shul. This anger—I hardly expected it—was expressed to me during a chance meeting on the street, several blocks from the synagogue.

In any case, as far as constituting the minyan the rabbi can be counted only once, and thus each man who comes in and brings the total closer to the minyan becomes a momentary focus. Sometimes the tenth man who comes in is referred to as "*der yidisher*

---

7. Paul Cowan (1986) has written in moving detail about Rabbi Singer's involvement as a social worker with the United Jewish Council. Yet Cowan presented that involvement as a saintly kind of self-sacrifice, rather than as a special mode of relation which, among other things, enables Rabbi Singer to maintain a minyan around himself.

tsenter." The Yiddish is a pun on "center" and "tenth." The bare
minyan thus mocks the pretensions of Jewish establishment and
monumentality inherent in the American idea of a "Jewish center," a place where Jews gather for secular socializing, recreation,
and mutual recognition. It also suggests that, at the moment he
compears, whoever walks in as the tenth man and makes the minyan is the center.

Thus the last becomes first. The honor of being tenth is a
barbed one: it implies as well that you've arrived late, that everyone's been waiting for you. Sam, a regular with a doctorate in
theater and a full gray beard, more often than not walks in as
the tenth man a few minutes after the services have begun. Evidently he has grown tired of having this pointed out to him.
One day when he walked in and someone said: "Sender,[8] you're
the tenth," he replied with just the slightest trace of hubris:
"Okay. . . . I always thought of myself as the first!" Another time
he took an opposite, self-deprecatory tack to mock the obsession
with constituting the minyan: "What's one Jew more or less?"
There was no response.

A theater critic working as a public school teacher, a former
Hebrew school principal working for the state government, an
unmarried middle-aged rabbi, a retired butcher, an anthropologist in his thirties—all of whom have synagogues closer to their
homes—what are these various people *doing* there? Trained after
all in a synthesizing, abstracting discipline, I insist on somehow
constructing their active presence in one way or another as susceptible to a distillable meaning, not simply an effect of sheer
inertia.

It is true that some recent voices in anthropology warn that
we can try too hard to avoid the theoretical embarrassment of acknowledging the force of inertia, as Sherry Ortner has written in
a discussion of the theory of practice:

> Either because practice theorists wish to emphasize the activeness
> and intentionality of action, or because of a growing interest in
> change as against reproduction, or both, the degree to which ac-
> tors really do simply enact norms because "that was the way of our
> ancestors" may be unduly undervalued. (Ortner 1984:150)

8. His Jewish name, used in the synagogue.

The way of our ancestors, yes. Sam, for one, joined the minyan only when he discovered that his grandfather came from the
same town as Rabbi Singer. Rabbi Singer—a flaming redhead as
a child, as some of his grandchildren are now—in the Old Country used to sit in Sam's mother's lap. And when Sam's grandfather
caught the future rabbi and his friends stealing pears from his
orchard, rather than scolding them he simply demanded, "Did
you say the blessing before you ate them?" Here are images of
extended family and what we could almost call a kind of primitive
communism—proper obedience to the Law being regarded as
more important than ownership of petty commodities. Indeed,
the anecdote is especially memorable because it seems to illustrate Blanchot's claim that the Jews are bound by "an ethical order that manifests itself in respect for the law." But such an order
entails, beyond singularity, a fidelity to memory and to an image
of community. In this case, such images of an earlier, intimate,
lost *relation* seem sufficient to have inspired the discipline of synagogue attendance, adopted only in late middle age, and sustained
early every morning for years now.

On the other hand, inertia is not only indulged in a nonre-
flexive manner. The way of our ancestors is teased even as its practice is confirmed. The tension of reiteration in a world where we
are instructed always to buy the new may be expressed when the
reiteration itself is unquestioned. Thus Morris, a plump older
man who comes every Sunday, complained one day: "Davening—
every day it's the same thing, over and over again. Why can't they
change it once in a while?" He was by no means seriously contem-
plating or suggesting a change, but rather highlighting by contrast the point that reiteration itself is the fundamental mode of
this particular scene of compearance.

There is flexibility and tension as well in the not-quite-simul-
taneous constitution of the minyan. Not everyone is there at the
same time. Occasionally someone recruited to fill out the minyan
who has no interest in praying or has urgent business elsewhere
will leave the second another person walks in. During the school
year I myself arrive early, pray by myself rather than keeping up
with the minyan, and leave early. Sam and Shmuel, the state
worker, come in late, and sometimes tease each other about
which one has arrived last.

One day Shmuel came in as I was winding my tefillin and preparing to go, and said: "Had enough, huh?"

I finished silently reciting the closing prayer of *Aleynu* and responded in the same ironic spirit: "Listen, I could daven all day, but I've got things to do."

Shmuel says, "At least you didn't say, 'I have important things to do!' "

Can this interchange be in some way commensurate with a philosophical statement about belief, irony, and solidarity? In principle, Jewish prayer is not simply a matter of taste or choice, of staying until you've "had enough." In practice, no one can be coerced into coming or into staying, and it is recognized that other demands affect compearance at the minyan.

The American political philosopher William Connolly, writing within a tradition of discussions of identity and politics that runs from Augustine through Michel Foucault, might treasure this remark of Shmuel's. Acknowledging the power of a historically constituted collective identity in a way that Nancy's formulation cannot, Connolly nevertheless holds out the hope of a reflexive shaping of that identity which would obviate the need for absolutist claims to authoritative truth. How, he asks, can people participate fully in a particular tradition without feeling compelled to reinforce that tradition through the silencing or elimination of others? His vision for such culture bearers is as follows:

> Its bearers may acknowledge a drive within themselves and their culture to naturalize the identity given to them, a drive discernible in the history of their previous relationships to external, internal, and interior differences. But they also struggle to ambiguate or overcome this drive because they think it is ungrounded in any truth they can prove and because they find it ethically compelling to revise their relation to difference in the absence of such a proof.
> (Connolly 1991:46)

Does Shmuel's question whether I'd "had enough" meet this criterion, or hint, at least, at this sort of ambiguated consciousness? Perhaps it remains within a traditional Jewish mode that itself is contained by some bounds of "faith" beyond which the philosopher is suggesting we must move. Or perhaps all this philosophy is too much of a burden to place on the back of the wisp of a joke, and they are two kinds of discourse, incommensurate, with what another philosopher would call a fundamental *differend* between them (Lyotard 1988).

It seems to me that Shmuel's remark is an example of precisely the kind of ironic yet unalienated identity Connolly is arguing for. In any case, if there is a larger cocoon within which the critical force of his joke is neutralized, it cannot be characterized by the word "faith." Certainly Shmuel's and Sidney's jokes are enough to indicate that the minyan does not compear in some Protestant-like, absolutized and unironical way "to worship God." Certainly that language per se would be alien to the members of this minyan.

And yet one of Nancy's commentators points out that *comparaître,* which we've translated as compearance, can also mean "to be cited to appear before judgment" (Van Den Abbeele 1991: xiv). Before whom—if not God?

Perhaps, to resort to an aphorism, God is the implied center.

IV. DEATH AND SINGULARITY

The ethnographer Jack Kugelmass has told us of another minyan, on the other side of New York City, stubbornly persisting to mark in its marginality the departure of Jews from the South Bronx (Kugelmass 1986). Yet there are still more Jews on the Lower East Side than in the South Bronx. And more synagogues: everyone who comes to Rabbi Singer's shul could walk to another, closer one. The congregations resist consolidation, the death of a synagogue; as Maimonides instructs us, upon seeing an abandoned synagogue we are to recite the blessing "Blessed be the True Judge," just as when we first hear that a person has died. Hence a congregation, an *edah,* a minyan will hold out longer than seems rational, and there are always several communities at loose ends on the Jewish Lower East Side.

Kugelmass describes the members of "his" congregation— both men and women—as a community of mourners saying Kaddish for each other. The irony is both a figure of speech and a condition of their isolation. Pierre Bourdieu (1972, 1977) explains that when social scientists collapse exchange—which has an element of time lag, and thus of discrepancy—into structure, the element of wager, of uncertainty that provides the dramatic tension of social life is lost. There's actually a deal here: I'll remember you if you depart first, since you agree to remember me if I depart first. On the other hand, the bargain can be fulfilled only as long as a minyan can be conjured, through a combination of organization and imagination; and a community of mourners is destined by definition to extinction.

Yet there seems no room in Nancy's articulation of community for a community of mourners. His singular beings seem to have neither history nor families nor memory. Indeed, this seems necessary for them to be able to "authentically" compear, to be adequate to themselves and to each other at the moment of simultaneous relation. Because for Nancy the common *creatureliness* of singular beings is what affords them the possibility of a nonimposed, nonhierarchical relation as community, he seems to fear implicitly that the possession of a memory would necessarily define them either as integral individuals, or as a stable collective. And yet Nancy relies on death, asserting plausibly enough that "community is revealed in the death of others" (1991:15).

Perhaps this is the too literal approach that might be expected of a Jewish ethnographer. It might be that when Nancy refers to death, he means "Death," the ultimate figure of resistance to the totality and eternity of Being or of presence. Listen to Nancy's commentator, Georges Van Den Abbeele, who sees the importance of the relation between death and community in Nancy's rumination but insists on idealizing it: "Death, which is *but* Nancy's metaphor of the day-to-day finitude that marks the singularities of our being" (xiv; emphasis added).

My death is but a metaphor?

It is not necessary to go quite this far in order to rescue Nancy's meaning. For Nancy death is the negative ground of community, around which each of us is able to recognize our shared singularity, not the socially established and recognized forms through which we accomplish our mourning, lay the dead to rest, and are reabsorbed back into the communal organism. Within the tropic range afforded by this rigorous negativity, the disappearance of a cultural form—Lower East Side Jewish sociality, for instance—would be a ground of community analogous to individual death. The awareness of this loss, of the part of "us" that is lost therein, would thus entail participation in the critical interrogation of community and its loss, a consideration beyond the retrospective provision of positive ethnographic materials for restorative nostalgia.

Nor is an outsider necessarily required for that critical interrogation to be acknowledged—though when it is produced inside the "community," its forms are as ephemeral or parodic as academic discourse is stolid and monumental. There are voices within Lower East Side Jewish sociality that recognize narcotic nostalgia as a threat and seek to counter it with humor. Some years ago I recorded a set piece recited from memory by my teacher—a man roughly my age—at Mesivtha Tifereth Jerusalem, the local yeshiva. He did not present himself as the author of this routine, which mocks an alienated Jew from the East Side reminiscing about his parents:

> I remember my mother. She was a real *eyshes ish.* She was so *frum,* she always wore a *kichl* on her head. And every Shabbes I'd come home, and she used to make the most delicious *khaloshes.* And my father—such a *tanis kholem, zeykher letsiyes mitsrayim!* Here—I have a picture of him—isn't that a real *azus ponim?* And the place he had in shul—every week they used to give him *nifter!*

"Eyshes ish," married woman, substituting for "eyshes khayil," a woman of valor; "kichl," a cookie, for "tichl," a modest kerchief; "khaloshes," fainting, for "holuptshes," stuffed cabbage; "tanis kholem," a fast after a bad dream, for "talmid khokhem," a learned Jew; "zeykher letsiyes mitsrayim," a memento of the departure from Egypt, for "zeykher tsadikim levrokhe," "the memory of the righteous is a blessing"; "azus ponim," brazen one, for "hodores ponim," a magnificent appearance; "nifter," deceased, for "maftir," the most prized section of the Torah reading.

Some of these substitutions—like the next to last one—are direct reversals of affective meaning, deriding the parents this straw figure wishes to honor through the misremembered signs of a lost common language. Others—like the first one—are simply evacuations into neutrality. The very last suggests that death—not the "Death" that forms the negative ground of community but the death of the very possibility of community—is what happens when those who once compeared around the sacred text have nothing to rely on but the emptied forms of the past. Yet the speaking of this set routine, the confidence that all of the substitutions are still recognizable, suggests a community watching, aware of its own death and still *resisting* its banalization into the Being of nostalgia.

V. A SINGULAR COMMUNITY

Van Den Abbeele's introduction confuses—following Nancy, perhaps, but that's not really clear from Nancy—two phenomena, the general validity of both of which may be putatively accepted, even as our discussion questions them. The first is the ubiquitous dissolution or destruction of community: this is "the world we have lost," "the vanishing primitive," even perhaps Baudrillard's "precession of simulacra" (Baudrillard 1983). This first is, really, the loss of an uncountable number of problematic, particular communities, which, whether or not they were ever "immanent," were certainly at least plural. The second phenomenon is what Van Den Abbeele calls

> the failure of communal models . . . linked to their embrace of the notion of human *immanence*, that is, of totality, self consciousness, self-presence. Nancy argues that such "failed" notions of community—communism, liberalism, Christianity, etc.—are tributary to a metaphysics that has largely been unable to think without recourse to the subject. (1991:xiv)

If indeed Nancy's authorizing text contains room for only the latter phenomenon—for the Hegelian idea of community, that is—then Nancy's work participates in precisely the immanent, ontological "work" that he sets out to escape, by crowding out the possibility of critical representation of our poor, fragmentary, and plural communities. Indeed a partial community like Rabbi Singer's minyan—partial in the precise sense that it does not *exist* continually and ubiquitously, but rather is repeatedly enacted at a very specific time and place, and is furthermore made up of people who don't have much to do with each other in other situations—provides an alternative to the metaphysics of community-as-totality. Without this the critique of philosophy remains contained within the limits of philosophy.

Nancy knows where his problems lie. Where Van Den Abbeele subsumes Christianity with modern movements, Nancy in fact recognizes the specific problematics of Christianity here, as

he writes: "Fascism . . . was the convulsion of Christianity . . ."
(Nancy 1991:17). Nancy must know that to level communism,
liberalism, and Christianity (or as Linda Singer has it, "Christianity and liberalism" [1991:124]) occludes the way Christianity
informs modern secularist-universalist ideologies. For he writes
as well that "the true consciousness of the loss of community is
Christian" (1991:10).

What exactly are the implications of this claim? Does this
mean that any consciousness of the loss of community that is not
Christian is not true, or that anyone who is conscious of the loss
of community is "in truth" a Christian? Nancy clearly wants to
identify a specific problematics of identity and subjectivity with
Christianity as the fading heritage of European dominance, but
the implicit assumption throughout his investigation is that "community" means universal community. Where Nancy himself would
presumably wish to be seen as post-Christian or not-Christian, the
assumption renders the framework implicitly Christian—a framework wherein nothing is ultimately valid if it is not valid for all
humanity. In this context it is not possible to speak of any communities of resistance, but only of "community" as "resistance."
Apparently this is what happens when the true consciousness of
community is Christian. (How free the philosophers make with
this word "Christianity," as if it were some natural thing or species, making its way through the course of "Western" history.)

Nancy has left adequate evidence to make it clear that his own
identity, the "we" whose conscience he lays claim to, is a specifically Greco-Christian one. When he writes that "our history begins with the departure of Ulysses" (10), he certainly doesn't have
the members of Rabbi Singer's minyan in mind! Nancy's rhetorical invocation of a remarkably exclusive "history" here is an apt
illustration of a pervasive danger acutely stated by the philosopher Judith Butler:

> How is it that we might ground a theory or politics in a speech
> situation or subject position which is "universal" when the very
> category of the universal has only begun to be exposed for its own
> highly ethnocentric biases? (Butler 1991:153)

The anecdotal use of a fragmentary Jewish community to
question a "universal" discourse that, upon closer examination,

clearly reveals its own ethnocentric biases is thus more than co-incidental.[9]

Yet among other things fragmentary community means that some people are irrevocably excluded. Such exclusions are sometimes taken as evidence that merely fragmentary communities have no place in a liberated world. One Sabbath evening nine men and a woman sat waiting for a minyan. Into the silence the president of the congregation called out: "Mrs. Wechsler, put on a pair of pants!" A few minutes later he repeated and added: "Mrs. Wechsler, put on a pair of pants, we'll have ten people!"

Ten people indeed! The minyan seems to be having some gender trouble. It takes pants to make a person. The Law is both instantiated and undermined here; the president's statement both reconfirms the woman's exclusion from the minyan and exposes its arbitrary construction. Is she not a Jew? Yet she is present. Inseparable from the tradition that excludes Mrs. Wechsler from the minyan while including her in the synagogue is the same resiliency that allows the anomaly to be acknowledged inside the synagogue.

For the moment, let me merely employ this anomaly to return to the question of perspective. How are we to define this phenomenon? Is what's going on here a minyan comprising ten male adult Jews, or a number of male Jews coming together each morning to fulfill a more-or-less shared desire for repeated action? Neither, Nancy suggests: it is precisely the relation, the compearance of singular beings that lies prior to a conceptual separation between the individual and the community. It is, Nancy might agree, a relation of "ec-stasy," a standing outside, a supplement to the discrete existence of the single organism that defines "the impossibility either of an individuality, in the precise sense of the term, or of a pure collective totality" (6). This is far from the usual sense of ecstasy as a transcendent joy in which we "forget ourselves," and so it is rather surprising to think of the minyan as defined by

9. Indeed, as Blanchot's response to Nancy makes clearer, the "universal" discourse is marked at more than one point by Jewish images: "The ideal community of literary communication. . . . If need be, one could gather around a table (suggesting the hasty participants at a Seder) . . ." (Blanchot 1982:21) and even more striking, "The Acéphale community [around Bataille in the 1930s] . . . felt obliged, as at Massada, to throw themselves into the nothingness that was no less incarnated by the community" (14).

ecstasy. The ecstatic "member" of the minyan may be miserable, or fervent, or asleep, yet still he stands, he counts, he is counted.

From a historical perspective, the minyan is an artifact attendant upon the loss of a state (inseparable from the loss of its ritual center, the Temple), whereas the polarization between the "community" and the "individual" (and hence the conceivability of their separate existence) is an artifact largely bound up with the invention of modern European states. As Van Den Abbeele comments, the first corresponds to "the organicist notion of the 'body politic' most colloquially linked with the name of Hobbes," the second to "the idea of social contract popularized by Locke and the Enlightenment *philosophes*" (1991:xi).

If there is something to the Jewish "freedom from myth," which Blanchot identified as the scandal provoking Hitlerism to genocide, is there a corollary Jewish freedom from the hypostatic dichotomy between the individual and the community? The modern European liberal state depends on the fiction that it is a particular instantiation of a universal principle, and the dichotomy between the individual and the community reflects the tensions of this fiction. Nancy attempts to work through or unwork the dichotomy by grounding the particular in the concept of "singularity." The echo of the material, the irreducible, the unallegorizable that we hear in "singularity" recalls the rabbinic midrashic resistance of ideal/typical allegorization (D. Boyarin 1990b). Midrash, like the minyan, is a response to the loss of a state and its totalizing communal forms: language in midrash is not a secondary reflection of some hidden meaning whose dispensation is entrusted to authorities backed by temporal powers, but is the historically constituted field within which singular beings compear as Jews.

Yet Nancy's formulation seems to imply that such a materialist approach to language is incompatible with community; he insists that there can be no community without mythmaking, *mythation* (51; also 57). Nancy suggests that the ultimate form of the insistence on myth in our day, of "the entire pretension on the part of the West to appropriate its own origin" (46), is Nazism. Again, does this mean that any religious collective practice that perpetuates "mythological" authority-identity narratives is necessarily tainted? Or is "the Jewish" inherently unmythical, because it does not couple "the logos" (the language within which the "truth" of the tradition is borne) with "being" or "nature?" If the Jews refuse myth, does this mean that Rabbi Singer's minyan is not a community, or that it does no mything?

Though Nancy cites Blanchot as affirming this Jewish genius for unmythicality, the affirmation is exceedingly ambiguous—largely because of the loose way in which the term "myth" is used. If Nazism is the ultimate myth (ultimate not only because the most grandiose, but also, Nancy suggests, because afterward we have lost our myths along with our communities), Hitler's notion of the Jews as free of myth could only be another myth—one that Blanchot and Nancy seem to share. Unless the old myths about Jews are really true, and we do have a secret, powerful knowledge: all along we've possessed the secret of the inoperative community.

This bizarre outcome is one potential reading of Blanchot's Kantian idealization of the Jews as the truly enlightened, as those who live with law rather than myth.[10] The search for an ethical community is realized in this image of the Jews—a trope that both eloquently eulogizes a slaughtered people and removes the identified ideal from close examination far away from "us," whose "history begins with the departure of Ulysses." It is necessary that there be a Blanchot, a Nancy, and a Lyotard to sketch the Jews this way, to attempt to understand what it is about Jews that arouses repeatedly the fury of Christian Europe. And it is necessary that there be a Jew, and the Jew must criticize this sketch.

The quote from Blanchot and Nancy's gloss on it suggest that *their* Jew has indeed been annihilated, that their Jew is the stateless Jew without power. After forty years of the State of Israel, can we really continue to discuss "the Jew" in terms separate from those of power? If we continue to insist on the rhetorical *figure* of the Jew, and refuse to complicate philosophical discourse with the recognition that Jews always have existed in history, whatever secrets of singularity Jews have kept will remain locked be-

10. "The gesture is not new. Kant's thought, whose Protestant descendance is so evident, has very rapidly been interpreted as a profound Judaism" (Derrida 1991: 69). The context of Derrida's essay on Hermann Cohen makes it abundantly clear that this interpretation has been shared by Jewish thinkers. More precisely, Maurice Olender notes that "Kant referred to the commandment 'Thou shalt make no graven image or idol' . . . as 'the most sublime passage in the Jews' book of laws' " (Olender 1992: 160). For a more general discussion of the "demythologization" of Judaism, see Eilberg-Schwartz 1990.

tween matching gates: on one side ethnic rhetorics of statist self-determination, on the other nostalgic views of the crumbling shreds of vanishing primitive community—such as the minyan at Rabbi Singer's synagogue.

From time to time in my dreams, this synagogue is whole, filled with people . . . Jewish men, women, and children, spilling out of the sanctuary and into the street.

(A pause.)

Gestures such as Blanchot's, along with the continuance of the fragmented minyan and—literally—the *dreams* of wholeness, may in our hopeful moments be seen to open up between the minyan and the open book of philosophy the possibility of a relation we might dare call . . . Shhh! . . . "community."

[Sof]

Before the Law
There Stands a Woman
In Re Taylor v. Butler
(with Court-Appointed Yiddish Translator)

Because texts do not reflect the entirety of their authors or their
worlds, they enter a field of reading as partial provocations, not
only requiring a set of prior texts in order to gain legibility,
but at best—initiating a set of appropriations and criticisms
that call into question their fundamental premises.
(Butler 1993:19)

Because relating Torah in the name of the one who said it is said
to help bring Redemption, I begin with a story I heard from my
Lower East Side rabbi, Rabbi Singer, about an East European sage
known as the Lemberger Gaon. My memory of Rabbi Singer's
story is imperfect, as is my understanding of his quick and somewhat mumbled Yiddish, but the gist of the story is this:

Once the Lemberger Gaon was asked to rule on a widow's
complaint that she had been inadequately compensated by her
dead husband's partners for her share in a piece of land. After the
ruling, the woman appeared weeping at the Gaon's home. When
the Gaon asked why she was upset, he was told that she believed
his ruling to be unfair. He was astonished: he was known for always judging such cases in such a manner that all of the litigants
went away satisfied. He sat down, reviewed again the stated facts
of the case and the relevant precedents in Jewish civil law, and
ultimately revised his ruling to the widow's satisfaction.

Now in modern fashion we would, I think, be inclined to interpret this story as a tale about the compassionate nature of the
best rabbinic judgments. But I do not think that Rabbi Singer
meant to tell a story about the flexibility of the Torah and the 87

compassion of the Lemberger Gaon. Rather his point concerned the wisdom of the Lemberger Gaon, by emphasizing the universally recognized aptness of his judgments; and there is also an assertion here about the Law: that the perfect interpreter can interpret the Law in a way that will be recognized by every litigant as just.

I cannot claim the wisdom of the Lemberger Gaon, nor the range of interpretive options his learning afforded him to reread the Law without traducing it. It is not clear—yet—whether I have been summoned as a judge at all. Yet the story about the Gaon seems to offer itself to an interpreter, a translator, someone who can make it speak the languages of identity, of "the Law," of the Differend. I have assumed the role of interpreter and translator of this and other stories, which does little to feed my family but helps me to balance on the tightrope of modern identity, clinging to the guy wires of a self-deprecating ethnic tradition and a modern ethos of self-invention.

One of those whom I cast here as litigants would tend to strengthen the legal-rhetorical force of an anecdote from the margins, such as this one about the Lemberger Gaon. This litigant is Judith Butler, as represented by her book *Gender Trouble: Feminism and the Subversion of Identity* (Butler 1990). Her voice speaks for a diffused power, inviting, for example, a dialogue between a rundown Lower East Side synagogue and academic critical theory. It insists: "The point is not to stay marginal, but to participate in whatever network of marginal zones is spawned from other disciplinary centers and which, together, constitute a multiple displacement of those authorities" (xiii).

I propose here to juxtapose Butler's voice with a different account of self-making, Charles Taylor's *Sources of the Self: The Making of the Modern Identity* (Taylor 1989).[1] A question immediately arises: What court, authoritative for whom and vested by whom, would need a Yiddish translator in a case between Charles Taylor and Judith Butler? I hope to answer that question more adequately below. But my fiction of litigation between the two books seems to be authorized by their respective subtitles: *The Making of the Modern Identity*, versus *Feminism and the Subversion of Identity*.

---

1. I will also refer to Butler's more recent *Bodies That Matter* (1993), and to an essay by Taylor on problems of identity and multiculturalism (1992).

Butler and Taylor are both fundamentally concerned with questions of selfhood, responsibility, liberalism, and autonomy; not only their conclusions but the rhetoric of their arguments vary starkly. In the context of a debate about identity and self-construction, the tone of a theoretical argument is obviously substantial (Derrida 1984). Are Butler and Taylor respectively trying to convince, to prove, to induce, to seduce, to bring the reader up, to bring the reader along, to move the reader in the same direction, to move the reader, but in another direction?

Significant differences surely, but since we're paying the translator, let's keep in mind a grosser point his presence keeps us from overlooking: Butler's and Taylor's books are written, in a fundamentally important sense, in the same language. No more than Taylor would wish us to take the notion of the autonomous self as given rather than achieved, nor Butler the finality of "male and female created He them," should it go without saying that English is a particular language of universal theory. I hope rather that the figure of the translator into and from a "minor" language (Kronfeld 1996) will echo, complicate, and reinforce Butler's notion of the *contingency* of gender construction (1990:38). That the reminder is both apposite and necessary is suggested by a passage in Butler's book criticizing "the *totality* and *closure* of language" (1990:40) within structuralism. The expense of paying the translator is also justified by Taylor's insistence that the language people use to speak about themselves and their identities is to be engaged and not simply dissected in explaining them (1989:57). But the gap between theorist and "people" Taylor has in mind here is one of class, philosophical obsession, or degree of self-reflection, not one of language; hence it may well be that other challenges to theory will be afforded by engaging other languages people use to speak about themselves and their worlds.

But will this plea stand up in court? What reasons other than sentimental (what harm can poor Yiddish do anybody now?) or nativist (Jonathan Boyarin is a grandchild of East European Jews, so Yiddish is presumably "his" language) to translate into or from a language so few speak now? Why not, say, Bengali? Perhaps the sentimental and nativist reasons have some value in themselves. In any case, as will become clearer when this court takes up Taylor's book, Yiddish is not arbitrarily chosen as a language of interrogation. My reliance on a nonnormative language (indeed, one that, more often than not, has failed even to be *recognized* as a language, and that might be referred to as "this language which is not one" [paraphrasing Irigaray 1985]) as a contingent ground of identity echoes Butler's reliance on the examples of "'incoherent' or 'discontinuous' gendered beings" to point out the constructedness of "the person" (17). The fugitive idiom, partaking of many territorial languages in its own diasporic fusion, bears out affinities with those who are not neatly "created" male or female. Both formations suggest the exploration of a range of differences within a more pretentious discussion of the transformations and possible futures of cultured and gendered subjecthood.

It is not clear how much intrinsic interest Butler wishes to grant to ambivalently gendered characters such as Foucault's Herculine Barbin; wary of fetishizing them, she insists that her focus on them primarily serves the purpose of helping us see "how the appearance of [normatively gendered, or in this case, dominant-language] naturalness is itself constituted" (1990:110). This demurral suggests that Butler might take Jews, if she spoke of them at all, merely "as an example." She writes in the dominant language, and like Taylor, though much more self-consciously, she addresses an elite of critical intellectuals. While recognizing the intellectual origins of the move, she retains the critical aim of sniffing out "false consciousness"—in this case what she calls "the epistemic regime of presumptive heterosexuality" (x). Her lingering confidence in the power of criticism to see through false consciousness to some underlying set of power relations is further betrayed by her reference to "the political stakes in designating as an *origin* and *cause* those identity categories that are in fact the *effects* of institutions . . ." (1990:xi)—a statement that curiously works to reinforce the mystified *sui generis* appearance of institutions.

Both books' subtitles are programmatic as well as descriptive. Butler wants to mark the subversion of naturalized gender identities and further it. Taylor wants to make us more conscious of our modern heritage through an account of milestones in its evolution and to encourage us to embrace that heritage more self-consciously and responsibly. But this does not just mean that Taylor is more "positive" or helpful than Butler. In fact, it might suggest that Taylor's account complies with the production of the modern identity through "certain exclusionary practices that do not 'show'" (Butler 1990:2) once the project is finished. Hence the political importance of revealing, of "repeating" once again those historical exclusions, one of which (still, in a surprising number of "enlightened" contexts) is the female body and gender, and another (still, in a surprising number of "enlightened" contexts) is the Jewish collective through history.

Butler is right to insist that focusing on anomalies such as hermaphrodites (or Jews) is not only an affirmation of the right to be different, but an important strategy for revealing what is taken for granted—what is precisely *self*-evident—in normative theories, especially when those theories take themselves to be at their most insightful and self-critical. Thus Taylor's recent essay "The Politics of Recognition" (1992) purports to consider the claims of various groups, especially in Canada, for academic or governmental recognition of the validity of their respective "cultures." Taylor assumes that demands for inclusion and diversification in the university are only intended to address wrongs done against those previously excluded. He summarizes his understanding of the rationale behind such claims as follows:

> [A] person or group of people can suffer real damage, real distortion, if the people or society around them mirror back to them a confining or demeaning or contemptible picture of themselves. Nonrecognition or misrecognition can inflict harm, can be a form of oppression, imprisoning someone in a false, distorted, and reduced mode of being. (1992:25; see also 65)

What this assumption "mirrors" is Taylor's language of distinct preexistent "selves" that are nevertheless dependent on each other (see below). Taylor implicitly assumes that the very impulse to demand recognition grows out of a philosophical dialectic internal to the dominant European post-Christian tradition, and he identifies the ideal of "authenticity" in Hegel as its main source (1992:36 ff.).[2] There is no "recognition" on Taylor's part that the dominant philosophical tradition may be subject to effective cri-

2. Butler, criticizing "identity politics" grounded in categories taken as natural or fixed, explicitly echoes this analysis (1990:144). Yet she is also extremely careful not to globalize her analysis and preclude analyses from other cultural situations, attempting thus to avoid the danger of "colonizing under the sign of the same those differences that might otherwise call that totalizing concept into question" (1990:13).

tiques rooted in other traditional or critical discourses, that critiques explicitly grounded "outside" need not only speak to or for themselves. In particular, feminist theory is not only a plea for "recognition" of women, it is perhaps the single most creative discursive field in critical thinking today, and hence vital to any "thinking in Jewish."

But all Taylor can see is the demand made of him, and he high-mindedly explains his refusal to be co-opted into an ultimately patronizing bestowal of such recognition, his refusal to surrender the critical faculty in the interests of a priori solidarity. Taylor somehow thinks that all those cultures out there are insisting that he be "on their side" (1992:69). He has little patience for the putative philosophical defenses of such demands, which he dismisses as "subjectivist, half-baked neo-Nietzschean theories . . . [d]eriving frequently from Foucault or Derrida" (1992:70). At this point in his essay, Taylor, who would presumably prefer "objective" reasons, has not yet granted the point that a "culture," in the traditional anthropological sense, is a way of being human, and hence, to the extent that the perpetuation of human life is deemed an ipso facto good (as Taylor might well agree), any culture is commonly accorded an a priori assumption of worth, if only in the same way that any animal species is commonly deemed to be of worth.[3] Moving beyond the traditional anthropological sense, Taylor's assumption of the stance of universal, unsituated arbiter—the gatekeeper of the Law, perhaps—allows him to continue writing of "cultures" as discrete and internally monolithic wholes. In the evaluation of different cultures he focuses only on their "creations," and not, for instance, on the kinds of distinctions and creative opportunities they afford to various of their members. The refusal to permit his monologic caricature of multiculturalist claims to be disrupted by any specific quotes or even citations could not be more thorough.[4] One

3. Taylor's assumption that what we are being asked to "evaluate" is another culture's "creations" betrays primarily the arrogance of a collector's attitude. For an exemplary essay that both dissects the attitude of the imperial collector and reappropriates meanings for collected objects on behalf of living bearers of the tradition in which those objects were produced, see "A Culture under Glass: The Pomo Basket" in Sarris 1993.

4. In *Sources of the Self,* Taylor occasionally makes references to hypothetical cultures that would offer counterexamples to the cultural universals he proposes. But

reference to another general "critique of both extreme camps" (1992:73) is all he provides.

Eventually Taylor does offer the apparent concession that

> merely on the human level, one could argue that it is reasonable to suppose that cultures that have provided the horizon of meaning for large numbers of human beings, of diverse characters and temperaments, over a long period of time—that have, in other words, articulated their sense of the good, the holy, the admirable—are almost certain to have something that deserves our admiration and respect. (1992:72)

Aside from the fact that this again focuses exclusively on the "sublime" aspects of culture rather than everyday life, since the bulk of his argument is aimed at an unspecified and caricatured straw multiculturalist[5] the force of the essay is against testing this last proposition. Taylor's defense of critical standards in explicit opposition to politics occludes the fact that critical dialogues in culture and identity are precluded when the hegemonic (and still commonly unmarked) cultural identity hogs the microphone.

Or take Taylor's acknowledgment that the self is not natural: "We are not selves in the way that we are organisms, or we don't have selves in the way we have hearts and livers" (Taylor 1989: 34). Taylor recognizes that what he would call the modern Western conception of the self is historically or culturally contingent in a way that the human organism is not. But within his language there is a reassertion of a preexistent "we" that "has" hearts and livers, something that on closer inspection, grounded in the examination of subjectivity by Butler and other feminist theorists, is not obvious at all. By assuming the "we" (as Lenny Bruce's Tonto

---

he seems quite uninterested in whether such counterexamples, e.g., to the proposition that there is "something like an a priori unity of a human life through its whole extent" (1989:51), do in fact exist.

5. A similar approach is evident in a recent essay on anthropology and multiculturalism by Terence Turner, who finds it apt to divide multiculturalist arguments into *critical* (read "good") and *difference* (read "bad") categories. As with Taylor's essay, presumptive proponents of the latter are not allowed to take the stand on their own behalf, but dismissed as those "for whom *culture* reduces to a tag for ethnic identity and a license for political and intellectual separatism" (Turner 1993:414).

says, "What do you mean 'we,' white man?'") Taylor opens and quickly shuts out the question whether "our" organismic identity is inseparable from some form of self-making, of identity construction. If it is, then does Butler's "subversion of identity," as a putative program to be carried out, suggest the end of the species? The specter of such a whimpering apocalypse, if usually unarticulated, might well be a fear underlying much of the "resistance to theory." It is articulated by Irigaray: "To wish to get rid of sexual difference is to call for a genocide more radical than any form of destruction there has ever been in History" (cited in D. Boyarin 1994:331, n. 14). Daniel Boyarin retorts that "even disaggregated bodies can get pregnant" (ibid.). Newborns must be nurtured, however, and it is not obvious that without some sort of structured differentiation—some cultural "aggregation of bodies"—in human society, such nurturing would take place. The link between difference and continuity at the level of the *group* rather than the *species* is briefly but pointedly alluded to by Butler, as I will discuss further toward the end of this chapter.

Has the feminist account of identity, then, simply progressed (in a fashion Hegel would applaud) to a level of self-awareness beyond the account of reflexivity available to Taylor's liberal, nongendered Western subject? Need more be said than simply that Butler has gotten the number of Taylor, among others? Taylor's effort to transcend the empiricist notions of the moral self as a supplement to the real might almost seem a preliminary to Butler, who for example quotes Michel Haar's claim that " 'The subject, the self, the individual, are just so many false concepts, since they transform into substances fictitious unities having at the start only a linguistic reality' " (quoted in Butler 1990:21). Butler also knows of course that this simplistic contrast between the prelinguistic real and a "merely" linguistic reality is inadequate; she lucidly insists that "to claim that gender is constructed is not to assert its illusoriness or artificiality, where those terms are understood to reside within a binary that counterposes the 'real' and the 'authentic' as oppositional" (1990:32). This might be brought back around once again to support Taylor's implicit insistence that just because the modern identity has a *history,* it is not therefore false to say it is universally valid (or more modestly, it is not correct therefore to say that it is illusory, as Haar would).

Which of these books should be translated first? That is, for a hypothetical Yiddish reader coming to study contemporary debates on the juridical subject, which of these books would be more approachable, more congenial, or more accessible?

Taylor's tome is massive in pages and relatively plain in syntax; its size and blurbs confirm its "definitive-work" status. Butler's book is elusive and dense. In format, then, a point favoring Butler for translation, which is usually paid by the page; in style, a point favoring Taylor, since straightforward language translates more quickly and reliably. Yet I would claim that Taylor's arguments, more than Butler's, discourage especially translation into the language I am here calling Yiddish, but that immigrants and their children of an earlier generation simply and colloquially call "Jewish."

Taylor betrays a certain reluctant progressivism when he asserts that in premodern cultures, the question of "moral or spiritual orientation" "cannot arise in the reflexive, person-related terms that it does for us" (1989:42). It is significantly unclear what he means by premodern here. Nor would it be fair to insist that Taylor, more than anyone else, unequivocally identify a single dividing point between epochs. The critical issue here is not the historical accuracy of one or another periodization, but rather the political implications of any such division.

In other contexts what Taylor means by "premodern" seems to be "pre-Christian," as much of a stretch as that would seem to most critics. To assign a figure like Augustine to modernity would clearly make "modernity" a transhistorical mindset, rather than even a very loose chronological account; and Taylor's history is eminently chronological and progressive, though he recognizes the persistence and reappearance of "earlier" forms (1989:496–97). Yet even without reading Taylor, the figure of Augustine—not to mention Koheleth—comes to mind as someone who, long before modernity, raised the question of moral or spiritual orientation in profoundly reflexive, person-related terms. The modernity of Augustine is cited as a commonplace by Krister Stendahl, who adds that Augustine's "*Confessions* is the first great document of the introspective conscience" (Stendahl 1976:85). And indeed Taylor offers support for this: "Augustine's turn to the self was a turn to radical reflexivity" (Taylor 1989:131), which he defines as the move in which we "turn and make this [our experience] our object of attention, become aware of our awareness, try to experience our experiencing, focus on the way the world is *for* us" (1989:130). On the other hand, one may well ask where the radical reflexivity is to be found in Taylor's account. There is no room in his rhetoric for autobiographical insights into the assumptions about identity and "the good" that he received as a personal heritage, through and against which he has been able to articulate his critical overview. His "I" is instead always the highly generalized, putative modern Western subject (also 1989:512).

Taylor's "modern Western" self, in any case, is eminently Christian or post-Christian in its modal form (see Taylor 1990; also Taylor 1992:62).[6] At various points he invokes the copula "Jewish-Christian" or "Judeo-Christian," and once mentions Hasidism as a form of early modern inwardness along with various brands of Christian Pietism, but never does he attend specifically to any possible Jewish *difference*. Western "religion" to Taylor effectively means Christianity; it is clear (e.g., Taylor 1989:343) that in speaking about the Enlightenment's rejection of "religion," he means Christian in a fundamentally unproblematic way. Taylor's conception of a universal moral imperative, far from exhibiting the radical reflexivity he values, instead exhibits and furthers a naturalization and dehistoricization of the founding Pauline critique of the relation between the Law and salvation. Stendahl states, in a stunningly precise formulation,

> In the common interpretation of Western Christianity ... [n]obody can attain a true faith in Christ unless his self-righteousness has been crushed by the Law. . . . [This] Law is not any more the Law of Moses which requires circumcision, etc., and which has become obsolete when faith in the Messiah is a live option—it is the moral imperative as such, in the form of the will of God. And finally, Paul's argument that the Gentiles must not, and should not come to Christ *via* the Law, i.e., *via* circumcision etc., has turned into a statement according to which all men must come to Christ with consciences properly convicted by the Law and its insatiable requirements for righteousness. So drastic is the reinterpretation

6. Partha Chatterjee's response to Taylor (Chatterjee 1990) affords the possibility of viewing Taylor as an implicit ethnography (rather than a history!) of elite Western selfhood.

once the original framework of "Jews and Gentiles" is lost, and the
Western problem of conscience becomes its unchallenged and self-
evident substitute. (Stendahl 1976:86–87)

Taylor, writing over a decade later, is a perfect example of this
syndrome, claiming precisely that "this isn't peculiar to Puritan
Christianity, but . . . all frameworks permit of, indeed, place us
before an absolute question of this kind, framing the context in
which we ask the relative questions about how near or far we are
from the good" (1989:45). Taylor's liberal framework does not
merely allow for a common human impulse (instead of restrict-
ing true humanity to Christians), it insists on it; but what he's saying more subtly is that "all frameworks" implicitly work in the
same way as Puritan Christianity explicitly does, hence suggesting
(again as the "making of" model suggests) a teleology in which
the unique realization of this human universal in the West implies
that we all must go in this direction.[7]

The effort to translate Taylor into Yiddish thus quickly runs
into a fundamental problem: the language of reception is not
recognized by the original text, and hence a certain complicity
with the text, which certainly facilitates the task of the translator,
is unavailable here. A larger and perhaps more feasible project

7. Here again, the essay by Terence Turner referred to above unexpectedly betrays rhetorical patterns similar to Taylor's. Turner, suggesting that anthropologists
may be able to articulate a radical notion of cultural rights that would empower
critical multiculturalism in a new way, suggests that "much as St. Paul revealed
to the Athenians the identity of the unknown god they had been worshipping anthropologists might play a useful role in helping multiculturalists realize the revolutionary implications of the course upon which they have embarked" (Turner
1993:428, referring without citation to Acts 17). Even granted that the reference is
not in fact to a text written by Paul, but to later writings whose naturalistic theology
may not be characteristic of Paul, still this kind of universalizing-appropriating
act is consistent with Paul's active dismantling of cultural/genealogical identities,
starting of course with that of the Jews. So do we *really* want to take Paul of all
people as the model for a message anthropologists are to convey about "the revolutionary principle that the protection and fostering of the human capacity for
culture is a general human right" (ibid.)? Combined with Turner's dismissal of the
claims of "difference," this would seem to devolve into a highly voluntaristic and
individualistic notion of culture, which is presumably not Turner's intent.

I would argue, but not elaborate, that the same line of criticism is pertinent
vis-à-vis essential aspects of the oeuvre of Jürgen Habermas.

would be a Jewish critique of Taylor's mono-Christian account of the rise of the modern Western identity—but the court's budget for translation does not afford that now.

Butler's book seems more susceptible to translation, largely because her lesbian standpoint actually does not rest at the subversion of dominant identities, but works to open up space for alternative identities without celebrating their oppression. Thus she provides a sharp critique of what she calls Julia Kristeva's "reification of motherhood" (1990:80): "Kristeva prefers to explain lesbian experience as a regressive libidinal state prior to acculturation itself, rather than to take up the challenge that lesbianism offers to her restricted view of paternally sanctioned cultural laws" (1990:83). The translation into Jewish not merely of the words, but of the sense here, might read something like this: Much as Kristeva identifies lesbianism as a state before culture, hence prediscursive and ipso facto unable to speak for itself, Taylor slides from the notion of the "premodern" to that of the "pre-Christian," making any contemporary non-Christian identity ipso facto premodern, hence without access to "radical reflexivity" and invalidated as an interlocutor of theory.

ACCUMULATION VERSUS REPETITION

Taylor's "making," despite the hint of exhortation to his readers to make themselves more reflexively, refers first and foremost to a massive historical project, the cumulative effort (it would seem) of several centuries of explicit philosophy. Butler's "subversion" refers to something that, perhaps, happens all around us every day, and perhaps to a much greater extent than we usually recognize (because the "making" of identity militates against such recognition). For Butler it is also something that should be done more, and if done more, will be done more partly through enlightenment as a result of books like hers, grounded after all in the same valuation of "radical reflexivity" that Taylor promotes. At the end of his massive history, Taylor gives substantial credit to Michel Foucault's pioneering archaeologies of Western subjectivity. Taylor seems to be aiming at an account of that evolution that would leave us more in control of ourselves without stripping us of our modern identities. Part of the reason the book is so long is that it aims not to be a simple reiteration of faith in modern individual dignity and autonomy. Still, while allowing the episodically disastrous consequences of various modern ideals, Taylor stops short of a Foucauldian analysis of what might be called the "repressions" those ideals engender, even though both he and Butler are well aware of the faith in a presocial and good human nature entailed by the putative identification of such repressions. A more sustained response to the disastrous abjections attendant upon modern self-making is the burden of much contemporary criticism, but it is more of an effort than Taylor seems to think necessary or prudent. Taylor does not wish to free us *of* modernity, but to free us *for* modernity: to clear the last barriers before we stand at the mountaintop.

Taylor protests that he does not see this modern identity as a purely philosophical product, but the bulk of his discussion belies the protest. Butler on the other hand insists on the notion of practice—perhaps making of it a fetish—appropriately enough, since she understands "culturally intelligible subjects [Judith Butler presumably included] as the resulting effects of a rule-bound discourse that inserts itself in the pervasive and mundane signifying acts of linguistic life" (1990.145). In other words, the act of saying "I" over and over makes the woman. It is only through a recognition of the inseparability of repetition and identity that we become aware of the only way in which a contestatory politics of identity becomes possible: through changes rung on the repetitions themselves, saying "I" with a slightly different accent.

Because liberal accounts of identity formation tend to speak in terms of the generic subject or the all-embracing and paternal "we," whereas feminist critiques of subjectivity tend to insist on the contingency of identity while still having trouble finding language that is simultaneously contextualized and authoritative, we tend to assimilate adherence to "the modern" with the universal, and "feminist" standpoints with a particularist, standpoint epistemology. But does that fit these two books? What in Taylor (aside from the blurb) suggests that his "modern," while historically localizable, is necessarily desirable for all humans henceforth? Butler's book, clearly recognized as a major articulation of feminist philosophy, is in the precise sense not "addressed to women" but rather addresses the status of the category "woman." The only sense in which Butler, with her emphasis on the deconstruction of dichotomies, is less universal than Taylor is that the general field of identity in which her rhetoric is grounded is more contentious and hence more marked than Taylor's.

It would be selling Taylor short to caricature him as a naive proponent of universal harmonization, theories of which he explicitly rejects. Taylor emphasizes (1989:480) the twentieth-century modernist recognition of the impossibility of a full reconciliation or harmonization, and there is indeed value for a "Yiddish speaker" in Taylor's insistence on an account that honors all of the "crucial goods in contest" (1989:497). But here again tone becomes critical: this impossibility, which Taylor seems to view in a properly modernist tragic fashion, is treated by Butler and those she draws on (especially Derrida) as a resource rather than a resigned recognition.

Butler and Taylor both know that they inevitably speak in the language of identity and selfhood, the one explicitly to refine it, the other to undermine and perhaps, through undermining, ultimately also to refine it. Both inevitably remain blinded in certain ways by the language they continue to employ. In an important and ambiguous footnote to her critique of Lacan's discussion of the repressive "Law of the Father," Butler seems to endorse Nietzsche's critique of the "Judeo-Christian" slave morality based on "the prohibitive law of the Old Testament" (1990:145, fn. 52). She thereby reinforces Taylor's effacement of a Jewish voice or strand. (The ambiguity is underscored by her teasing comment on Lacan's "unnamed 'organ,' presumably the penis [treated like the Hebrew *Yahweh*, never to be spoken] . . ." (1990:48).

The story about the Lemberger Gaon's revision of his ruling perhaps reinforces the claim that the Law in life has not been nearly as univocally repressive as Nietzsche claims, even as it reasserts a claim about the ideal human perfection of a perfectly interpreted law. Indeed, Butler goes on to point out that this Lacanian account of the links between gender construction and the Law (she calls it a structure of religious tragedy in Lacanian theory [1990:56], without making any further distinctions within the "religious") is an unnecessarily tragic one, that indeed there is a possible "flexibility of the Law itself" (ibid.). There is a profound ambivalence to this passage, revealed by the likely predisposition of a Yiddish speaker to think specifically as neither Lacan nor any other in this psychoanalytic tradition seems willing to do, of the Law not as a Christian-identified "Old Testament" but as the oral and written Torah, which is the raison d'être of continuing Jewish community. Again, she uses the general and I think suspect term "theology" in referring to the subject of a necessary critique (1990:57), while citing with evident approval Nietzsche's echo of the young Hegel's point about the Jews having invented a God and then slavishly submitted themselves to that God (see J. Boyarin 1992b:93–94).

In her new book Butler returns to this confused and productive question of the relations among Nietzsche, Lacan, and "the Law": "In this way, the symbolic law in Lacan can be subject to the same kind of critique that Nietzsche formulated of the notion of God: the power attributed to this prior and ideal power is derived and deflected from the attribution itself" (1993:14). She continues in a footnote to that sentence:

> Nietzsche argues that the ideal of God was produced: '[i]n the same measure' as a human sense of failure and wretchedness, and that the production of God was, indeed, the idealization which instituted and reenforced that wretchedness [Butler cites *On the Genealogy of Morals*, section 20]. That the symbolic law in Lacan produces 'failure' to approximate the sexed ideals embodied and enforced by the law, is usually understood as a promising sign that the law is not fully efficacious, that it does not exhaustively constitute the psyche of any given subject. And yet, to what extent does this conception of the law produce the very failure that it seeks to order, and maintain an ontological distance between the law and its failed approximations such that the deviant approximations have no power to alter the workings of the law itself? (1993:247)

One preliminary response to this is grounded in Stendahl's insight into the abstract generalization of Paul's discourse on the Law "into a statement according to which all men must come to Christ with consciences properly convicted by the Law and its insatiable requirements for righteousness" (1976:87, quoted above). Thus Nietzsche's critique, if valid at all, should not be aimed at an unlocated "production of God" but at the simultaneous production of abstract idealism and a priori human wretchedness in Protestantism, from Paul to Luther via Augustine (see also Connolly 1993). This suggests what Butler may not have noticed: that the same critique of Lacan can be mounted vis-à-vis Nietzsche's formulation of the nature of God! Nietzsche's comment is left in

Butler's account as a model of truth. In line with the historical European Christian tendency to see living Jews as fossils, the critique "of [Jewish] law" may "produce the very failure that it seeks to order" in various ways, such as by conceding authority over the "authentic" tradition to a congealed Orthodoxy and then damning that Orthodoxy as immovable.

I would argue, in fact, that far from Jews having invented God and then been left wretchedly inadequate slaves to that alienated and alienating concept, there is in Jewish discourse a recognition, fundamental if rarely explicit, that God and the Jews exist in and only in mutual articulation, or as Butler puts it, that in contrast, she claims, to the "biblical rendition of the performative, i.e., 'Let there be light!' . . . discourse gain[s] the authority to bring about what it names through citing the conventions of authority" (1990:13). One of the places where this is made relatively explicit is in the traditional custom, at the beginning of the weekly Torah reading in synagogues every Sabbath, of having the entire congregation recite or murmur the biblical phrase *ve'atem hadveykim b'adonoy eloheykhem khayim kulkhem hayom*—"and all of you who cling to the Lord your God are alive today." Not merely a reaffirmation of the life-giving properties of Torah, this is also an assertion of the subjecthood of those who in turn give voice to the Torah "today," and of the inseparability of the biblical day on which that statement was "first" articulated, and every Sabbath, every "today," on which it is enunciated again.

Butler rightly does not strive for a place beyond the Law, since she claims that the only possible subversion is one "from within the terms of the Law" (1990:93): but implicitly she assumes that such subversion is a revolution to come, detached from strategies of cultural survival. The Yiddish translator is in an excellent position to note that for a diaspora community, performance *and* subversion of law and gender are necessarily linked strategies of cultural survival. Only a hegemonic culture can or would need to indulge consistently the fiction of static law and identity. One problem in translating Butler is that she consistently presumes a situation in which there is one hegemonic epistemic regime and takes no account of persistently resistant counterhegemonic epistemic regimes, which might not only be, for example, Jews in a Christian or post-Christian society, but "religious" Jews in a secular Jewish society (see the afterword to El-Or 1994). When the same critique is allowed to be carried over to a nonhegemonic cultural identity, the effect is one in which the presumption of culture as essentially repression is generalized and hidden; the effect, ironically, is to reinforce the hegemonic identity as the one that permits greater freedom.

More documentation is needed of such strategies of nonhegemonic cultural survival that have at times occasioned the kind of subversion Butler seeks to identify and promote. But meanwhile it is eminently attested to by a certain rabbinic misreading. "*Eys la'asos l'adonoy, heyfeyru torosekho*" stands the verse (Psalm 119:126), and it is read to mean "It is time to work for the Lord; they have violated your Torah." However, after citing this verse, the Talmud suggests changing the vowels to read the first word *hafeyru*, as a radical authorization: "Rabbi Nathan says [to read the verse] Violate your Torah, for it is time to work for the Lord" (Babylonian Talmud, Berakoth 54:A; my translation).

The example of Torah, a discipline that is both thoroughly prescriptive and also dialogic, places into question Butler's Foucauldian claim (1990.64) that gender "'dispositions' are traces of a history of enforced sexual prohibitions which is untold and which the prohibitions seek to render untellable." I submit to the Court that here she relics too heavily, as she points out that Wittig and Foucault also do, on the "Marxist notion of reification." Is it really the case that cultural dispositions, e.g., toward a certain gender or ethnic identity, most prominently always use self-masking as their primary mechanism of continuity and stability? It seems to me that the Torah contains a quite explicit account of the history of the enforced sexual prohibitions, and indeed that the forgetting of a tradition of learning Torah—which is in large part the tradition of reciting the history of the institution of prohibitions—has accompanied the forgetting of Yiddish.

Against this it should be argued that women even when they speak/spoke Yiddish do/did not have much to speak of in the way of access to Torah! Indeed, the unequal access of women to Torah—a repression that is general but far from historically universal or inevitable—must be addressed at least briefly here. The seriousness of the issue, for Orthodox Jewish communities as for Jewish cultural studies, is indicated by the language of one rabbi opposed to women's Torah study, "even if it is justified by 'violating his Torah for His sake'" (Rabbi Shmuel Halevy Vazner, cited in El-Or 1994:76). Rabbi Vazner is saying that his respected rabbinical colleagues may invoke the Talmudic injunction to overturn the Torah for God's sake in a time of crisis—first invoked to permit the oral tradition to be written down so as not to be forgotten, and here invoked to permit women, against the weight of centuries of rabbinic opinion, to be taught so that they will not defect from the community. He does not accept the justification, but grants that the analogy is rhetorically permissible.

Both the Talmudic and contemporary invocations of "[Let us] overturn your Torah; it is time to act for the sake of God's name" have to do with crises in the transmission and dissemination of authoritative knowledge, linked to the continuity and reproduction of the group for whom that knowledge is constitutive and authoritative. But even those within the Orthodox world who, unlike Rabbi Vazner, argue that tradition must be overturned for its own sake in such a crisis are not reaching for the kind of revolution implied by an ethic that focuses on the creative tensions between intersecting difference and genealogical filiation. Indeed, at the conclusion of Tamar El-Or's ethnography of "ultraorthodox" Jewish women's literacy in the contemporary Israeli state, she states that in this particular counterhegemonic social world, "Haredi women have learned to be educated (and to educate) in ignorance, in order to survive as educated women" (1994:202). Still this paradoxical formulation preserves a measure of indeterminacy, and the discursive possibilities opened up (even?) within this highly separatist group by the dilemma of change for the sake of tradition are documented throughout El-Or's study.

The point, then, is not necessarily to defend Torah scholarship as "liberating," but rather to question whether this repression of a constructed history is always the mechanism of construction, or whether (as in the published internal debates about "ultraorthodox" women's literacy that El-Or analyzes) the history can be very explicitly presented in the service of another, greater identification—here that with "a people," the story of whose very tangled and far from autochthonous birth is also presented within the explicit and authoritative tradition.[8]

8. And, although this is not an explicit concern of most Jews, "a people" whose survival is one cornerstone of the possibility of criticizing naturalized domination in the so-called "West."

After these animadversions, these muddled weighings of the scales, what connections could be suggested between a possible notion of "Jewish identity" in relation to Butler's account of identity formation and to Taylor's account of "the modern identity," linked to the general issue of the subject of justice? Once again, the asking of this question as a Jewish question is not as parochial as the conceit of translation into Yiddish would suggest, since the modern experience of Jews has been taken by some as the exemplary case of the impossibility of a justice recognized by all litigants *as* justice (Lyotard 1988). But if the rules are those of philosophy, then the "court" is academia with all its implicit and explicit standards and regulations. The Yiddish speaker present in court is neither plaintiff nor defendant, but merely present to offer evidence from a certain perspective that may serve to edify the court. Were the Yiddish speaker a litigant, she might not expect justice or even comprehension from a court whose language is English, whose default Bible is the Gospel, and whose etiquette demands that men remove their hats.

This stands in some contrast to the ideal suggested by Rabbi Singer's story about the Lemberger Gaon, and not only because that story is told in Yiddish. The Lemberger's revision of his judgment in a fashion that, according to the storyteller, satisfies not only all the parties but implicitly the Law as well seems to suggest an ideal of distributive harmony much more in line with the tenor of Taylor's account than with the insistence on tensions and disruptions that characterizes Butler. And Taylor hints at his own loyalty to some unspecified Law, as when he argues in what he calls his "thesis" against the presumption that the extreme secularism of the Enlightenment was motivated by nothing so much as simply a braver recognition of reality (1989:324). One thing that makes Taylor's book so puzzling is that on the one hand it insists on situating itself (he even refers to himself, albeit ambivalently, as a believer), and on the other the situation in which he places himself is one that he treats in an almost-universal guise—the modern Western male within the Christian discursive tradition.

Butler similarly says nothing explicit about her own cultural situatedness, even while insisting on the cultural situatedness of the theorist (1990:147). My *chutzpadik* hypothesis that it would enrich her account to "identify" as a Jew comes from certain phantom gestures she makes in this direction, along with a brilliant and unelaborated claim she makes about the link between gender and cultural genealogy: "Gender is a project which has cultural survival as its end" (1990:139). By contrast, Taylor's "self" (e.g., 1989:462)—for all his occasional talk about the "family"—is always disconnected from generation.

Nevertheless—or perhaps because of this, since it might be reasoned that a lessened demand for cultural survival would lead to a loosening of the bars in the prison house of gender—cultural survival as a value gets little consideration in Butler's account. Indeed, the moral sources of Enlightenment naturalism, which Taylor explicitly attends to (1989:351), seem to echo almost beyond the range of hearing in Butler's reliance on the masking through which normalized identities are enforced.

A major difference between the two is that Taylor is supremely in command of his "own" cultural idiom, which is the master one. There is something generally Pauline in Taylor's faith in the rightness of universal values. He says that "to talk of universal, natural, or human rights is to connect respect for human life and integrity with the notion of autonomy" (1989:12), but it is precisely this "notion of autonomy" that Butler diagnoses. Although Taylor insists that "a self can never be described without reference to those who surround it" (1989:35), there's a reassertion of the insistence on autonomy (1989:47) that draws us back once again to this overriding framework of the individual. That, in the framework of gender, is what Butler tries to undo, trying to help shape a new language beyond the antinomies in which Taylor is trapped.

So confident, so comfortable does he appear to be with the rightness and generalizability of this identity that despite a single passing mention of Emmanuel Levinas, Taylor is utterly oblivious to recent discussions of the construction of the Self through the construction of the Other. Indeed, Taylor seems to have little use for contemporary French ideas in general, seeing them as a faddish change on subjectivism rather than a fundamental critique of the Western subject: "Decentring is not the alternative to inwardness; it is its complement" (1989:465; see also 481). The charge certainly does not hold against Butler, who knows (as Taylor perhaps does not) that " 'inner' and 'outer' constitute a binary distinction that stabilizes and consolidates the coherent subject" (1990:134).

My appropriation of Butler, my "translation into Yiddish,"

might seem a gentle form of "outing." But it is not intended simply as an entry in the game of "Guess who's Jewish," and even less as an attempt to reclaim Judith Butler's soul! Beyond the question of any one critic's articulation of a personal identity, it is intended to foster Butler's program attendant on her insights about repetition and subversion, namely the identification and mobilization of a field of "local intervention" (1990:148). I do it perhaps first and foremost for *me,* in an attempt to expand the possibilities of my own primary cultural identity.

The conceit of casting myself as a translator may be labored, my diction flawed, my paragraphs stumbling, lacking Taylor's encyclopedic, emeritus-like sweep or Butler's ability to float like a butterfly and sting like a bee. Awkwardness and lack of transparency sometimes mark a translation that chooses to respect the difficult difference of the original language over the elegant composure of the language of reception (translators are always paid according to the market of the language they are translating into!). They are more a device than a price here, if the metaphor of translation serves to mark well that supplement, that situatedness, that both Butler and Taylor call for, but, still responding to the particular conventions of the academic disputation, fail to articulate in their own writing. My point has been not so much to sniff out what their respective situations really are, let alone to "fix" what their situations should be, but rather to limn a story that might someday be told in a minor language about the making and subversion of modern identity.

From Derrida to Fichte?
The New Europe, the Same Europe, and the Place of the Jews

To this we must add the influence of great fateful events that completely upset the international community insofar as, through them, the general faith in the idea and the practical ideal of Europe, that of a harmonious unity of the life of nations with its sources in the rational spirit, has been undermined.

At present we are faced with the imminent danger of the extinction of philosophy in this sense, and with it necessarily the extinction of a Europe founded on the spirit of truth. (Husserl 1970:xxvii)

If man loses this faith, it means nothing less than the loss of faith "in himself," in his own true being. . . . True being is *everywhere* an ideal goal, a task of epistēmē or "reason," as opposed to being which through *doxa* is merely thought to be, unquestioned and "obvious." (Ibid.:13)

Showing how Europe was never that much Greek, nor that much Jewish, nor that much Christian even but only attempted to define itself in relation to these different *caps*, never quite achieving an *absolute* distinction, the more showings of these inevitable failures there will be the quicker we close in onto other *horizons*.

—Gil Anidjar[1]

. . . the academic left's current dream [is] that history will somehow save one from the complacencies of humanism, that it is better to confront the historical roots of conflict than to comfort oneself with the fraudulent fantasy of a shared humanity, that "difference" and "otherness" are more progressive, more

1. In a lengthy set of comments on an earlier draft of this paper, which have helped me immensely in producing this final version.

hopeful, than "the illusory goal of wholeness." But why should
we believe any of this?

—Stephen Greenblatt (1993:120)

By way of introduction to this essay, I offer a prospectus written in
response to Michael Herzfeld's first request for abstracts.[2] At that
uncertain but earlier date, it still seemed that 1992—marking
neatly the fiftieth anniversary of the midpoint of World War II,
the departure of Columbus's first voyage, and the expulsion of the
Jews from Spain—was indeed to be the year of the New Europe.
Events during 1992, including the refusal of certain countries to
sign the Maastricht agreement and the backlash against foreign
workers and refugees in the reunited Germany, belied that expectation. This essay too has developed in its own fashion, growing
much more introspective and less grounded in the concerns with
social history enunciated in the prospectus. The original prospectus, then, offers a convenient summary of the extratextual framework away from which the analysis shies. That demurral in turn is
justified by a series of initial critical responses to the prospectus.

Here, then, is the original prospectus:

THE NEW EUROPE AND THE PLACE OF THE JEWS

Looking at the evolution of "Europe"—as a cultural and economic entity—from the standpoint of Jewish history has many ad-
vantages. Arguably, one of the most powerful motivations for the
transcendence of narrow nationalisms is the terrible legacy of
Nazism. Nazism, in turn, rested to a considerable extent on the
specter of an international Jewish society that—scandalously—
was not confined within the "proper" boundaries of various
nation-states. To the extent that, in the early twentieth century,
there were significant levels of practical and communicative interaction between Jews in different countries, this reflected not only
traditional patterns of Jewish social organization, but also broader
intra-European patterns of trade and communication that pre-
dated the rise of discrete nation-states.

2. This essay was originally drafted for a conference on "European Identity and
Its Intellectual Roots," sponsored by the Social Science Research Council and held
at Harvard University in May 1993.

In a very real way, in fact, traditional Jewish society can be taken as a model of European transnationalism. Both Jewish learning and the livelihood of Jewish communities were dependent on long-distance, "international" trade networks, as documents from the early modern period clearly demonstrate. Thus, collections of moral parables printed in Yiddish in High Holiday prayer books contain stories of sons of Russian Jews caught by the secular temptations of the Leipzig fair. The memoirs of Glueckel of Hameln, an eighteenth-century matriarch and businesswoman, detail the interaction of marriage and trade connections between North Germany and Holland (1977).

This Jewish culture area bore the name Ashkenaz. Over the centuries from the Middle Ages to the modern period, Ashkenazic Jews were spread from Amsterdam to Odessa. Today, especially when contrasted with the rubric of "Sephardim"—popularly taken to mean Mediterranean, North African, and Middle Eastern Jews—the term "Ashkenazi" is considered synonymous with "European." But clearly the borders of Ashkenaz are not identical with those of the New—northern, southern, and central—Europe. The idea of Ashkenaz, while clearly not "local," is just as surely an indigenous one, and its scope therefore affords an excellent perspective for delineating the historical and cultural specificity of the notion of Europe. Precisely the gap between "Ashkenaz" and "Europe," however, reminds us of the expulsion of the Sephardim proper—the Jews of Spain—and thus of the deeper roots of Christian European identity in the exclusion of Jews (J. Boyarin 1993).

Modern Jewish liberal thinkers enthusiastically embraced the European Enlightenment, which they depicted both as consistent with core Jewish values and as offering Jews a chance to be recognized as equal human beings. Jews may also have suffered ideologically from some of the prophets of European identity, such as Ernest Renan, who argued in his essay "What Is a Nation?" for solidarity among the "advanced" European peoples (i.e., the Germans and the French) against the backward races and nations (Renan 1990). Because Jews are an excluded group who have nevertheless been present inside Europe for so long, focusing on the discourse of Jews and about Jews should prove an unusually opportune way to distinguish the inclusive from the exclusive aspects of the idea and program of a new, united Europe. For example, it would seem that whereas opposition to anti-Semitism is generally consistent with a liberal view of the new Europe, such liberalism is not necessarily free of chauvinist discourse vis-à-vis other "minority" groups. On the other hand, anti-Semitism, racism, and anti-immigrant sentiments are almost invariably linked on the part of nationalists resisting the idea of a broader Europe.

The Jewish presence in contemporary Europe is not solely historical or theoretical. On the one hand, there has been a reconstitution of thriving, face-to-face Jewish communities in various countries of Western Europe, especially France. On the other hand, the question of virulent anti-Semitism in Eastern Europe is an important aspect of the evolving relation between the former Communist bloc countries and the new Europe of the EEC. Is it possible that a new trans-European Jewish identity will be created? The safety of Jews in the new Europe may prove to be a remarkably accurate test of how thoroughly the murderous contradictions of the old Europe have been resolved.

With a lapse of time, various rhetorical slips and indeed false implications in this text all appear to demand criticism. I number these points for convenience.

1. The pious reference to "the terrible legacy of Nazism" as conferring a privileged standpoint to "Jewish history" might be seen as an exploitative victimology, making cultural capital out of the death of ancestors—a problem, of course, which belies a vast amount of work in critical cultural studies, and which perhaps cannot be transcended, but always only pointed to. In any case, at least one of the texts to which I respond in this essay indirectly but powerfully criticizes the use of anti-Semitism as a justification for the generalization of Jewish perspectives in critical hermeneutics.

2. Jews are not the only example of a group that refused to confine itself within modern nation-states. The Romanies, called "Gypsies," have suffered for that sin as well, and the ways in which they function like and unlike Jews vis-à-vis the construction of "Europe" will be briefly alluded to here.

3. I have learned to beware of phrases of insistence and reassurance, such as "certainly," "to be sure," and the one that ap-

pears here, "in a very real way." To assert that a tradition can serve as a model in changed circumstances even for those who owe no allegiance to that model is a very dubious move, and the phrase "in a very real way" seems mostly designed to convince the author. Not that the assertion is necessarily wrong; but the sentence as it stands seems to cut off the issues of chronology, determination, and exemplarity that will be central to this paper.

4. There is an apparent non sequitur between the first and second sentences of the fourth paragraph. Did Jews suffer from modern Jewish liberal thinkers' embrace of Enlightenment? Perhaps Jews only suffered from the failure of all Europeans to embrace Enlightenment! In any case the implication here of a *betrayal* of the mass of Jews by a modernizing intellectual elite, or by the modern regimes of thought to which that elite aspired and often gained access, is hereby made explicit and will be interrogated below.

5. The mock-innocent verb "to be," here declined as "Jews are an excluded group," precludes the very historicization of Jewish exclusion, a process I want to claim as integral to the invention of Europe.

6. Once again, despite a series of distressing incidents, especially in France, at the time this prospectus was written it seemed that the main contemporary problem with European anti-Semitism lay in the East. Today, in March 1993, that is no longer clear, and it is possible to invoke the relevance of anti-Semitism without referring to Eastern Europe at all. In any case, the paper as it stands focuses on the "idea of Europe" that still centers on England, France, and Germany. As to the rest, I will content myself with citing (and refrain from interpreting) the suggestion of my friend Konstanty Gebert, a Jew, a Pole, and a critical journalist, that this essay might as well be called "The Jew Europe and the Place of the News."

7. Finally, the safety of Jews in Europe might prove to be unrelated to the dynamics of tolerance and diversification as they concern the vast majority of native Europeans, immigrants, and refugees. Studying the security of Jewish lives and the freedom of expression of Jewish identity and culture is important not only for the role Jews play as a litmus test. On the other hand, this essay will insist that Jewish identity is indeed marked by a constant ten-

sion between self-identification, and identification by and as the Other.

It will be noticed that the title has become both more precise and more obscure since the prospectus was written. There are at least three explanations of this:

1. The arrival of a massive and disturbing new book has helped shift the focus of this paper toward an examination of European critical discourses on identity and the place of the Jews. Being an anthropologist, albeit one who poaches freely in the domains of history and literary theory, I am led to characterize this examination as an interpretive ethnography of a peculiarly (although now by no means exclusively) European practice of theory. By a "practice of theory" I do not necessarily imply a "theoretical practice" in the curious sense latter-day Marxists have given to that phrase, which redeems theory as revolutionary action. I simply mean that theory can be dealt with in the same way anthropologists deal with any product or discourse of any culture.

2. The sense of deception or at least uncertainty about the lowering of national tensions and differences within the New Europe leads to the question mark after the connection of the late-twentieth-century thinker Jacques Derrida and Johann Gottlieb Fichte, who wrote around the turn of the nineteenth century. A commonsensical chronological account, of course, would trace the relations among nationalism, capitalism, and philosophy "from Fichte to Derrida." My hypothetical reversal of this chronology promotes the tragic sense that, far from the question of personal, ethnic, national, and "European" identity having grown progressively less rigid and chauvinistic and more open and contingent in the course of the last two centuries, we are experiencing a regressive flow back toward a "primitive" ego and ethnocentrism. The question mark represents my own interrogation of this tragic gesture, that is to say, of merely placing the shopworn idea of progress in a reflecting mirror. Few gestures of academic criticism are as ready to hand or as futile as that of standing aside and noting the growing darkness.

3. The question of the same has been added, and it will be explored here in three senses. First, is the proper goal of criticism of European identity today the reestablishment of a liberal and

tolerant vision of Europe that has somehow been derailed, perhaps through the loss of a demonic Communist Other and the renewal of economic crisis? Is our goal the same Europe; "is this the *same* Europe, then, that is being unified for a second time" (Naas 1992:xxxv)? Second, a stock theme of poststructuralist criticism is that the project of Europe defines itself *as* the self-same, and its mission as the remaking of the world into the same, into a Europe writ large. Indeed, when 1992 still loomed hopeful ahead of us, much was written about whether the entire world was destined to become like the expected Europe of 1992, or rather to move "backward" toward barbarism. Finally, the Jews are sometimes cast as the paradigmatic Other that, more than any other Other, has made it possible for Europe to define its identity, its sameness. Is there a Jewish place in Europe, beyond Otherness? Should we continue to argue for, to hope for, a Europe constituted with rather than over against the Jews? Should we abandon the Jews to their (our) fate among the nations, and thus abandon the latter, liberal idea of a small continent and its identity? To ask the questions again implies that there is still hope and desire for that "other" Europe, and I will not try hard to dispel that hope and that desire.

I.

It is notably through the common exclusion of Jews—later Arabs—by all the nations, even though born from the dissolution of the former politico-theological unity of the Middle Ages, that the signifier "Christendom" has come to mean "Europe" or European civilization. Naturally some intellectuals have also forged the idea according to which Europe as such does not exist *without the Jews* and the Jewish tradition: thus the Jews, who have no territory of their own in Europe, no national *status*, would be the catalyst of the community of European peoples and of the "consciousness" of their destiny. Thus we are presented with a myth mirroring the myth of Christendom. And the game of mirrors can go on: when the "Judeo-Christian dialogue" is begun, the essence of Europe is at stake, etc. (Balibar 1990:n.4, p. 293)

This is a tremendously concise and insightful statement. It neatly overcomes the dehistoricization of Jewish exclusion that I have just criticized, carefully notes that Jews were not the only ones subject to such exclusion, and marks the contingent identification of Christianity and Europe. It further observes that in a certain liberal conception, because the Jews have no geographical particularity within Europe, and can (or could once) be found throughout Europe, they are the truest "Europeans." This, Balibar suggests, is merely another way of enforcing the identity of "Europe," as is a third alternative, emphasizing the interactive dialogue of Jews and Christians.

Tremendously insightful, except that this statement does not in itself dismantle any of the three "myths." Nor is it clear what the term "myth" is meant to denote here; all the term carries is a vague connotation of false consciousness. It may well be that "Europe as such does not exist *without the Jews*"; it only needs to be made explicit that "Europe as such" is itself a contingent construct. Deliberately or no, Balibar's use of the phrase "as such" is altogether ambivalent; for we are so accustomed to thinking with the concept of Europe, so accustomed to taking Europe as a given entity, that even where he is paraphrasing the views of "some intellectuals" and not expounding his own constructive notions, the "Europe as such" here is reinforced as well as interrogated— at least on a first reading. Is he indeed suggesting that, contrary to the tropes he is identifying, there is a "Europe as such" that could or does exist even without the Jews? Presumably he is not, and Balibar is at least as aware as I that "Europe as such" is a historical and cultural product, one in which debate about the place of the Jews has been a major ingredient. Then he is saying, correctly, that these liberals want to insist against the chauvinists that the only true Europe, their "Europe as such" (Husserl's "Europe founded on the spirit of truth") is the one that has room for the Jews and imagines itself in interaction with Jews.

Balibar's footnote points obliquely at another insight, that the obsession with the role of the Jews in European identity can serve to keep the idea of Europe and the criticism of its effects confined to the territory of Europe, and hence to keep the formerly colonized world in the background. But, if I achieve nothing else in this essay, I will not permit once again the Jewish question and the colonial question to obscure each other's role in making and remaking Europe. After all this essay, this conference on European identity are being invented beyond Europe, in that other headland of England where the phenomenon of nationalism arising out of European colonization first appeared.[3] What is the ground of a discourse about European identity, carried on outside Europe, at the "other" Cambridge that is at the *same* time the headland of the idea of the university in the United States—the Harvard of Cambridge, the Harvard of Harvard? Insofar as my academic and intellectual identity is that of a Jew in America, to what extent is *my* or rather "my" identity European? Are Americans European? Clearly so for some purposes, but the question is too large to deal with here. Are Jews per se European—especially if "Europe as such does not exist *without the Jews?*" The move is tempting: to adopt the professional stance Walter Benjamin feared as his fate, to survive in America as "the last European" (Arendt 1969:18). Certainly it is valid to ask whether the appeal of Jewishness for certain young Jews in America is quite unconnected with the idealized image of a certain European culture. As you will read below, a certain critique of European bourgeois hermeneuticism will suggest that to identify a Jewish ethos with "Europe as such" is to perpetuate an exhausted and intellectual liberal discourse of emancipation, though that critique does not suggest an effective replacement for an emancipatory hermeneutics. More straightforwardly, even to raise the question of the American Jew as imaginary European (and hence disrupt that identification) turns us toward that "other" Jew whose Jewish genealogy is not European. For this essay, the Algerian-born Jackie Derrida (Derrida 1993) will serve.

II. AN AGONISTIC TRIAD: FICHTE, LAMBROPOULOS, DERRIDA

In a recently published thin volume called *The Other Heading* ("L'Autre cap" in the much more suggestive French) (Derrida

---

3. I do not mean that there can be a pure notion of Europe that would grant such a perspective, but rather I intend to mark in passing two notions: first, that the relation of North America or of the United States to "old," geographic Europe, to Valéry's "'appendix' to the Asian continent," *might* fruitfully be thought of in terms of postcoloniality; and second, that the questions of centrality, of the putative responsibilities of declining colonial powers, that Derrida raises in the text I analyze here evidently could be brought to bear on the confused issue of the United States' relation to colonialism in the 1990s.

1992), Derrida attempts to acknowledge the history of European domination through capital while refusing the complete abdication of a certain notion of European centrality.[4] The central essay of the volume was itself written for a conference on European identity, and as I will discuss, for Derrida the notion of identity seems connected willy-nilly to some degree of centrality. Hence his formulation of the question:

> I will deduce the form of all my propositions from a grammar and syntax of the heading, of the *cap*, from a difference in kind and gender [*genre*], that is, from *capital* and *capitale*. How can a "European cultural identity" respond, and in a responsible way—responsible for itself, for the other, before the other—to the double question of *le capital*, of capital, and of *la capitale*, of the capital? (Derrida 1992:16)

As is his custom, Derrida has chosen to explode a kind of pun, a nucleus in which he sees a highly effective but unstable union of material and moral power. To the extent that Europe both remains *la capitale*—setting attitudes and policies that will vitally affect the situation of those living on other headlands as well—and disposes of *le capital*—the accumulated wealth of centuries of colonialism—the question of responsibility cannot be escaped for anyone who enjoys or claims a European identity. But in his new book *The Rise of Eurocentrism: Anatomy of Interpretation* (1992) (completed too soon for the author to have addressed *The Other Heading*), Vassilis Lambropoulos attacks Derrida in particular and the asking of this kind of question in general, a habit that he at-

---

4. Gil Anidjar has asked me whether it would be possible to talk about Europe and at the same time completely abdicate from "a certain notion of European centrality." The question is complicated. In principle, why would the speaker have to identify "with" Europe or "as" Europe? What if Derrida were to work for a moment as an anthropologist, and attempt speaking about Europe from, say, an "Islamic" center—as I, implicitly here at least, attempt to speak about Europe from a "Jewish" center? On the other hand, what would happen if one were to propose a conference titled "Islam and Its Others?" It seems that for now at least, the terms of art at such a conference would necessarily be derived from European or at least post-[European]colonial theory. See the critique of Charles Taylor by Partha Chatterjee (1990), where the latter argues that even if the only language we have for speaking about universal questions of identity is "European," that language still has a local European specificity and history. For another suggestive seed of a possible ethnography of European universalism, see Asad 1993, esp. pp. 200–208.

tributes not so much to the Jewish tradition of close interpretive reading as to a dominant discourse of Protestant "Hebraism." Lambropoulos might suggest that whatever the response to a question based on the difference between a word's masculine and feminine declensions might be, it will have little political import; but we need not concur with that judgment too hastily.

Remembering the Jews (which Derrida barely does in *The Other Heading*), this brief question of Derrida's can be questioned in turn from another unexpected direction. Invoking "responsibility," isn't Derrida thereby reinforcing the proper, decent, and even paternal "Europe as such," that which duly and dutifully attends to the Other before itself, in an empathy that, paradoxically, founds Europe's sense of itself? Not quite, for Derrida immediately goes on to specify the *kind* of responsibility he is talking about, a responsibility for the maintenance of contingency, of "an opening and a non-exclusion" of the other, such that European identity never would be fixed and defined, once and for all, but would always and in different ways at each time and place be reworked and interrogated by its encounter with the other heading. This may indeed be a sharp way to specify Europe, though in my reading Derrida betrays the limitations of his own questioning of European centrality by an almost reflexive subsequent move to link this notion of Europe to "every history" (17). The specificity of Europe, of the trope of identity, is partially lost when Europe becomes once again the prime example of "a history" or "a culture." What of those inside Europe who would fail to see themselves as perpetually self-questioning and "open" in this way, who would define themselves in a different way than through a bracing encounter with the Other, indeed, who might have no particular interest in whether or not they are "Europeans?" When the job at hand is the definition of Europe, are such internal others merely an irritation? In the revealing case of Fichte, the Jews did indeed constitute such an irritation.[5]

As suggested already, it is tempting to "just do" Derrida and Fichte in this paper, to move from Derrida to Fichte in an attempt at rhetorical reversal of linear chronology, either as a tragic expression of the failure of Enlightenment or as a plea for a return to premodern "transnational" links of trade and culture as a

5. As the historian Karl Morrison notes (1988:xii–xiii), only to drop the point.

model for post-1992 Europe. Such a rhetorical reversal, as we all know by now, would tend to reinforce rather than dismantle the time-line progressivism of modernity. I choose instead to counter the temptation by concluding the paper with a serious consideration of Lambropoulos's book, since one of Lambropoulos's themes (especially in his long chapter on Horkheimer and Adorno's *Dialectic of Enlightenment* [Horkheimer and Adorno 1972]) is precisely the political resignation implied by the tragic take on the failure of Enlightenment.

Still, the question mark does not mean that the hypothetical return of Fichte is posed only to be dismissed. One reason it should be kept in play is precisely because so many responses to contemporary European intolerance are couched in the language of the return of the repressed that we might want to add our own candidates for previously unconsidered returned repressions. A strikingly concise example of this kind of response is contained in a recent article on anti-Semitism in the post–cold war world: "With the end of the bipolar world order," writes Henri Zukier in the *New School Commentator*, "all the congealed forces erupt again, unfettered and with renewed identity. Our ever-shrinking world condemns all societies to become progressively multicultural" (1993:2). The language here bears close scrutiny. "Congealed forces" suggests some sort of undifferentiated, primeval ooze, from which we were only temporarily made safe by the vigilant maintenance of fetters; the *production* of chauvinist and intolerant ideologies under Communist or advanced capitalist regimes is obviated by the insistence that it is the collapse of such regimes that allows such naturalized forces to wreak havoc on civil society. Similarly, the image of the "ever-shrinking world" seems like something that no longer offers us adequate room to breathe or to move around in, alone and self-identical; inevitably, unfortunately, and against our will we are all "condemned" to "progressive multiculturalism." For our own good, even though we naturally hate it, we're going to have to resign ourselves to the co-presence of people who are different from us. The tone, though not the immediate content, is much like the French Ministry of Foreign Affairs document cited by Derrida: " 'It is the task of *culture* to *impose* the feeling of unity, of European solidarity' " (1992:51; emphases Derrida's). Zukier seems to assume on the one hand that the primitive, unrepressed state is one of egoism and intolerance, and on the other that it is only in our century that groups have experienced significant mixing.

In one sense this view of multiculturalism as an unfortunate discipline is analogous to the Fichte who will be cited below, in the full flower of an early articulation of organic and autochthonous German cultural identity. On the other hand, it no longer assumes, with Fichte, that such organic identities are something we can afford. Echoes and difference together; or, as Derrida puts it, "We must be suspicious of *both* repetitive memory *and* the completely other of the absolutely new" (19). At least this would help us remember that cultural diversity is not in any way a peculiarly postmodern phenomenon, nor something that should be dealt with through a mere disciplined restraint of the expression of intact identity, a giving way to share space with the other. I will allude briefly to Yiddish as another model of intercultural creativity (see Weinreich 1980)—yes, another example, a model offering perhaps the possibility of a *minor centrality* (cf. Kronfeld 1996)— only to return quickly to Fichte.

III.

The contrast between Yiddish and the notion of a "lingua franca" is instructive. Its development was conditioned as fundamentally by the core Jewish cultural tradition of collective and oral textual study as by the range and sequence of intercultural contexts in which its speakers lived. Before the Nazi genocide that drastically reduced the number of its speakers, there was never a great concern with maintaining the purity of its word stock. Yiddish was the language of a nonstate, diasporic group bound together by links of trade, marriage, mutual aid, shared textual obsessions, and shared practices. Its reach did not constitute the supranationalism of an intellectual or diplomatic elite, but rather the tenuous extent of a network that operated around, through, and largely despite the establishment of principalities and nascent national states. Yiddish is geographically defined as a language of migration, its word stock defining it as a Germanic tongue, the demography of its speakers centering its use, until the Nazi genocide, far to the east of "Germany." Yiddish has never enjoyed legitimation as a state language, and it has never served as the cultural double of a military power, in the way that English is tied to England, French to France, and German to Germany.

Not that the ideological history of Yiddish is entirely free of attempts to harness it to state allegiances. In an article published a year before *The Other Heading,* Derrida analyzes an essay by the German Jewish philosopher Hermann Cohen, titled *Deutschtum und Judentum,* published in 1915 during World War I, and as Derrida observes (1991:74), aimed at convincing the American Jews that they should not support a war against Germany and *its* Jews. In the course of his argument, which purports to show a distinctive affinity between Jewish and German ethics, Cohen attempts to cancel the transnationality of Yiddish and claim the Germanic loyalties of its speakers. Cohen does this indirectly, through an attack on the French Jewish philosopher Henri Bergson, whom he attacks as an unloyal son both of his biological father and of his Germanic-Jewish heritage: " 'He is the son of a Polish Jew who spoke Yiddish. What may be happening in the soul of this Mister Bergson when he remembers his father and denies Germany its ideals!' " (quoted in Derrida 1991:74).

The notion of a special affinity between Jews and Germans was by no means an idiosyncrasy of Cohen's at this time. The legacy of German Enlightenment was still very much present during the first decades of this century. During World War I, the czarist regime assumed that the Jews of the Russian Empire would support the German invaders, and caused a great deal of suffering by forcibly evacuating masses of Jews from the western provinces further into the interior during the course of the war. The German philologist Beranek pursued studies in Yiddish dialect geography between the wars, partly in support of German colonial claims in the East (Beranek 1965).

It is not necessary to denounce these co-optations in retrospect. Variants of Yiddish and different spoken German dialects clearly do enjoy a high degree of mutual comprehensibility. On the other hand, any talk about a supposed unique compatibility between the essential spirits of Jews and Germans is obviously and painfully anachronistic now.[6] The very notions of national

6. Gershom Scholem was understandably quite severe on this point: "It is true: the fact that Jewish creativity poured forth here is perceived by the Germans, now

essences and of linguistic (sometimes along with racial) purity remain current and powerful, however. Yiddish still survives as a vernacular among a shrinking community of elderly secular Jews (J. Boyarin 1991) and continues to evolve among the thriving Hasidic communities in Israel, the United States, and elsewhere, where it remains viable as an example of a successful mediation between the desire to preserve group specificity and the reality of regular intergroup communication.[7] It gives the lie to the theses about the desirability of an integral and unbroken community of speakers of a given language, offered by Fichte in the fourth of his *Addresses to the German Nation,* titled "The Chief Difference between the German and the Other Peoples of Teutonic Descent." First noting a fundamental distinction between words referring to perceptible, "sensuous" images and those that denote "supersensuous" concepts, Fichte states that the latter can only be named through metaphorical reference to the former, and he continues:

> if . . . we make the assumption that the people of this [i.e. any] language have continued in unbroken communication, and that what one has thought and expressed has before long come to the knowledge of all, then what has previously been said in general is valid for all who speak this language. To all who will but think the

that all is over. . . . But it no longer changes anything about the fact that no dialogue is possible with the dead, and to speak of an 'indestructibility of this dialogue' strikes me as blasphemy" (Scholem 1976:64). My concern here however is not with the moral problems of German intellectuals but with the whole notion of national "essences" or "spirits" and their putative compatibility or lack of same. Nor do I have any wish to claim that the Jewish participation in modern German culture and a fortiori in the shaping of European modernity was illusory or unfruitful, or that there were no distinctive elements in German-language cultural production (the *Trauerspiel* perhaps, or as even Scholem concedes, Johann Peter Hebel's openness toward difference) that gave this fruit a unique character. On the contrary, the "German-Jewish" encounter and its tremendous creativity constitute a fundamental aspect of a certain notion of Europe to which I still owe allegiance, and that I cannot (yet?) see how I could possibly disavow.

7. For East European Hasidim at the turn of the century, a *daytsh* referred to a Reform or modern-style Jew, at least as much as it referred to a non-Jewish German (see J. Boyarin 1994c). I might add here that the ethnography of contemporary Hasidic communities, which in the last decade or two has focused on their successful negotiation of modernity, might be enlivened by insights from the current debate about comparative diasporas.

image deposited in the language is clear; to all who really think it
is alive and stimulates their life.

Such is the case, I say, with a language which, from the time the
first sound broke forth among the same people, has developed
continuously out of the actual common life of the people, and into
which no element has ever entered that did not express an observation actually experienced by this people, and, moreover, an observation standing in a connection of wide-spread reciprocal influence with all the other observations of the same people. It does not
matter if ever so many individuals of other race and other language
are incorporated with the people speaking their language; provided the former are not permitted to bring the sphere of their
observations up to the position from which the language is thereafter to develop, they remain dumb in the community and without
influence on the language, until the time comes when they themselves have entered into the sphere of observation of the other
people (Fichte 1979:61-62)

Several assertions contained here need to be underscored by
paraphrase. Sound—language—originates in nature, and that
language closest to the original eruption is the most authentic
and the most "alive." The group progresses if it enjoys unbroken
continuity, since "what one has thought . . . [inevitably becomes]
the knowledge of all." Thus, for instance, a German philosopher
speaking in German could claim that any insights he had would
inexorably become the shared heritage of all the German people.
Any such genuine insights must rest on what is "actually experienced": despite Fichte's supposed romantic turn, there is still
reference here to some ground of experience that authenticates
claims to authoritative discourse. The ideas are not racist per se;
although Fichte clearly links genealogy, linguistic continuity, and
collective wisdom, he is ready to admit that outsiders could come
to share in that collective wisdom. But it is imperative that until
they gradually do so, they must "remain dumb in the community," not infecting the immediate relation between language and
experience that grants it—and the case in point here is of course
the German people—an access to reality and Enlightenment
superior to that of any other people. Since Fichte gave these
addresses in the course of the academic year 1807-1808, during

the Napoleonic occupation of the Germanic states, the "other people" he has in mind here are the French, whom he designates by the term "neo-Latin peoples"—thus combining the discretion of the occupied with the suggestion that, unlike the Germans, the French have betrayed their authentic Teutonic heritage and hence stand at a more confused, less enlightened stage than the Germans themselves. Thus Fichte writes that the "German . . . above all other European nations, [has] the capacity of responding to such an [enlightening] education" (52) . . . because "the German speaks a language which has been alive ever since it first issued from the force of nature, whereas the other Teutonic races speak a language which has movement on the surface only but is dead at the root" (68).

This is by no means an anti-Semitic analysis, then, whatever uses may have later been made in anti-Semitic ideology of the notion of organic national culture adumbrated here; it is rather anti-Gallic. Earlier in a career that was otherwise free of anti-Jewish statements or acts, Fichte published the four viciously anti-Jewish pages to which Morrison refers in his book on empathy. To move from Fichte in 1808 to Fichte in 1793 need not be an exercise in trying either to exonerate or to accuse some construct called "Fichte" of some complex called "anti-Semitism," but to flush out an unexpected link between these passages. In the course of his early "Contributions to Correcting Public Opinion on the Rightfulness of the French Revolution," Fichte wrote that

> "Through almost all countries of Europe spreads a powerful state which is hostile to all others, is continually at war with them, and in some states presses very heavily upon the citizens: it is Judaism. . . ." The separation of the Jews from the alien surrounding, commanded by their religion and deepened by their national pride, prevented them from developing friendly relations with their host nations. . . . [Fichte continued] "Far from these pages be the poisonous breath of intolerance as it is from my heart. . . . They must possess human rights, although they do not acknowledge ours, for they are humans and their injustice does not excuse our becoming like them. . . . But to give them civil rights, I see no other means than that of cutting off all their heads in one night and of placing others upon their bodies in which there is not even one Jewish idea. To protect us from them, I again see no other way than of

conquering their beloved country for them and to send all of them
thereto." (Low 1979:144–46)

What runs consistent in the two excerpts from texts written
fifteen years apart is the positing of an ideal and uniform entity
enveloping the national language, culture, and state. In the earlier text the Jews are noted as an obstreperous and unreformable
flaw in that unity; by the time of the latter, Fichte seems to imagine ways in which Jews and others could be gradually integrated
into the organic group. Fichte is by no means the originator of
the idea of the Jews as a state within a state, but here the state of
shared *affect*—of a capacity for empathy limited to fellow Jews and
hence disrupting the concentric empathy of the state proper and
all the citizens within it—is made to mark the Jews irredeemably.
Indeed, the notion of the ethnic nation-state seems so powerful
here that Fichte's conclusion is Zionism *avant le lettre*. The association may be a painful one for some; perhaps that is why Morrison's
paraphrase of this passage has Fichte calling for "the conquest of
a homeland for the Jews and the deportation of them all to it"
(1988:xii)—i.e., not "*their* homeland"—emphasis mine.

Alfred Low argues that in the essay from which this quote is
drawn, Fichte was primarily arguing for the expansion of the right
to form associations within the state, and concluding from the
example of the Jews that such associations "were perhaps harmful
but did not actually undermine the existing state" (Low 1979:
144). I would not want to conclude from that context that this
exemplary rhetorical use of the Jews was inconsequential. Which
brings us to the next theme raised by the juxtaposition of this
agonistic triad, namely the politics of the example.

IV.

The question of examples is explored at length by Michael Naas
in his introduction to *The Other Heading* (Naas 1992). The critical
point is that the use of "examples" in European rhetoric is not
neutral, but a highly charged topos in European culture. It is not
only that the question of which examples are selected for an argument about the best way to understand or to rectify a given
situation are inseparable from the question of power over that
situation. More than that, part of the lingering legacy of Euro-

pean hegemony is the very idea that it is proper and possible to set an example, to compare examples, to be at liberty to take an example, to make an example of someone or some country. Exemplifying is an act of rhetorical and of material power.

Jews are thus examples of different notions of Europe. In addition to specifying the Jews as a uniquely and unequivocally demonic force, Hitler made an example of them as well. They were the example of what had to be eliminated in order to produce a New Europe. Anti-fascists and other liberals, as Balibar suggests, also take the Jews as exemplary Europeans, those without whom there can be no "Europe as such." The Nazi genocide of the Jews is commonly taken as the paradigmatic example of intolerance (as in the new Museum of Intolerance in Los Angeles) and of genocide, and there is constant political tension over the generalizability of the term "holocaust," which has somehow become attached to that particular genocide (Patraka 1992).

The point can be made clearer by contrast with a different example. Katie Trumpener has recently written an eloquent article, "The Time of the Gypsies" (Trumpener 1992), analyzing numerous literary uses of the Romany people as a figure for freedom from the constraints of bourgeois domesticity and routine. It is first of all significant that Trumpener finds the emphasis on the image of the Gypsies as living in "another time" to be salient, whereas so far I have been focusing on the Jews as a *spatial* disruption of the European state system. Nevertheless, the very fact that in English at least these people are called "Gypsies" means that they are associated with the Orient. The identification of these people as non-European, combined with their presence throughout Europe, makes them available as a sort of pan-European theme in romantic and modernist literature. Though they are even more transnational than the Jews, they do not share the primitive capitalist image of thrift, domesticity, and industry. Few elite thinkers would imagine taking the Romany as an exemplary premodern people useful as a resource in the reinvention of Europe. Perhaps someone like Gilles Deleuze (the theoretician who, along with Felix Guattari, highlighted notions such as "nomadism" and "deterritorialization") might do so (Deleuze and Guattari 1986); although again, he would be more likely to figure the Gypsies in the prospective dissolution of Europe rather than in its reinvention. The counterexample helps to highlight the particular ways in which the more common example of the Jews (or as Lyotard 1990 styles them, the "jews") functions in respectable European critical theory.

It would be easy to say, especially if one is an admirer of Derrida, that it is inadequate now to take the Jews as an example in this fashion. Nor will we learn much by taking once again the French model of liberal, assimilative tolerance as an example, as Julia Kristeva has been doing of late, traveling North America touting good French Enlightenment against bad German Romanticism. Perhaps we could combine the two, taking as our example contemporary discussions by French Jews about Judaism in France—discussions marked by their simultaneous expression and interrogation of diasporic ethnic identity and liberal values (see Friedlander 1990; J. Boyarin 1992a). These debates instructively mark the current status of discussions of universality and difference. In order to avoid once again idealizing or vilifying "France" as the particular instantiation of universal culture, they need to be situated within the history of Jews in France, of France within Europe, of the twentieth-century doctrine of national self-determination, and of France vis-à-vis Germany, especially German philosophy—the kind of relationship binding Husserl to Derrida, for example.

Thus, notably, a certain strain in contemporary French thought identifies an enlightened opposition to myth with Judaism (Nancy 1991; see also Boyarin and Boyarin 1993) and, in the name of the Jews as exemplars of suffering, readmits Kant through the back door. "Kant's thought, whose Protestant descendance is so evident, has very rapidly been interpreted as a profound Judaism" (Derrida 1991:69). This identification may help to explain a problem I have raised elsewhere (J. Boyarin 1992b), namely the way the critique of anti-Semitism is commonly divorced from the critique of imperialism. If critics of imperialist ideology likewise read an idealized Judaism in Kantian-Protestant terms, they may agree that Jews are properly Europeans, and hence the treatment of Jews, while perhaps scandalous, is a European family matter. For this reason as well we must avoid the temptation to resolve the question of the place of Jews in Europe too quickly by insisting that not only are Jews Europeans but they are the exemplary Europeans!

The temptation to view Jews as proto-Enlighteners, and hence at least complicit participants in the workings of European imperialism, is reinforced by the common dichotomy between an Enlightenment devoted to a purified individualistic universalism and a Romantic movement identified with an unalloyed organic nationalism. The example of Fichte, whose presumptive turn from Enlightenment to Romanticism was accompanied precisely by an abandonment of his early willingness to indulge in easy anti-Jewish rhetoric and a principled defense of Jewish civil rights, should help to dispel that assumption. In fact Derrida refers precisely to Fichte on this point, arguing that "nationalism and cosmopolitanism have always gotten along well together, as paradoxical as this may seem. Since the time of Fichte, numerous examples might attest to this" (1992:48). *The Other Heading* does not refer to Hermann Cohen, but the possible analogy between the supposed German-Jewish synthesis and the evident caution with which we should approach a putative new French-Jewish synthesis lead us to recall Cohen as another example of this combination. As Derrida explains (1991:49), Cohen argued for Judaism's "essentially cosmopolitan" character starting with Philo.

Cohen was thus able to couch his argument about the affinities between Jewishness and Germanness in a long tradition of German philosophical discourse on the (paradoxically) unique universality of the German culture, language, and spirit. Unintimidated by the possible charge that national chauvinism begins with the Jewish Bible (Akenson 1992), Derrida proceeds to cite Fichte's own use, in the third *Address to the German Nation*, of Ezekiel's vision of the restoration to national greatness of "those in captivity, not in their own, but in a foreign land" (Derrida 1991: 78). Here Fichte identifies the Germans with the Jews; in 1793, he had called for the separation of the Jews from the Germans, perhaps because he sincerely thought that the only solution was for the Jews to be where they *belonged*, in their own land. For that Fichte, and in this the early essay indeed sounds the note for a long tradition of anti-Jewish writings, the Jews disrupt the very idea of Europe. They do not fit into any of the existing states that have the potential for internal identity and hence mutual harmony. It is *that* idea which Derrida, here and elsewhere, repeatedly comes to disrupt, and by no means only for or "in the name of" the Jews.

V. IDENTITY AND THE SAME

A cardinal point contained in Derrida's strategy of disruption is that the disruption must and inevitably will be contained within the language in which the disruption is staged. Thus it is difficult, "even" for Derrida, to escape the idea of a transhistorical, hence eternally identical, Europe, whether the mood that idea calls forth is nostalgia for liberal tolerance or pessimism about eternal intolerance.

Even granted the brevity of *The Other Heading*, Derrida seems remarkably willing to use "Europe" as a stable, unchanging reference. It is not that he fails to see Europe as a question as well; rather he claims that *all* cultural identities, and as it seems Europe in the purest form, constitute themselves by the kind of self-questioning that he exemplifies in *The Other Heading*.[8] Thus he finds himself writing that "Europe . . . has always given itself the representation or figure of a spiritual heading" (Derrida 1992: 24). Certainly this has not "always" been true; to be charitable to Derrida, we might read this sentence as meaning "Inasmuch as there has ever been something that explicitly thought of itself as Europe (and how long that has been the case is a subject surprisingly open to historical debate), it has always understood itself in this way." The sentence as written obscures the critical point that this representation is a project largely propelled by differentiation from Jews, Muslims, Indians, and others. Derrida only has time in *The Other Heading* for "the Other," not for any particular, historically existing, named non-Europeans. Despite a Levinasian

8. Again my reading of Derrida's important questions is dogged by the impression that for Derrida, Europe is both the model of cultural identity and the only example of it: "What announces itself in this way seems to be without precedent. An anguished experience of imminence, crossed by two contradictory certainties: the very old subject of cultural identity in general (before the war one would have perhaps spoken of 'spiritual' identity), the very old subject of European identity indeed has the venerable air of an old, exhausted theme" (1992:5). How great is the difference between Husserl's Europe, "founded on the spirit of truth," and Derrida's, constituted by "an anguished experience of imminence?" I realize that, as Michael Naas says in his introduction, Derrida is trying to acknowledge the Other without pretending to abandon the universalist and modern values, the European identity, which we never fail to employ despite ourselves. It is a balance that no one can maintain perfectly, nor should one expect to, and in reading Derrida against himself here, I am in the main endorsing the sense of his effort.

insistence on the primacy of the Other here, the absence of historicity and the presence of the little term "always" combine to convey a *sous-entendu* of geographical determinism.

The Other Heading is inevitably Eurocentric inasmuch as it is about "Europe" and the possibility of a Europe that need not see itself "always" as the world's spiritual head. While criticizing the way such presumptions purport to universal validity, Derrida remains as always on guard against easy resort to the mere opposite of that which he criticizes. Thus he warns against an uncontrolled *droit à la différence:* "It is necessary not to cultivate for their own sake minority differences, untranslatable idiolects, national antagonisms, or the chauvinisms of idiom" (1992:44). Clearly Derrida is warning against egotistic separatism here, whether on the part of the individual or any group, but it is not clear what these four specifications mean. "Minority differences" seems so broad as to include any perpetuation or invention of a cultural practice that does not explicitly and indeed theoretically proclaim the priority of universal human identity. "Untranslatable idiolects" sounds like a person mumbling to herself in public, or the secret languages children invent. Everyone likely to read Derrida or accord him any authority agrees that "national antagonisms" are not to be cultivated for their own sake. "Chauvinisms of idiom" could mean Fichte's defense of the autochthonic purity of German as against the putative inauthenticity of French, or the attempt to defend and preserve the use of Breton or Yiddish. Furthermore, what does "for their own sake" mean, and how could the judgment whether such distinctions are being made "for their own sake" possibly be made from outside?

Derrida, famous (or, as we shall see, notorious) for his criticism of the Greek valuation of the same, here implies that there is a certain inappropriateness, an unpresentability about any cultural formation that does not adhere to a universal ethos. Thus he writes further on in *The Other Heading* that

> No cultural identity presents itself [to whom? Derrida does not ask; to itself? to the world? to the philosopher?] as the opaque body of an untranslatable idiom, but always, on the contrary, as the irreplaceable *inscription* of the universal in the singular, the *unique testimony* to the human essence and to what is proper to man. (73) (emphasis in original)

In effect, this is to claim that all identities rationalize themselves in the terms of liberal cultural anthropology. Which might be true, or it might be true only of such cultures that themselves embrace, that take as one of their constitutive themes the concept of identity itself! In any case, Derrida has chosen—and claims that the example is "just as typical or archetypical as any other" (73)—an essay by Valéry that Derrida sees as the quintessential expression of *Frenchness* as *universalness*. France is the prime example of a cultural identity insofar as it presents itself as a particular instantiation of universal values. Now Derrida's little book is all about the problem of European identity, and Derrida knows that the problem of identity is what constitutes the idea of "Europe," but he does not consider any other possible terms by which what we cannot help but call "a culture" or "a tradition" might recognize itself, other than as a particular "*inscription* of the universal." Despite the interrogation of the European dialectic of identity, by failing to acknowledge any other possible logic than Valéry's "archetypical" one Derrida is in effect claiming that the whole world is French!

The only alternative is, once again, to read Derrida not against Derrida but in support of Derrida: to take the range of cultures covered under the injunction "no cultural identity" to mean all *European* cultures, all those that take identity as their reflexive theme. This would *still* mean that there is no "presentable" (articulable, recognizable) cultural identity other than those modeled on the European French example. Whether or not Judaism or "Jewish culture" is presentable in these terms is a question Derrida does not even raise in *The Other Heading*.

VI.

The work by Vassilis Lambropoulos that I have so far repeatedly darted at and will now consider at some length dances almost constantly around this question of Jewishness as a model for European identity. Lambropoulos repeatedly insists that he is talking about the appropriation of a certain image of the Jew in a Eurocentric "Hebraist" ethos, but then again he focuses overwhelmingly on twentieth-century critics who are in fact avowedly Jewish. Especially when discussing the remarkable presence of Jewish intellectuals in German-language culture in the first decades of this century, Lambropoulos risks the claim that "Jewishness was elevated to a cultural idea . . . and Judaism became the new counter-politics, oppositional culture" (1992:303).

All this is contained within the framework of an attempt to explain how politics—activist democracy, about which Lambropoulos has very little to say of substance—became derailed by a neoreligious domain of critical hermeneutics. In his basic thesis, blending insights from Weber, Nietzsche, and Foucault, Lambropoulos insists that the core solution of European modernity to the problem of how to discipline bourgeois man once his basic autonomy has been proclaimed is the interiorization of an ethic modeled on the disciplinary exercise of biblical interpretation. Interpretation, subsuming its origins in Renaissance humanism and Reformation polemics, has become secularized as the esthetic pole of the Judeo-Christian ethos of emancipation. Both because the ultimate text on which interpretation is exercised remains the Bible, and because Jews are taken as the model interpreters, this "Hebraism" has generally been dominant over its dialectical pair, Hellenism, which has in fact been for the most part denigrated. Since we are all suffering under false consciousness, it is not surprising that this argument runs counter to common assumptions; the real regime is a hidden one:

> Hebreophilia and mis-Hellenism [are] the twin ideologies that the post-Reformation world has most strongly repressed (cultivating the impression that they are rather impossible) and can never admit, since their function is cardinal to Western religious identity, the catholicism of civil rites (fn. 91, p. 375).

The argument is almost a gnostic one: Lambropoulos has discovered a fundamental truth that undermines and overturns everything we have been taught as critical truth at least since World War II. For Lambropoulos, it is not the Greek legacy with its burden of the "same," the "mythical," the "ocular," the "logocentric," and the "spatial" that is the ground for Eurocentric and colonialist ideologies, but rather the monotheistic and text-centered Hebraism that has invented that demonized "Greek legacy" as its foil. Lambropoulos rests his case for mis-Hellenism (the term he wishes to bring back into currency as a needed counterpart to anti-Semitism) on the vilification of myth that he sees running throughout twentieth-century criticism, especially Auerbach's *Mimesis,* Horkheimer and Adorno's *Dialectic of Enlighten-ment,* and Derrida's entire body of work. Lambropoulos also in-cludes a clutch of grossly anti-Greek generalizations issued by such boorish intellectuals as Harold Bloom and Cynthia Ozick. Unfortunately the argument as a whole is rather weakly made; thus, for example, a footnoted list of titles indicating the recent "unabated interest in myth" (fn. 93, p. 376) hardly proves that "mythology identifies its subject with the irrational, and proceeds to discover its operations in socio-political turmoil and conflict" (173).

Yet Lambropoulos has certainly flushed out quotes in which Derrida seems to abandon his prudential wariness of embracing the opposite of that which he wishes to deconstruct, or of demon-izing the source of the Same in the course of celebrating differ-ence. He has discovered Derrida writing of a heroic thought that

> seeks to liberate itself from the Greek domination of the Same and the One (other names for the light of Being and of the phenome-non) as if from oppression itself—an oppression certainly compa-rable to none other in the world, an ontological or transcendental oppression, but also the origin or alibi of all oppression in the world. (Lambropoulos 1992:229–30, citing Derrida 1978).

It is not necessary to make this the linchpin of a claim that Derrida's entire project rests on a demonization of the Hellenic and a concomitant avoidance of politics, as Lambropoulos does; *that* denunciation recalls the charges that Fichte was an anti-Semite on the basis of the one vicious document we have already discussed. Nor should such an example be ignored. Lambro-poulos's focus on a certain demonization of the Greek might in-deed help open our thinking. Certainly the careless use of the vague pejorative "Greco-Christian," which I have used in public speeches if not in print, is less likely to appear in my own work from now on.

One thing that makes Lambropoulos's argument simultane-ously infuriating and compelling is his claim that Jews have been willingly duped into submitting Judaism to a "Hebraist," actually Protestant-Modernist, interpretation: being co-opted and at the same time selling out (whatever it is that a Judaism free of this co-optation might have developed into). Again, Lambropoulos defines Protestant Hebraism as "civil interpretive governance through self-rule" (316). This is certainly one insightful approach to the "identity of Europe." If it is permissible to free it of the monotonous and almost paranoid tone with which Lambropoulos pursues it, I see it as complementing the focus I am trying to develop elsewhere on the role of specific historical others—Jews, Muslims, and "Indians"—in the invention of a Christian European identity. Lambropoulos's argument has at least one advantage over discourses on Othering that assume that identity always works through a brute exclusion of the Other, since it explains how at least at times there could be room for the Jews not only within the territory of Europe, but within the idea of "Europe" as well.[9]

Nowhere is Lambropoulos explicit about the consequences of his argument for his title, *The Rise of Eurocentrism.* Like Derrida, he problematizes the notion of Europe but somehow fails to historicize it, leaving us to guess that Lambropoulos indulges in the historically implausible notion that while Jews are integral to Eurocentrism, Greeks are totally outside it. Lambropoulos purports instead to historicize the Jews. Thus he writes, in a certain Sartrian reflex, that "as far as Western culture was concerned, there were no Jews before modernity, only Hebrews" (182).

This claim is so fraught with ambiguities that some potential misreadings (or even "intended" readings that are nevertheless misguided) must be articulated and refused before its provocative value can be specified. It is fairly clear where the claim fits into Lambropoulos's scheme, enabling him to attack "Hebraism" as a preexisting cultural form that becomes prominent in modernity, so that the vaunted encounter between Christians and Jews in modernity serves only to co-opt Jewish intellectuals in the service of Protestant Hebraist Eurocentrism. But the implication that Jews were merely left alone by premodern European Christians, or that there was no intellectual interchange, is a flat historical falsehood (see, among a vast number of works on premodern cultural

9. One implication of this (as of Derrida's insistence that Europe has always constituted itself by interrogating its identity), with regard to the crucial Iberian experience of dominance and difference that I hope to explore further over the coming years, is that the long period of more or less secure *convivencia* under both Muslim *and* Christian regimes must not be overshadowed by the processes of exclusion and "purification" that generally, though not exclusively, accompanied the *reconquista* (see Menocal 1987).

interaction between Jews and European Christians, Dahan 1990). Similarly puzzling is the claim that it was "probably first in England"—the country from which Jews were most decisively expelled and then readmitted after the Reformation and the putative beginning of the rise of Hebraism—"that the West met 'real' Jews" (41). According to Lambropoulos's conception, where the Jew is constructed as a trope of the West's self-imagination, "real Jews" could only be encountered after they had been invented, and that was most clearly done in their absence. The entire approach seems to relegate Jewish existence to a choice between exotic but irrelevant curiosity and the narrow and dangerous space of the Western imagination.

It is not even clear what the quote from page 182 is supposed to mean. Does it mean that before modernity, Western culture knew only of Hebrews, not of Jews? But this is once again to dehistoricize Western culture (which Lambropoulos elsewhere specifies as "the only culture there ever was"),[10] and to rob the idea of the West of any specificity it might have. Or does it mean that in the retrospective imagination of Western culture once constituted, there were only Hebrew interpreters, not even Jewish usurers and child-killers, let alone undemonized, living Jews? If this is Lambropoulos's thesis, it leaves precious little space for understanding hostility toward Jews in European modernity. There is something bracing about Lambropoulos's refusal to ground his critique of Hebraism in the horror of Jewish experience in twentieth-century Europe, but there is also something too disingenuous about his equation of Jews and Greeks in the parenthetical observation that "(The tremendous cost for the two peoples and the respective results . . . cannot be examined here)" (83). Indeed they cannot—not, as some readers might be tempted to respond, because it would be wrong to imply a possible comparison of the different modalities of victimage, but rather because the totalizing strain of Lambropoulos's deconstruction precludes considerations that would be consistent with his critique.

But Lambropoulos's critical insights should not be lost. Let me try to interpret the quote from page 182 as sympathetically as

---

10. Meaning, correctly I think, that the West knows itself to be a true culture through its elaboration of the *concept* of culture, much as it identifies itself by ceaselessly worrying the concept of identity.

possible. Then Lambropoulos would be saying that "Western culture" (modern Europe) only had room for the "Hebraic" cultural stereotype. This would put us on guard against an easy dichotomization of the Western and the Jewish, as in the quote from Levinas cited by Lambropoulos, where the philosopher warns that

> our belonging to a religious or national or linguistic Judaism is not something purely and simply to be added to our Western inheritance. One or other of the two factors becomes discredited. We must ask ourselves if there is not a permanent risk of the traditional aspect of our existence sinking, despite what affection and goodwill may attach to it, to the level of folklore. (Levinas 1989, cited in Lambropoulos fn. 145, p. 388)

I think I know what Levinas means. On one level, which is not to be dismissed, the point is valid. Any group identity suffers a seachange as its adherents come to be accepted (provisionally or permanently) within the tenuous fraternity of "Western" citizenship. It is tempting to retain a sentimental space for that particular identity, to domesticate it and thereby make sure it will not be able to serve as a source of troubling questions about the very value of universal humanity. For our own sakes, there is a tension that must be maintained, an awareness of a "permanent risk" that (contra Lambropoulos) need not be quietist or paralyzing but can serve as a creative and indeed politicizing impulse. On the other hand, precisely that creative possibility is undermined by a dichotomization between the tradition and the West. Indeed, to assume—as Levinas and Lambropoulos both do, in their different ways—that the two worlds have been innocent of each other before the encounter of modernity is virtually to doom the particular tradition to at best the folkloric conception against which Levinas warns. Despite the fixation of center and margin implied by my earlier question about the place of the Jews *in* Europe, the more fruitful debate is not about whether Jews are Western or not, but about the role of the Jews as both actors and image in the construction of the West and of "Europe."

VII.

Lambropoulos's previous book, a critique of the criticism of modern Greek literature, makes clear that neither Hebraism nor the

Jews is his only target (Lambropoulos 1988). At the beginning of this new book Lambropoulos disarms criticism by insisting that he is just "playing the game" (1992:xii)—but not in a dialogic sense: "To play a game is to exercise one's will to power against one's opponents in order to win. . . . The ultimate aim of communication is not self-expression but domination" (1988:238). Aside from an enthusiasm for a certain Nietzsche, it is not clear why Lambropoulos, even as recently as 1988, would have fallen back on these two stark alternatives, with their philosophically naive assumption of the ego-centered individual. In the new book, the moral bitterness of his evaluation of those he criticizes seems especially incommensurate with his weak concluding suggestion that we, in effect, think of something else to do.

I would not presume to guess how any Greek intellectuals will respond to this book. But from my point of view it is far from clear what Lambropoulos has in mind when he writes that "the exhaustion of Hebraism and Hellenism may finally allow Jews and Greeks to live and create like every other people" (1992:331). What is this entity called "every other people" that Jews and Greeks could or would want to be like? Perhaps, to refer to Derrida again, the French? The unthinking autonomist ethos here carries us further yet, all the way to Fichte. In fact, "every other people" lives with and through its own set of contingent reifications held by and about its own people and those with which it is contingent. There is every reason for a critical examination of Hebraism and Hellenism, and none that I can see to assume in Enlightenment fashion that liberation lies in overcoming them.

On the other hand, there is probably even more to be learned from comparing the situation of groups such as Jews and Greeks than what Lambropoulos has already offered. The more limited thesis proclaimed in the jacket-cover endorsements of Lambropoulos's book by Michael Herzfeld and Edward Said—to the effect that the Hebraism-Hellenism duality defines the motor of philosophical Eurocentrism—seems more promising than the gnostic one about the dominance of a repressed anti-Hellenism. Even this thesis forces me to rethink the determination of my own intellectual direction toward adulthood, where it was a stunning thing to read Edmond Jabès, to see that the Jew could be taken as a universal figure, rather than seeing Jewishness as something that merely needed to be overcome. I remain unconvinced by the claim that such figures as Auerbach, Horkheimer and Adorno, and Derrida operate on a more elite level of cultural criticism and therefore represent vestiges of a more profound and powerful regime of knowledge than the conservative public school and college education that led me to believe that European universalism was indeed Greek in inspiration and Christian in effect.

The obvious advantage of polemics like Lambropoulos's is that they force the questioning of intellectual pieties grounded in historical, social, or cultural embarrassments. The disadvantage is that inasmuch as they attempt to present a radically new thesis and in doing so distort or silence fundamental issues, they tend to reinforce something very like the pieties they question. Taking together Fichte's combination of an early rejection of a demonized figure of the Jew and his later organic cultural nationalism, Derrida's attempt to encompass the question of European exemplarity without totally discrediting the promise of Europe, and Lambropoulos's call to Jews not to let themselves be pressed any longer at their own expense and risk into the ideological service of Eurocentrism, how *should* a Jew respond to the question of Europe and the place of the Jews?

My response begins with a caveat and a suggestion.

The fact that the place of the Jews in Europe can still be a current question (as it evidently is) suggests that, for reasons that are contingent but remarkably durable, debate over the place of the Jews indicates not an immaturity in the liberal conception of the state, but part of its constitutive discourse (J. Boyarin 1994a; Halpérin and Lévitte 1989). Generous statements by liberal German politicians, or even an official French government act commemorating the suffering of Jews under Vichy, do not necessarily indicate a direction for "Europe," but rather a move in a game of European identity and power. This caveat also suggests an even stronger questioning of the claim made in my prospectus, that the Jews are still a bellwether for European tolerance in general. Certainly we should not be too optimistic about the cultural and political inclusiveness of this decade's New Europe. To the extent that this New Europe is conceived as a superstate, rather than in some measure an abandonment of statism, the place of Jews in Europe is likely to oscillate among suspicious rejection, cosmopolitan tolerance, and creative appropriation.

The suggestion is that Jews resist confinement to a purely textualized space, and that Jews along with others insist on the maintenance of social spaces that cannot be neatly confined within the bourgeois concentricity linking individual, nuclear family, and state. The maintenance of such spaces includes "folklore"— Jewish languages, domestic practices (Bahloul 1992), rhythms of time; contingent political associations with others threatened by an exclusive conception of European identity; and *also* an anamnestic interaction with texts that need not and should not be reduced to games of interpretation. Only through an informed exercise and constant reinvention of Jewish identity and practice, along with the reinvestigation of earlier cultural interactions that serve to question the dichotomy between Jew and Greek (e.g., D. Boyarin 1994) is it possible for Jews to be more than just the "Greek's," and hence "Europe's," tragically absent Other. The new Greek and Jewish creations that Lambropoulos wants to see, the other horizons that Anidjar wants us to reach beyond the reification of Greek, Jew, and Christian as competing idealized ends for Europe, even some sort of redemption of Husserl's desperate faith in a Europe defined by its devotion to reason may, as Greenblatt wonders and Derrida seems to insist on believing, be possible in a decentered Europe beyond its own exhaustion.

At Last, All the Goyim:
Notes on a Greek Word Applied to Jews

"What are you doing out here in the ruins?"
(Miller 1959:14)

August 1, 1994

Dear Richard,

It will be immediately obvious that what follows is not the work of a specialist on Jewish apocalypse, but rather a set of reflections on the various associations that have come to hand in response to your request for an essay on Jewish apocalypse. In fact, though I'll have nothing more to say about them, the first thing that comes to my mind (still) when you say the word "apocalypse" is the figure of the Four Horsemen of Revelation. I know them, of course, not from having read that book but rather at the same level of popular imagery that leads, for example, to a further mental association with the Four Horsemen of Notre Dame.

Since it may seem at points in what follows that I'm straining to draw a sharper distinction between "Jewish" and "Christian" apocalypse than the textual history seems to warrant (which would necessitate exaggerating not only the differences between the two, but also the extent to which they are internally coherent), let me state clearly that I do so only in order to reopen questions about notions of resolution and completion to which "we all" (by virtue not least of being people capable of reading this volume and inclined to do so) are heir. On the other hand I would not want the terms "Jewish" and "Christian" to dissolve into mere tokens of the twin horns of a Western dilemma about the particular and the universal. One indication of the continued or renewed distinctiveness of what we have learned to call textual communities (Stock 1990) is that this is virtually the first occasion on which I have opened, let alone cited, the Christian Bible! On the other hand, the Jewish prophetic texts I cite below are also new to me, since in the early modern "traditional Judaism" on which my own Jewish practice is loosely modeled, they are not a standard part of the curriculum.

Let me fortify myself for this journey with some definitions. One who has spent decades working on the Jewish apocalyptic texts of late antiquity and their early Christian heirs and contemporaries confirms the gloss of the term *apokalypsis* as "revelation" (Collins 1987:3). What such texts purport to disclose is "a transcendent reality which is both temporal, insofar as it envisages eschatological salvation, and spatial insofar as it involves another, supernatural world" (ibid.:4). It needs to be pointed out that this division into temporal and spatial is *our* grid, but it nevertheless serves as a useful reminder in this context that the relation between revelation and resolution for "the Jews" and for the entire human species on earth is a question about both the time of the Jews and the place of the Jews.

As to the name apocalypse itself, the "genre label is not attested in the period before Christianity" (Collins 1987:3), and the first book designated as such is Revelation. From the beginning, however, the revelations the genre has in mind imply not only a Gnostic doctrine of the secret nature of the universe, but also always "the inevitability of a [future] final judgment" (7). Furthermore, there is an ancient type of apocalyptic literature that lays out a narrative of Divine intervention giving sense and direction to human suffering and affording eventual redemption, and this "historical" type of apocalypse does contain an end-of-history scenario (ibid.:9). This scenario in turn entails the destruction of those who, depending on the ideological context of the particular apocalyptic text, either have unwarrantedly harassed God's people and failed to acknowledge Him, or failed to recognize the advent of His Son. In recent usages of the notion of apocalypse, this element of destruction has come to the fore, and thus in the present context it is not inaccurate to note that the two "dominant senses of *apocalypse* [are] revelation and destruction" (Fenves 1993:3).

Yet if the element of destruction is there from the "origin" of apocalyptic, as it were, it is also important to mark the slide from this original sense of uncovering, revealing, a secret knowledge to the common modern notion of *the* apocalypse as a cataclysm leading to an "endtime." There is a near-reversal in the dramatic chronology of the dominant sense of apocalypse, from the emphasis on the first man enlightened, the first "Christian" to whom the true and heretofore hidden promise of God's word has been revealed, to what Derrida calls a motif of "apocalypse without apocalypse" (Derrida 1984:35), which here is not merely a rhetorical or philosophical figure of presence-in-absence, but is rather transcribable as endtime-without-revelation: the ultimate evacuation of any hope of meaning.

Since the "historical" ancient apocalypses, as suggested above, fundamentally include an aspect of judgment leading to reward and punishment, the notion of apocalypse without apocalypse could also mean endtime-without-judgment. Phrasing it this way gives us, I suggest, a startling characterization of the postmodern turn, revealing both its Jewish and Christian roots in the vision of an endtime, and how much of a break with the modern transformation of traditional hope it represents, since Jewish and Christian apocalypse both entail final judgment.

Here the first relevant distinction between Jewish and Christian ancient apocalypses comes into play. "In all the Jewish apocalypses the human recipient is a venerable figure from the ancient past, whose name is used pseudonymously" (Collins 1987:4). The technique of assigning authorship to a revered figure from the past is actually a standard characteristic of Jewish writing down to the medieval mystical classic called the *Zohar* at least. It is consistent with the general Jewish tendency to view citation as more authoritative than originality. Thus there are noncanonized Jewish texts known as the Apocalypse of Abraham, the Apocalypse of Adam, and so on. This kind of "firstness" is quite different from the firstness of revelation to the self-named Christian authors, which proclaims the revelation as new and contemporary, the authority of its authorship not borrowed but boldly proclaimed. Thus "A man appeared, sent by God, whose name was John" (John 1:6). Susan Noakes has recently analyzed other scenes in the Gospel to show how this rhetorical habit of self-ascription as author/interpreter informs the Western Christian reading tradition down to the present (Noakes 1993). We have tended therefore to take self-ascription as the norm, ourselves as the font of authentic interpretation, and the practice of ascription to a respected legendary ancestor as anomalous. At the same time we question our own authority now, when the confidence of modernity is exhausted, and seek to interrogate once again the legendary ancestors.

In the formative visions of the ancient apocalyptic, the meaning of life is to be found in a resolution after death. Our own sense of living in the shadow of apocalypse might be translated as a sense of being already located beyond or after death. The specific event I am thinking of as casting that shadow is indeed the Nazi genocide, the funeral pyre of the Enlightenment and of a certain culminating vision of Europe as the problem of difference resolved, the death of the attempt to solve the problem of the Other by the incorporation of this founding other. The future has collapsed upon itself, and we are burdened more by what we come after than by what awaits us. The postmodernist task is not so much any longer to offer hopeful or terrifying visions of the future (we, more conclusively than the moderns though perhaps as Derrida suggests not ultimately, having lost faith in retribution and reward), but to stand ourselves as the goaltenders, offering retribution and redemption to those who still, before apocalypse/endtime/holocaust, that is before the time of the last of the just, of the last European, of the last man, of the last Jew, still lived their lives in some sense under the sway of faith in redemption and retribution. (And is it possible that I really do not?)

Hence the first broad theme of the essay focuses on a series of individual and implicitly pathetic, if not properly tragic, male figures, which will eventually be contrasted with a notion with very different affect and implications, the collective and quite properly and literally genealogical concept of the *genos*—or, as we will call it here, following Derrida, the *goy*. Now I want to articulate a series of final figures that, I propose, serve as postmodern counterweights to the emphasis on originality, presence, and universality in Christian revelation.

The "last of the just" is the character of Ernie, the righteous son murdered by the Nazis in André Schwarz-Bart's novel of that name (Schwarz-Bart 1960). The title is drawn from the legend of the thirty-six concealed saints (in Yiddish, *tzaddikim*, or, more specifically for the legend, *lamed-vovniks*, literally meaning "members of the thirty-six") on whose existence the continuity of the world depends. The figure has a particular valence vis-à-vis visions or ideologies of the endtime. Marking the novel's hero as the last in a line of such saints clearly does mean that his death is in some sense the end of a cultural world. More generally, since the designation of the thirty-six refers essentially to their saintly behavior toward others, the act of translating "just" back *into* Yiddish as *tzaddik* signals that the death of the last *tzaddik* is the end of a *moral* universe, the end of the time in which just behavior was the ultimate determinant of fate. What makes *The Last of the Just* a novel rather than a legend, and gives it an extraordinary human pathos, is that it is also a family chronicle, the end of the world and also the death of Ernies.

The "last European" comes from an even wispier source: Hannah Arendt's remark, in her introduction to the collection of Walter Benjamin's essays called *Illuminations,* that part of his ambivalence about coming to America to escape the Nazis (and hence one motivation for his suicide) was his fear that "people would probably find no other use for him than to cart him up and down the country to exhibit him as the 'last European' " (Arendt 1969:17–18). With its echo of sad and isolated Eskimos, Indians, and Pygmies caught on display and destined to die (Kroeber 1976; Bradford and Blume 1992), the phrase indicates an astonishing flash of empathy with the colonized in this indeed most European of thinkers. It reminds us, at least momentarily, that such figures of the end or of the last person are not limited to Europeans, to Christians and Jews—or, at any rate, that the West has often pressed the Rest into the service of its apocalyptic vision. Furthermore, by envisioning the putative asylum of America as a sideshow in which he would be trapped, Benjamin marked this New World as an ironic anti-paradise, a place one goes to not so much to escape disaster, but *after* the catastrophe has already hit.

It is Maurice Blanchot who offers a portrait of the last man. The portrait begins with an acknowledgment of the startling and portentous responsibility of the title, and a suggestion that something has happened to make the narrator conscious that this is indeed the phrase he wants to use now: "From the time it was given to me to use this word, I expressed what I must always have thought of him: that he was the last man" (Blanchot 1957:7). This person whom the narrator confronts and describes is a troubling, demanding, and uncertain presence, who always responds to every proffered idea with an understated demand, a tone of dissatisfaction: "Why do you only think thus? Why can you not help me?" There is something childlike about the last man's eyes. He has always been somewhat reclusive, "outside of us." Indeed, his very existence is in doubt—which seems hardly surprising, for how certain could a narrator who comes after the last man, who is hence not a "man" himself, be of his own cognition? "I think today that perhaps he had never existed or perhaps that he no longer existed. . . . Perhaps he had changed everyone's condition, perhaps only mine" (Blanchot 1957:8). What I find most striking, aside from the evocative mood of Blanchot's prose, is how easily it could be taken to be the words of a French intellectual, immediately after World War II, trying to figure a surviving Jew, surviving simultaneously as "the last Jew" and as "the last man," phantomlike. The point is not to establish whether Blanchot, in whose oeuvre the name "Jew" has occupied a significant place (Mehlman 1983), had a Jew in mind here, but to note that for a certain strand of high modernist European thought, it is after the great European catastrophe that the problem of Jewish difference can be resolved in its dissolution and idealization. Only after Auschwitz, as we say, has it been "given to" Blanchot's narrator "to use this word."

Regarding the last Jew, two texts draw my attention here. The most recent is Jacques Derrida's autobiography cum commentary, "Circumfession." Here, citing a diary excerpt from 1976, Derrida doubts the evidence of his own circumcision: "Last of the Jews, what am I [. . .] the circumcised is *the proper*" (Derrida 1993:154 [ellipsis and emphasis in original]). The "what am I" signals a profound puzzlement, already: can one be the last of the Jews, the last in a series and still a member of that series? The circumcised (male Jew, or Jewish penis) marks the property of generation. Thus when Derrida meditates on the meaning of that mark, as other Jewish critics have been doing recently, he does not see it as symbolizing a rounding continuity of generations. For Derrida the circumcised penis is nothing so much as a point, a "head" or *cap* of individual finality associated (through the titillating mention of the practice of *metzitze*, or the sucking of the blood of cir-

cumcision [152]) with a generalized exchange of fluids, hence
(inevitably now, and he refers to this elsewhere) to death through
the exchange of a deadly virus. The finality is also expressed
through a *reversal* of the emphasis on circumcision as continuation, fertilization, and generativity, a reversal through which
circumcision becomes literal self-absorption, or as he coins the
concept, "autofellocircumcision" (158). A further association of
death with circumcision comes through his association of the cutting of the foreskin to the tearing of the clothes in mourning (specifically, here, for his mother, 167–68). That cutting away of the
bond to his living mother is extended further into a death of collective identity; eventually, after hesitantly claiming the proud
title of the last Jew, Derrida decides that he is "one of those *mar-
ranes* who no longer say they are Jews" (170). Denying the physical identification of circumcision and opting for a spiritualized
carnal filiation, he insists that he "has a Christian body, inher-
ited from Saint Augustine in a more or less twisted line" (170).
Indeed.

How pretentious, properly speaking, to refer to oneself in
writing as the last Jew, even when this identification is presented
as an embarrassing revelation, the blow softened by distancing the
author of "Circumfession" from it, citing it instead as a diary ex-
tract. But note well that to say "pretentious" is not to say phony
or inappropriate. I would claim by way of anecdotal evidence that
it is fairly common enough for (male?) Jewish intellectuals these
days to fall occasionally into the apocalyptic mood of thinking
themselves the last Jew. Yet this is the first time I have ever seen
the sentiment, even equivocally, *written.*

The other case of the last Jew comes from Walter Miller's wonderful novel *A Canticle for Leibowitz* (Miller 1959). The novel is set
in and around a Christian monastery in the Southwestern desert, many decades after a nuclear holocaust. The collective identity of the monks centers around a shopping list attributed to
the blessed "Saint Leibowitz," the kind of normal, middle-class
American Jew who has been made legend by the likes of Bernard
Malamud and Stanley Elkin. But the beginning of the book also
presents another character, literally the last Jew—a hermit, living apart, and distinguished from the expectant and recuperative
community of monks by his stance of crotchety survival.

The first major scene of the book describes a dramatic encounter between the novice Brother Francis, sent into the desert for a period of fasting and solitary, silent meditation as part of the process of initiation into his order, and the aging Jewish hermit. One gets ready for an allegory of the youth of Christianity versus the dried-up old age of Judaism. Miller might be said to be working off the legend of the wandering Jew—precisely a non-Jewish story about the Other—and this could be contrasted to Schwarz-Bart's deployment of the *Jewish* legend of the thirty-six hidden saints upon whom the world's existence rests. Indeed the picture of the Jew could be read as hostile: he is suspicious and ornery. Yet to this Jewish reader his very appearance in that post-disaster landscape—his remarkable survivorhood—comes across as affectionate, the "nasal bleat" in which he intones his recognizably Jewish blessing over his bread a moment of ethnographic familiarity rather than stereotyped caricature. Miller also grants the pilgrim a remarkable degree of cultural autonomy and even isolation, more than any American Jew today would be expected to have: "Still writing things backward!" (15), he says in response to Brother Francis, who chalks a note on a large flat stone to avoid speaking. When he finds just the stone that Brother Francis needs to complete his temporary shelter, he marks it with two Hebrew letters printed in the novel and left untranslated and untransliterated. The two letters spell the word *lets*, whose meanings range from "clown" and "joker" to "trickster" and "devil." Miller even provides a gentle mockery of Christian suspicions of Jews; the hermit offers Brother Francis some bread and cheese (Miller does not say whether he knows Brother Francis is bound to fast). Brother Francis in turn sees this as the temptation of Satan and himself rescued by the vision of the Blessed Martyr Leibowitz, a parody of Christianity's historical demonization of Jews and deification of a Jew.

No clear difference in the experiences of nuclear holocaust of Christians and Jews is implied by Miller's characterizations. But in postmodern apocalyptic generally, there is a powerful imbrication of the feared *vision* of nuclear holocaust—that disaster which has indeed already happened, but in a place that is *elsewhere* for most Christians and Jews—and of the memory of the Nazi "Holocaust," as the genocide "here" is commonly styled. The conjunction of the two is most clearly present perhaps in Don DeLillo's bitterly funny novel *White Noise* (DeLillo 1985), which describes both a shameless professor who has made a name for himself by developing a Department of Hitler Studies, and a mushroom-like cloud of poison gas euphemistically referred to as "the airborne toxic event." The title of DeLillo's book could be taken to suggest precisely the absence of meaning that absence of a vision of ultimate judgment implies in our culture. Against this, *A Canticle for Leibowitz* seems to combine or in a kind of sad comedy almost resolve the genres of messianic vision and endtime apocalypse, inasmuch as there is a coming back together of the Jewish and the Christian, the abbey itself being named for Leibowitz (Miller 1959:14), significantly without the collapse of identity implied by Derrida's references to his circumcised yet "Christian" body.

The second question I want to raise concerns something like the double relation between visions of the end of the Jews and the end of the species or "world" on one hand, and between visions of the redemption of the Jews and the redemption of the species/world on the other.

When the question is phrased in this way, one would expect a neatly symmetrical, Aristotelian exposition of all of the various relations. But there is a very interesting disruption of the symmetrical balance between chosen people and "humanity," and between the right hand of reward and the left hand of punishment. That is, there is something that fundamentally cuts against the grain of anything that could roughly and broadly be conceived of as traditional "Judaism" in the notion of apocalypse as an end in oblivion. There seem to be powerful strains in Christianity that envision the destruction of all nonbelievers, all non-Christians. License for such rhetoric comes first of all from the Gospel of John, who states at the very beginning of his book that all those who receive the Light will be saved, but those who are sinners will be afraid to come into the light and, so to speak, "be revealed" and saved. (Hence the theme of revelation is double-edged, its very logic seeming to call forth interrogative impulses in Christian institutions, and it is tempting indeed to read back the origins of the Inquisition into this move of John's.) Jewish visions of endtime, including the destruction of all non-Jews, existed in the first century. The rabbinic Judaism that has been "normative" for the past millennium and a half, however, rejects such notions. The issue of redemption is very much contested in Judaism—subject to both differing philosophical/speculative accounts at different times and places, and to a wide variety of communal practices and disciplines very often closely akin to those of Christian or Islamic neighbors. Yet the idea of the extinction of the Jews (and a fortiori the extinction of the rest of the world) is explicitly refused consideration by the Bible, which would seem to preclude the possibility of the extinction of the world within the context of a recognizably Jewish thought system.

Scholars and others sensitive to the powerful ethnocentrism present in most of the Jewish biblical literature may doubt this claim. The prophet Zephaniah declares the imminent destruction of all the nations that surround Israel, who have brazenly defied God by harrying his people, along with most of the sinners in Israel, who have in effect called forth such destruction upon themselves. Remarkably (or perhaps predictably enough, given the legacy of centuries of diaspora and the lessons in discretion granted thereby), only the last verse of his book is part of regular religious Jewish currency:

> At that time will I bring you in,
> And at that time will I gather you;
> For I will make you to be a name and a praise
> Among all the peoples of the earth.
> When I turn your captivity before your eyes,
> Saith the Lord. (Zephaniah 3:20)

Whereas the burden of the entire book has been focused "on the region," as it were—on the behavior of the people of Israel and its immediate foreign relations—this opens up to a vision of "all the peoples," oddly doubling back on everything the prophet has raged about before, making it clear that *somebody* has to be left around to admire the saved and glorified remnant!

Still, if Zephaniah is a muted or "minor" Jewish canonical text, there is another brief passage that, for thousands of Jewish families, is a dramatic high point in the Jewish ritual calendar. The following verses from Psalms (79:6–7) are recited as part of the Passover seder:

> Pour out Thy wrath upon the nations that knew Thee not,
> And upon the kingdoms that call not upon Thy name.

> For they have devoured Jacob,
> And laid waste his habitation.

The drama of this recitation and the anticipation of redemption that it carries are both accentuated by the custom of sending a child to open the door for the Prophet Elijah, traditionally regarded as the harbinger of the Messiah, for whom an extra cup of wine has (always already!) been set out beforehand.

To whom do the verses refer? Precisely which "nations" (goyim) are Jews—some ignorantly, some triumphantly, some with profound ambivalence—praying God to punish at every Passover seder? A popular Yiddish encyclopedia states that "the content of the verses is a prayer that God take vengeance on the people who torment the Jews" (Petrushka 1949:896), which is indeed the conventional and colloquial understanding. A commentary to this passage based on the teaching of Reb Chaim Soloveitchik, the Rabbi of Brisk, connects the presumably metaphorical "eating of Jacob" to the punishment meted out for those who improperly eat that which was set aside, made *kodesh*, separate, holy, to be eaten in the Temple (Gerlitz 1983:230). Through this expanded commentary, the conventionally understood historical plea for punishment of unjust historical action is reconnected to an emphasis on the *raising* and *separation* of Israel: the nation Israel is *kodesh*.

In any case, the "original" context of these two verses in the psalm powerfully attests to a particular situation where the Land and the Jewish kingdom are being attacked. In a modern literary reading, the "devoured Jacob" there seems to be a metaphor of Jacob (a famous shepherd who identified with and protected his sheep) as a lamb being devoured by wolves coming out of the mountains. The language clearly does identify these people to be punished as those who do not acknowledge God (recalling John's admonitions against those who do not acknowledge his Revelation), but the emphasis is on the failure to respect Israel that comes out of that lack of acknowledgment. Furthermore, the context is a plea for God to stop punishing Israel for its sins, and the subsequent challenge to God, as it were, is a reminder that such devastation *encourages* the "goyim" to mock Israel's pretension to have a saving God.

It can safely be said of all these biblical texts that at least they know who Israel is, and who the goyim, the nations, are. Another text by Derrida suggests that such may not be clearly the case any longer. Certainly with the advent of Christianity, a troubling confusion—troubling to Jewish discourse as well as Christian—arises. Christian identity disrupts this dichotomy between inside and outside. Thus, especially perhaps vis-à-vis this theme of apocalypse, contrasting Jewish texts or ideas to Christian ones is not the same as contrasting Jews to the entirety of humanity!

The early Christian writers—often, as with Paul, addressing themselves to churches throughout the Empire modeled on the diasporic institution of the synagogue—borrow the insider's "we" of the Israelite self-conception, even while explicitly combatting Jewish ethnocentrism. Hence perhaps the striking turn of phrase in the passage of Derrida's essay "Of an Apocalyptic Tone Recently Adopted in Philosophy" where he is paraphrasing the stance of John on the relation between his identity (his justification for being himself, as it were) and the revelation only some share with him as yet: "We are going to die, you and I, the others, too, the goyim, the gentiles, and all the others, all those who do not share this secret with us, but they do not know it" (Derrida 1984:24). The use of the consummately Jewish word "goyim" covertly but inescapably intimates an "us" that is the Jews, here not so much ancient Israel as contemporary, post-genocide Jews, and along with them—along with *us*, I Jonathan Boyarin can show off and say—any other literate person who is hip enough to have Jewish friends who will tell him what the word "goy" means (cf. Gilman 1986). But, precisely because it is the Apostle John whom Derrida is ventriloquizing here, the "you and I" who are not "the goyim, the gentiles" cannot unambiguously be all Jews transhistorically, but rather the primitive Christian community. Derrida's words here would then be an ironic description of the unfulfilled apocalyptic aspirations of this primitive community, with its resentment at the failure of the Gentiles to recognize "our" apocalyptic truth, compensated for by the booby prize of knowing the end, a death sentence, beforehand. Yet Derrida's catachresis— the semantic contradiction of borrowing an ethnic insider's term for an apostle of the bursting of the ethnic boundaries—remains unfulfilled and unexplored as well. At the very beginning of the essay in question Derrida refers to a (then) just-released new translation of the Hebrew Bible, affording him the opportunity to mention casually that it would be worthwhile comparing the range of meanings of the Hebrew *gala* to those of the Greek *apo-kalupsis,* but he hastens to add that he certainly has no intention or time or competence to carry this out.[1]

After this initial discussion of the difficult "task of the translator," "a task I will not discharge" (Derrida 1984:3), Derrida drops the Hebrew *gala* and proceeds using the Greek-derived and "European" "apocalypse." His resort to the Hebrew "goyim" here is indeed significant, deliberately teasing and provocative. It flaunts Derrida's own Jewishness (was he still taken by the notion of being "last of the Jews" when he wrote this?) to seduce a philosophical *community* or club—I write "seduce," because the word "goyim" is "taboo," impolite, obviously not totally so but sufficiently so to titillate when used outside a Jewish idiom. At the root of its inter-Jewish colloquial usage, its commonly but not inevitably dismissive *tone* does not refer to the Gentile's failure to possess an apocalyptic "secret" that we alone share amongst ourselves, but rather their failure to embrace and possess the Torah, which makes us smarter than they are, which lifts us into a more heightened, more fully realized *human* interaction with the world, God, and history.

There is yet further irony in Derrida's deployment of the Jewish term "goyim" just once, here, in this philosophical text. "You and I" not only *are* the community of early believers in Jesus' Godhood; we are also, manifestly and pointedly, not the collectivity of the people Israel. In fact John expresses, right from the start, resentment at the failure of the Jews to recognize Jesus as the Messiah: "He came to what was his own, yet his own folk did not welcome him" (John 1:10). So the contrasting pair us/goyim could not for John mean Jews versus the other nations, but must always be translated into "we the believers" versus "everyone who is not Enlightened." Indeed, the covenant with God by birthright, the ethnic or tribal covenant, has been superseded in the vision of John: the new "children of God" are those "who owe this birth of theirs to God, not to human blood" (John 1:12). Genealogy, the connection of generation that underlies the contrast between Is-

1. Unremarked by Derrida is how prominent translations are in the beginning of John (see for example the three terms "rabbi," "messiah," and "cephas" translated in 1:38 and 1:39).

rael and the nations, is explicitly delegitimated as a mark of distinction here.

As the above sentences about present and ancient contexts of the term "goyim" intimate, Derrida's "goyim" shocks a(n apocalyptic?) constellation not only between Christian and Jew, but between "past and present." Even ripped out of their colloquial context, the "Jewish" associations of the word are strengthened by its deployment to emphasize insiderhood. Maybe Derrida uses the term because, imagining that we have spent enough time either being Jews or empathizing with Jews, he sees the term as offering us powerful empathetic access to John's paradoxical reinvention of a new privileged and threatened insider identity. The catachretical use of "goyim" reminds us once again that much of the murderousness between the two names, "Jew" and "Christian," has to do with the underlying awareness of their connection and fear of their mutual contamination.

Immediately preceding the paragraph in which Derrida speaks "goyim" as John's line is a discussion of the concept of *Verstimmung*, by which he means to identity all the hazardous chances and possibilities of intersubjective communication, especially here the interruption and potential disharmony of apocalyptic messages between sender and receiver. There is indeed a rich and troubling disruption of the potentially unproblematic reciprocity between "you and I" when the other terms are introduced: "the goyim, the gentiles." Who are all the others? I still don't have a clue; perhaps, as yet, a place marker for the recognition that dichotomies are not worlds.

Again Derrida is pretentious! Daring to speak as and for the apostle, daring to appropriate—*after all they've done to us,* the vernacular Jew in me mutters *sotto voce*—our word and try to make us sympathetic to a false Christian prophet! It works. He makes me interested in John. The word "goyim" sets in motion a sort of double helix here, one strand of which is the constellation joining past and present (on which more immediately) and the other, intercontamination of the Jewish and the Christian.

The temporal strand is, of course, inadequately described as a linkage of past and present. Its complexity in this context is indicated by the multivalence of the term "recent" in Derrida's title. Since he chooses to substitute the word "apocalyptic" for the word "elevated" in the essay by Kant he echoes and discusses, his "recent" could refer to the first blossoming of Christian apocalyptic—the time of the book of Revelation to which, as cited above, the genre label was first applied, the time at which Jewish apocalyptic also blossomed. But since he alludes to Kant, he could refer to the period of the Enlightenment or more specifically the decline of high Enlightenment, the first period in which it was necessary to criticize popularized Enlightenment. And, since the paper was delivered during the second half of the twentieth century, "recent" could refer to the tone of philosophy since World War II. It might be objected that in the first case, the literature under question was not "philosophical." But this is not as powerful an objection as it might seem, because even in the third and most recent of the possible "recent" periods, philosophy is weakened and has little of the force it seems to have had in Kant's day.

Ironically, there is something in the new tone of the Christian apocalypse that works against the panchronic strand of all these pressing and urgent "recents." As I discussed toward the beginning, John's speaking of his apocalypse in his own name signals a *present* orientation. "Now," retrospectively as it were, two millennia later as we are wont to say, this self-ascription makes John's apocalypse a *past* revelation, a revelation that happened in a certain sense "in history" and is repeated now. By contrast—although the point is difficult to articulate and I am not altogether certain of its validity at this point—a pseudepigraphical "Apocalypse of Abraham" probably did not have the same quality of chronological pastness at the time it was first disseminated and, for whatever reasons, certainly has not taken on the quality of a "past" revelation two millennia later. Apocalypse thus becomes not only a future-vision theme (a vision thing?), but an event in Western religious history, outside of whose shadow, Derrida suggests, we cannot stand to speak or write. Here the periodic necessity to question the inclusive "we" appears again, for since the revelation to John is one that non-Christian Jews obviously *missed,* their or rather our relation to the chronology of apocalypse is likely to differ from the dominant one, even if the ways that relation differs cannot be adequately specified yet.

One might begin specifying this different relation to apocalypse by noting that Jewish visions of the endtime tend to be associated with the vision of a future Messiah. Here we could rely on the scholarly distinction between apocalyptic literature proper and more general (and, for Jews, more canonical) prophetic visions of redemption and judgment. It is not obvious why, in our post-catastrophic situation, there has not been a greater turning toward an apocalyptic eschatology defined by Paul Hanson as

> a religious perspective which focuses on the disclosure (usually esoteric in nature) to the elect of the cosmic vision of Yahweh's sovereignty—especially as it relates to his acting to deliver the faithful—which disclosure the visionaries have largely ceased to translate into the terms of plain history, real politics, and human instrumentality due to a pessimistic view of reality growing out of the bleak post-exilic conditions within which those associated with the visionaries found themselves. (Hanson 1975:11–12)

One speculation this perhaps overly sharp contrast suggests is that a twentieth-century experience of Nazi genocide without the realization of Zionist dreams in a state might have produced a renewed emphasis on this sort of hermetic apocalyptic among a much more consciously isolated "remnant" of faithful and practicing Jews seeing themselves as the "elect." Such hypotheticals are too awesome for me to contemplate at length. Given the world as it is, the distinction between hermetic and prophetic apocalyptic is useful precisely in helping us to understand why, throughout the modern period and continuing into the last decade of the twentieth century, messianism has tended to be associated with Jews, apocalypse with Christian discourse. This tendency has been reinforced in twentieth-century literary criticism, which once again identifies millenarian, political, and public visions of the endtime with a primitive and outmoded Judaism, and sublime, inner-directed visions of redemption with Christianity (Goldsmith 1993:10). Furthermore, inasmuch as "the canonical work of apocalypse persists in imagining the end of history to be the end of historical differences" (Goldsmith 1993:21), such a characterization seems much more apt vis-à-vis Christianity than Judaism. While biblical visions of all peoples coming to acknowledge the God with whom the Jews already have a special relationship, and coming to bring sacrifices at God's Temple in Jerusalem, may point toward a *reconciliation* of difference, once again the vision does not see the whole world becoming Jewish.

Not that even a public and this-worldly form of messianism has in fact gained hegemony in mainstream Jewish discourse after the genocide. As it stands, despite the messianic trends of movements such as Lubavitch and Gush Emunim (the Bloc of the Faithful who have struggled to gain the whole of the historical Land of Israel for the Jews and for the Jews only), the dominant tendency has been to cast the events that shatter the Jewish world in the twentieth century in terms of a this-worldly, yet still progressive, secular history of nations—and on the popular level, as stated, to cast Jewish distinctiveness in terms of a privileged teaching and acuity rather than an esoteric revelation.

By way not so much of a resolution or even restatement of the questions about authority, identity, ethnicity, and teleology I have raised in these pages, but rather of an indication of the directions they might lead to in a dialogue with you and others, Richard, let me state in brief a notion that occurred to me years ago, but that I have never attempted to put in writing before. The question is whether it is possible to harmonize the notion of Nazi genocide as divine retribution against the Jews (a *Jewish* notion, let me hasten to clarify, that bears the weight of millennia during which a series of Jewish disasters were interpreted as the result of the collective covenantal failures of the people of Israel) with the notion of a secular history in which the Jews have no particularly important place. My bold proposal is to recast the notion of an inseparable link between moral action and historical fate, to rescue it as it were from an ethnocentrism that, at this level, has little purchase on me, by the move—odd perhaps for someone who sets such store by difference—of positing a *generalized* human moral responsibility for human history. In this way "humanity" (a term we have come to know and mistrust, rightly) would be responsible for what Blanchot calls "the disaster" that indicates but is not limited to the Nazi genocide (Blanchot 1986). The problems with this suggestion are doubtless legion, but one of the reasons it appeals to me is its contingency. Unlike, for example, Hegel's progressive unfolding of the World Spirit, it does not posit any necessary *progress* in the relationship between morality and history.

In a sense that ironic resolution of the tension and confusion between Jewish and Christian identities that the very title of *A*

Canticle for Leibowitz points toward is echoed here: I cannot live in a world that revolves so totally around the Jews, nor is all of me willing to accept a morally arbitrary universe. It is not that I have "faith" that God doesn't play dice with the universe. Rather the nihilistic assumption seems to place too great a strain on my Jewishness.

Is that a good enough reason? Perhaps a further articulation of my investment in Jewishness is necessary in turn, by way of relating a post-genocidal mistrust of all pretenses to universal redemption, universal community, such pretenses having been shown, convincingly I think, to be intimately related to the possibility of a genocide rationalized in the Western terms of collective identities and destinies (Nancy 1991). Yet it is significant that the very text I cite in support of this claim—Jean-Luc Nancy's *The Inoperative Community*—still insists on an articulation of the possibility of such community in universal terms that inevitably privilege clean slates and a lack of prior or outside commitments on the part of those "singular beings" who are to constitute and be constituted through the community. Nancy's emphasis on a lack of constraining or distorting formalized attachments recalls Paul's prejudice against marriage, an institution that only hampered the freedom of the believers to come together in the Spirit that had been revealed to them.

As Daniel Boyarin has argued, there is a link between Paul's sense of "speaking in an extreme eschatological situation" (D. Boyarin 1994:177) and his criticism of those who "bear fruit for death" (Romans 7:5), that is, who bear children destined to die. He contrasts the link between the apocalyptic sense in Paul and Paul's opposition to generation to the quite normative vision of established families in the Land of Israel that is a stock element of Jewish messianism—to which we might add Steven Goldsmith's dry observation that "after predicting imminent doom, Jeremiah, with his flair for symbolic action, buys land in Israel" (Goldsmith 1993:29). There is a sense in which, contrary to my identification of Blanchot's "Last Man" with the figure of the "Last Jew," the two tropes are in fact mutually contradictory. Unlike the Romantic genre of "Last Man" poems written in England between 1823 and 1826, Mary Shelley's novel *The Last Man* denies "the mind's power to dictate its own transcendence" (Goldsmith 1993:267).

This Romantic notion of an all-encompassing male conscience that absorbs the universe in its transcendent solitude is the individual analogue of the apocalypse of Revelation, which, "by programmatically imagining a world rid of the *feminine* . . . imagines as its most general social ideal a community rid of *all* differences" (Goldsmith 1993:72). The Jewish vision of redemption referred to by Daniel Boyarin and by Goldsmith, on the other hand, entails precisely the continuation of Jewish specificity, grounded both territorially and generationally—hence with the continuing presence of not just "the feminine," but women as well. Rabbinic Judaism cannot conceive a world rid of the feminine; because Judaism has so much difficulty containing a vision of nihilistic apocalypse, there is an inherent slippage between the vision of the last Jew and that of the last man, already conceived as autonomous and isolate. Outside of a secularized and individualized, modern or postmodern literary sphere, there can be no last Jewish man, and no last Jew, as intimated, "properly," by Derrida's "last of the Jews, what am I. . . ." To echo Kafka, who said that the Messiah would always come on the day before the last day, the "last Jew" can always only be the next-to-last Jew. Hence the refusal of nihilism, "realistic" or not, might serve to guard against the Romantic impulse toward solipsism in this world, and the very *specificity* of the Jewish vision of redemption might serve as a building-block for that sense of generalized human responsibility I referred to above.

We are approaching what the West calls the millennium, all of us "last Europeans," but not with the anticipated sense of an event-to-come. *After the last word has been said, can I hold out the vague notion of a provisional identity beyond a certain extinction?* Let me call it here post-Judaism, not only because it comes after Judaism in a way analogous to postmodernism following modernity, but more specifically because it comes after the catastrophe as the betrayal of the hopes for redemption central to Judaism. The question is not rhetorical, and I myself wonder at the paradoxical tone of apocalyptic resignation I seem to have worked myself into today. Too much reading Derrida!

Your response would be welcome of course, since any possible post-Judaism would apparently be articulated not only by "real Jews." Yet I would not yet relinquish the insistence that my question is most urgent for, and hence in the first instance addressed to, those of "us" who are still, rather dazedly, attempting to constitute ourselves as a *generation of Jews.*

Warmly,

Jonathan Boyarin

SEVEN

Jews in Space;
or, The Jewish People in the Twenty-first Century

For Judith Friedlander and Jay Geller

Schick dich in die Welt hinein
Denn dein Kopf ist viel zu klein,
Dass die Welt sich schick' in ihn hinein

—Johann Peter Hebel (n.d:397)

The most powerful and concise expression I know of the sense of living after the end of the world is Georges Perec's *W or the Memory of Childhood*. The book alternates chapters of a resolutely un-melodramatic memoir of the author as a hidden Jewish child in Nazi-occupied France with fantasy chapters describing the social system of an imaginary society centered on sporting competitions. Perec's description of the Olympian social structure established by Northern European colonists on the island of W starts out in-nocuously enough, reflecting not only Greek athleticism but also the modern state system that the modern Olympics are intended to idealize, representing in sport the ideal *coherence, neatness, stability,* and *fairness* of states. In the course of the book, inevitably and in a horrifying manner, the two narratives approach each other, such that a fantasy allegory of Fascism informs the depiction of a childhood spent in the shadow of its terror. In the last pages of the book Perec makes it quite explicit that the world of W is the concentration-camp universe. Furthermore, by remind-ing us that his fantasy world grows out of childhood drawings done by the orphaned Perec immediately after the war, the mem-oir merges into the fantasy, with the latter becoming a sort of me-morial to the unknown horrors suffered by Perec's mother after her deportation to Auschwitz. She "saw the country of her birth again before she died. She died without understanding" (Perec 1989:33). Even diaspora is denied: the emigrant from Poland to Paris is shipped back "home" to her death. The two narratives spiral in upon each other, on the author, and on the reader: there is no timespace left: "No beginning, no end. There was no past, and for very many years there was no future either; things simply went on" (ibid.:69) But not quite, since Perec did write, and wonderfully. So I begin with Perec's book, taking near-suffocation as a starting point, looking for potential openings afforded by books like his, written after world's end to confront Fascism, rescue childhood, and remember the dead.

. . . Which might make my title sound frivolous, especially since it is made up of a double allusion. The first allusion is to "The Muppet Show's" show-within-a-television show, their parody of space operas, starring Miss Piggy and titled "Pigs in Space."[1] This comic and primarily hopeful *sous-entendu,* aiming to implant something like the image of a minyan on the Enterprise, will signal one of my key concerns back here on Earth: the effort to begin to imagine a future for Jewish communities beyond the vision of a closed world of contiguous, monocultural nations.[2] That effort is unthinkable without a critical sense of the current transformation of global social space. It entails in turn a reopening of the question about the *possible* futures of Jewish communities, implied by the partial dismantling of the assumption that Jewish and other "minority" distinctiveness is doomed to disappear as a structurally significant factor in the progressive rationalization of nation-

1. For more on the association of Jews with pigs in European Christian culture, see Fabre-Vassas 1994.

2. See the title question of Wladimir Rabi's *Un Peuple de trop sur la terre?* (1979). Rabi, a French Jewish community activist who repeatedly contended against the organizational consensus in tones simultaneously pragmatic and prophetic, points out in that text the irony that sometimes this "extra" people seems to be the Jews, sometimes the Palestinians. In the decades after the Nazi genocide, Rabi refused the twin illusions that only the Jewish state offered the possibility of security and continued creativity for Jewish communities, and that the world was now a safe place for Jews. He insisted simultaneously that anti-Semitism is a permanent phenomenon (and thus that it is vain to combat solely against anti-Semitism; ibid., 174) and that the last has not yet been heard from French Jews. *Anatomie du judaisme français* (Paris, 1962).

states. In this sense the logic of "secular" identities must be thought through once again: an effort this essay is intended to stage, but not explicitly to carry out.

The second allusion, much more general, is to an immense tradition of Jewish historiography that shares two broad characteristics: a totalizing rhetoric of corporate national identity (the Jewish people) and a confident chronological periodization (not always numerical, but always with ultimate reference to Christian millennial divisions, as "in the High Middle Ages," "in the modern world"), placing the subject *in the past*. There is an implicit and highly subtle contradiction between strictly chronological designations such as "the nineteenth century" (even more so than broad epochal ones) where they appear in such historiography, and the rhetoric depicting the Jews as somehow remaining intact and integral.[3] Indeed it is difficult to speak of "Jewish history" without reference to a Christian chronology inaugurated by a movement that saw rabbinic, normative post-Temple Judaism as at best obsolete and at worst satanically misguided. Hence the surprising and encouraging *possibility* of even considering the existence of Jews in the Christian twenty-first century suggests prima facie evidence that the continued presence of not-for-Jesus Jews is still a problematic phenomenon for Western/Christian/European modernity. Indeed, one aspect of global modernity that seems to have caught relatively little attention in cultural studies is the hegemony of the calendar sometimes called "secular," but more properly Christian.[4] Much as we are all caught in the discursive "space of Europe," so too, if to varying degrees that should

3. The contradiction is squarely acknowledged in a recent text on the Jews in Christian Europe: "Since dating by regnal years is not a serious option, it is necessary to decide between the traditional Jewish date of the creation of the world by the Lord and the Christian date of the birth of Jesus Christ as the basic reference point. For practical purposes, however, the decision has already been made by the western dominance over the history of the world, which has been achieved, largely in a Christian tradition, over the last four or five hundred years" (Edwards 1991: 1). See also the opening pages of Halevi 1987.

4. The various suffixes appended to years numbered according to the Christian Messiah's birth reveal much about the shifting inflections of that calendar. We still sometimes write "A.D." for Anno Domini, the Latin "Year of Our Lord"; but only B.C., the English "Before Christ." The idea of a significant history before Christ datable according to the same system, evidently came later. The still more recent, "nondenomnational" "B.C.E." and "C.E." for "(Before the) Common Era" reflect

be debated and compared, we are all caught in Christian temporality.

The word "space" on the left of my title, and the word "century" on the right, might be taken to refer to distinct considerations of time and space. Such a conventional divide so pervades our analytic habits that it cannot be dispensed with, but its conventionality should be borne in mind; otherwise this Cartesian distinction disables our critical thinking about memory, practice, and identity. Thus the repetition of the "in" on the right side of the title is yet another reminder that the answer to the question "Where?" can also be a "time," that whenever we name a century we are identifying a location of culture.

To what extent can any group, let alone one living in the post-Christian West, resist the homogenizing effects of that calendar? Even if Jews now live predominantly in a post-Christian society rather than a Christian society proper, as with modernity and colonialism the continuing power of historical Christian social formations must be made infinitely more explicit than it has to date in criticism. In ways that can only very partially be articulated, it may be that speaking of post-Christianity also implies post-Judaism. Will Jewish discourse and community *continue* to be framed predominantly within a post-Christian, that is dualist and universalist, milieu, or will a reconfiguration of Jewish difference be part and parcel of a more profound epochal shift from Eurocentric modernism and colonialism? The following is not meant to answer, nor even necessarily to address directly such questions, but merely to provide some signpoints toward a developing discourse.

Homi Bhabha's recent call for papers for a special issue of *Critical Inquiry* quotes without citation Walter Benjamin's famous invocation of memories that flash up at a moment of danger (Bhabha

---

an attempt to neutralize the Christology of the calendar, while insisting much more explicitly on its generality.

The French revolutionary calendar might be closer to the idea of secularism, but it has vanished without a trace—almost. Recently I was moved to learn that the first name of a Haitian taxi driver who picked me up one day was "Thermidor," one of the months of that calendar. In this case, a revolutionary interruption of the dominant calendar was retained within a familial tradition of transgenerational identity. On Haitian history and the French revolution, see James 1963.

1993:597). The reference isn't needed; Bhabha assumes, correctly I imagine, that most readers will know where the phrase comes from. Thus it seems that Benjamin's *Theses* have become canonical for theory, in the specific sense that they are regarded by theory as "citable in all [their] moments." Though obviously there are other twentieth-century canonical *names*, I don't think there is any other elite critical text of our century that has entered "our" language in this way. Indeed it is easy to imagine an impressive scholarly oeuvre that would consist entirely of books and articles using as their titles fragments of the *Theses*. In addition to my *Storm from Paradise*, Robert Alter's *Necessary Angels* and Stéphane Mosès's *L'Ange de l'histoire*, there could be *Moments of Danger; How Sad!; Making Things Whole; The Strait Gate; The Secret Agreement; Soothsayers of Enlightenment; Liberated Grandchildren, Enslaved Ancestors*. Along slightly different lines (and from a perhaps unexpected quarter) Daniel Boyarin has suggested an oratorio whose text would be the *Theses*. Or we could institute an academic ritual, having a scribe write the *Theses* out on parchment, gathering each Saturday to hear a different thesis chanted and to ponder together what its meanings are.

This observation about Benjamin's canonicity provides a starting point from which we can begin to specify one of the interstitial spaces of Jewish discourse at the end of the second Christian millennium—an interstitial space unstably located in and around the critical pole of the secular academy. What draws us so to Benjamin?[5] "We," to some extent, but certainly I, live and doubtless will continue to do so under the sign of Walter Benjamin—if for no other reason than because he more than anyone else showed us how to work with fragments of culture without the need to reinvent a fantasized whole.

Such reinventions have been of great scholarly interest lately,

5. I do not want to mystify or iconize Benjamin, as, for example, the presentation of Yosef Haim Yerushalmi's recent review of Walter Benjamin's correspondence in the *New York Times Book Review* did, with its reproduction of the famous photo of Benjamin's head and the forbidding "pull quote," "Benjamin, vastly praised, is little understood; to grasp his deepest thought one has to read all his work in context, and few dare attempt that" (Yerushalmi 1994:13; these words do not appear in the body of Yerushalmi's review). Such iconization of Benjamin's image, along with the fetishization and mystification of his texts, is not what I mean by "canonization." Nor would I want to silence critics who might remain unimpressed by Benjamin. Let us hear from them!

particularly in ethnographies of nationalism and the state. These critical ethnographies, in turn, are closely tied to questions about the politics of memory. Alain Finkielkraut's recently translated *The Imaginary Jew* (1994) appeared in France in 1980, during the first wave of "revision" of the revolutionary moment of 1968. One of the great strengths of the book is precisely its refusal of a tragic, heroic, self-righteous, and delusive identification on the part of children of Jewish survivors of Nazism with the victims themselves. Even more important for me, Finkielkraut's "imaginary Jew" phrase first led me to attend to Benedict Anderson's *Imagined Communities* when I saw it on my editor's bookshelf. Anderson's book, well known and thoroughly discussed by now, deals with the institution of collective identities in the modern, secularizing nation-state, and shares to some extent a critical ethos aimed at dismantling the illusive totalities of nationalism. Seeing his title, however, I associated it positively with the Jewish diaspora, a community whose creative work consists precisely in continuously reimagining itself. Finkielkraut's French title, *Le Juif imaginaire*, preserves an ambiguity that is similar to the double valence of the notion of "imagined communities." The burden of Finkielkraut's discussion centers on the simple sense of the English title: a confession that, as a radical youth thinking of himself as a persecuted Polish Jew and hence as enjoying privileged revolutionary access with other oppressed peoples, he had only been pretending: he hadn't been a "real Jew." Yet because the French term *imaginaire* also means a consequential cultural space of self-invention and world-invention, the original title also implies a space of the imaginary within which "Jewish" is constituted. This is the road not taken by Finkielkraut.

Finkielkraut's critique was the beginning of wisdom. Evidently, however, Finkielkraut was so taken with his retrospective discovery that he and his generation were not "Polish Jews born in France" (see Goldman 1977), but relatively privileged and thoroughly "acculturated" French citizens, that his subsequent career evinces no critical reintegration of recuperated fragments of his annihilated ancestral culture. He subsequently embraced philosophical enlightenment and mourned its retreat from the world stage in a brief and resentful book called *La Défaite de la pensée* (*The Defeat of the Mind*) (Finkielkraut 1987 [1995]). Meanwhile the absence of integrated fragments of Eastern European

Jewish culture in his subsequent work suggests that, having once dismantled the illusion of a total identification with his ancestors, he still imagines identity as an all-or-nothing affair. Certainly Finkielkraut remains actively concerned with Jewish politics and history, writing and polemicizing on topics such as the media representation of the Israeli invasion of Lebanon, the Faurisson affair, and the Barbie trial (e.g., Finkielkraut 1982). Yet there is little of a distinctively Jewish inflection in these engagements. Finkielkraut imagines the world of the "real Jews" to be an actual whole, irretrievably in the past. He has made himself an imaginary "not-Jew," and the fantasized whole continues to bar him from an engagement with his parents' native idiom.

As Finkielkraut understands it, with *Le Juif imaginaire* he "faced the reality" of his generation's situation. He woke up. He got real. This suggests, by contrast, that Walter Benjamin's famous obsession with fragments of the past is a sign of "not waking from history,"[6] and perhaps of the wrongness of imagining that our goal ever should be waking. One way to summarize the essence of Benjamin's appeal is that his work is driven by the paradox of revolution without progress. Inevitably, then, one of the major unresolved moments in Benjamin is a tension between nostalgia indulged and defended, and a claim that liberation is an overcoming of nostalgia (cf. Jankélévitch 1974). How stable is the distinction between "melancholy"—an affect, as Max Pensky claims, central to Benjamin's entire ethos—and the historicist sadness Benjamin denounced in citing Flaubert? Benjamin was manifestly mistrustful of confident socialism and rhetorics of "revolutionary hope." He might well have thought that everybody really needs to get depressed about the situation before anything will really change. How different is this from collective fasting and reading of Psalms, the classic Jewish response to a situation of potential disaster?

Unlike Finkielkraut, Benjamin could not make such neat distinctions between a finished and irretrievable ancestral world and contemporary reality. Certainly his desperately urgent mission to communicate with the dead should help open us more toward our contemporary "traditionalists" who imagine themselves shar-

---

6. On the importance of dreaming and waking in Benjamin's notion of history and politics, see the chapter on Benjamin in *Storm from Paradise* (J. Boyarin 1992b).

ing the world of their ancestors. Benjamin, that is, does more than help us to avoid what Ella Shohat acutely identifies as "an anti-essentialist condescension toward those communities obliged by circumstances to assert, for their very survival, a lost and even irretrievable past" (Shohat 1992:110). Without Benjamin, we might be misled by a plausible misreading of Shohat's statement, one that would render it ineffective. In this misreading the statement would imply that "we," unlike "they," know that the past really is lost and even irretrievable, and that only our awareness of the "circumstances" that constrain those communities to insist on such illusions leads us to a generous attitude. By contrast, Benjamin's insistence (at the eve of *his* world's end, in 1939) that nothing can be truly accomplished without concern for rescuing the dead, more fully overcomes the lingering progressivist prejudice that insists that the past is "lost and even irretrievable." This suggests that a refusal to wake up, a refusal to get real, may well be characterized as a form of *resistance*—in this context, resistance to the homogeneous time of a secularized, nationalist version of Christian supersessionist temporality.

One important way of maintaining the fantasized, reinvented whole is the postgenocidal reinvention of Hasidism. Most Hasidic groups after World War II have concentrated on the construction of closely knit Torah communities in the image of their own ancestors, while muting the messianic and, to put it anachronistically, somewhat "anti-Orthodox" urgency that characterized early East European Hasidism. Within that world, the most spectacular irruption of a messianic impulse, simultaneously radical and traditional, is the recent experience of Lubavitcher Hasidim, especially events following their leader Rabbi Menachem Mendl Schneerson's second stroke in March 1994 and his death on the third of the Hebrew month of Tammuz,[7] a few months later.

7. According to Henry Goldschmidt, who conducted ethnographic fieldwork with the Lubavitcher community in Brooklyn in 1994, members of the community only refer to the Hebrew date of the Rebbe's death. Goldschmidt's ongoing project is so far primarily captured in an unpublished paper titled "Spreading the Wellsprings of the Torah: An Ethnography of Torah Reading in and around Habad Hasidism" (University of California, Santa Cruz, 1994). Much as my tangential and anecdotal account of Lubavitch is based on my association with the Lower East Side, Henry's more sustained projected involvement has to do not only with the ambivalence of his own secular Jewishness, but also with his attachment to Brooklyn as a native of that borough.

The Lubavitcher Hasidim, seemingly one of the most visibly and successfully resistant countercultures of Euro-American modernity, are famous for their "outreach" to Jews all over the world, for their sometimes violent clashes with other ethnic groups in the neighborhood of Brooklyn where they stubbornly maintain their headquarters, and, recently, for their militant messianism. Though Rabbi Schneerson never proclaimed himself the Messiah, by the time he died the belief that he was indeed the Redeemer of the World held sway at least among a large segment of his followers. The response within Lubavitch to his inevitable death is developing in fascinating directions. Indeed, between now and January 1, 2001, there will be ample time to prepare for comparison of the disappointment and ideological regrouping within Lubavitch to similar reactions among the vastly greater number of Christians who will be disappointed when the second millennium has come and passed without the second coming of Jesus.

At least one response on the part of some Lubavitcher Hasidim is to declare their faith in the imminent and triumphal resurrection of Rabbi Schneerson. Once again, and in startling ways, the question of "What is 'authentically' Jewish?" has become actual, within the crisis of a group that had dedicated itself to reconstituting an integral and "traditional" corporate Jewish community. The explicitly postmessianic and resurrectionist brand of Lubavitcher theology rapidly being developed since the Rebbe's death[8] may be characterized as a form of post-Judaism. As a resurrectionist post-Judaism it is doubly analogous to Christianity. As adherents of a messianic hope that has been dashed, but not quite irretrievably, both professing Christians and Lubavitcher Hasidim are also in an analogous situation to that of those postrevolutionist, post-Marxist, critical or philosophical Jews with whom I would tend to identify myself.

All three of these collective formations (and given their very different frames and registers)—Christianity, Lubavitcher Hasidism, and critical theory—show that the nonadvent of the expected redemption that explicitly underlies the collective identity need not lead to the collapse of the collective. The rationalization

---

8. Rabbi Shimon Schneebalg first alerted me to this phenomenon and urged me to attend to it more closely than I actually have so far.

of the nonadvent becomes a powerfully motivating project in itself. I suggest that, for many "Jewish" critics, an identification with Benjamin serves as a melancholic articulation simultaneously of post-Judaism and postrevolutionism. It is a means of keeping faith after "faith," or in the phrase of Rudy Koshar, a formation of memory "under the sign of mourning" (Koshar 1991:71). I hope we are not each, separately, as melancholy characters as was Benjamin; but he, after all, lived *before* the end of the world. Ours, like his, is a rather melancholy sign. Max Pensky quotes Adorno's comment on Benjamin:

> "Sadness . . . was his nature, as Jewish awareness of the permanence of danger and catastrophe as well as the antiquarian tendency to see the present transformed into the ancient past, as if by enchantment." (Pensky 1993:71)[9]

Such "awareness," however, does not constitute Jewishness for all Jews—indeed, the Hasidic master Levi Yitzkhak of Berdichev stated categorically that "a Jew must always be happy." But this awareness is indeed a characteristic gesture of identification for European-oriented Jewish intellectuals, like Adorno . . . or for that matter, Woody Allen! Beneath it lies a frequent lurking suspicion—though my thrust here will be to deny it ultimately—that all we know how to do anymore is abstractly keep faith, and at the same time the suspicion that at bottom, being Jewish isn't about keeping "faith."

9. Compare Gershom Scholem's reference to traditional Jews as compelled by messianism condemned, between mourning for the lost homeland and anticipation of the always-delayed Messiah, to a "*life lived in deferment*, in which nothing can be done definitively, nothing can be irrevocably accomplished" (Scholem 1971: 35; emphasis in original). Scholem's word "compelled," however, suggests a kind of paternalistic generosity toward the past (we are not so compelled, and hence can comprehend them without being limited in the way they were), which I warned against in reading a citation from Ella Shohat above. There I used Scholem's friend Benjamin as a corrective to such a possible paternalistic reading. Here, against those such as Yerushalmi (1994) who would still insist that Benjamin turned against his true nature in rejecting the ideology of Zionism and the physical refuge of Palestine, I insist that Benjamin's solidarity with the dead has much to do with with the tradition of Judaism that can sustain us beyond the nation-state. Scholem's sensitivity to traditional Jewish *suspension* is related to the temporal dimension of *difference*, a notion embraced much more widely now as a condition we all share and not necessarily one from which escape must be sought.

This diagnosis is not merely a *Rand-Bemerkung* incidental to our ideas, to what really counts. It is intended as a preliminary *situation* of a discourse of Jewish criticism. I want to resist a likely first impression according to which the Jewishness of secular critics is merely a tag of identity, an inert or nostalgic name to which these "imaginary" Jews are not really entitled. Nor do I mean to establish a school or draft a manifesto. By hereby coining (I think) the phrase *critical post-Judaism,* I mean to name an already-existing but unidentified commonality, a way of being Jewish "otherwise than Being." This is not quite a school of thought, nor yet does it exist only in thought. This kind of identity formation is not enabled solely through its own intellectual passion and inventiveness, but on the contrary, only within or at the margins of academic institutions and academic culture (and even then generally outside the disciplinary boundaries of "Jewish studies"), and certainly at the margins of Jewish institutional life in the United States. As a post-Judaism, it is marginal to the would-be "Jewish community" monolith. As criticism, it is subject to centrifugal pressures. It finds its creative tension in an unstable mixture of accommodation and resistance to the centrifugal spin toward the margins, and it need not be its members' only Jewish world.

Necessarily so, for critical work in and around the academy is always subject to *two* incompatible senses of "the critical." As Louis Marin points out,

> A critical question, in the Kantian sense, is a question intending to found in a rational metadiscourse (historical and theoretical a prioris) the processes acknowledged and described by social sciences; in other words, critical in the sense that it establishes the limits or the frontiers of a specific scientific discourse within which that discourse is scientifically validated or legitimated (Marin 1993:399).

Critical research of this kind occupies the place of the "master science" once pretended to by philosophy, a place recognizable within slowly evolving and legitimated divisions of academic labor. Alongside and opposed to this is the militant urgency implied by a second notion of the critical stance or perspective: the critical as fundamentally oppositional.[10] When they are paid and

10. Masao Miyoshi, for example, stakes his claim to "really" occupying this latter critical stance by denouncing studies in postcoloniality, New Historicism, and the

given official positions and recognition, critical academic scholars
are recognized as doing critical work in the first sense, whereas
often they justify themselves to themselves and to each other in
terms of the second: "I'm not hiding in the ivory tower, I'm
undermining the reigning epistemé/articulating an alternative."
What seems never to be acknowledged is that the two concepts can
only be held together—that critical work can only be simultaneously legitimate and oppositional—where it is jointly assumed,
as part of the institutional raison d'être, that progress provides
the ultimate resolution of these seemingly divergent understandings—that everything will be known in the end. Such an assumption hardly seems warranted at present; hence whatever my spec-
ulations about the place of Jews in the twenty-first century may be,
they should not be taken as an expression of *hope.*

The recent critical phrase "late capitalism" seems to betray
some critics' lingering progressivism, a residue of—again—faith
after faith that, even though Marx's clock may have been fast, the
schema was accurate and capitalism is always soon to pass. Such
broad epochal schemata seem hardly useful in trying to analyze
what is alternatively perceived on one hand as a remarkable opening up of academic life to contentious diversity and critical perspectives, and on the other as a vicious retrenchment of conservative ideologies. Better understandings of the relation between
the dilemma of theory and the marginalization of the universities
in bare-bones, post–Reagan and Thatcher Western capitalism are
still desperately needed—if nothing else, so that professors can
act responsibly toward their graduate students!

Attempts at more midscale analyses of the links between particular academic openings and emphases on the one hand, and
the implicit legitimation or expansion requirements of current
capitalism on the other, seem more promising, as with Christopher Newfield's recent essay on the political economy of politi-

---

like as "efforts once again to distance political actuality from direct examination"
(1993:750). Presumably this assertion is based on the idea that if such discourse
fails to help overcome the inequalities underlying cultural "epiphenomena," then
it is covertly complicit with the transnational corporations that really pull the
strings. The frustration is shared by many, and so the imperiously dismissive stance
is understandable. It seems fair to ask, however: What "real" battles has Miyoshi
won lately?

cal correctness (Newfield 1993). There is likewise a political economy of academic Jewish studies, grounded first and foremost in the fact that unlike many other ethnic studies programs, Jewish studies are generally funded not by government money or general institutional budgets, but by wealthy alumni, local individuals, or even Jewish community organizations. To scholars outside the discipline, this seems to make Jewish studies appear as a growth field. This, along with the historicist philological tradition in which secular Jewish studies are still largely grounded, helps to explain its isolation from the other "minority" or "ethnic" studies establishments and would-be establishments. Thus unlike such fields as gay and lesbian studies or cultural studies *tout court,* Jewish studies is not a predominantly critical discipline in either sense outlined above. *Jews* are not marginal in American academic institutions, but Jewish criticism is at home neither in cultural studies nor in Jewish studies. Hence one of the limitations of this interstice I am calling Jewish criticism is precisely its narrowness and instability. Ironically, those who most fully enrich this space, attempting to articulate its possibilities as fully as possible, may find themselves ultimately silenced by the agentless process I call "discipline and exclude." Homi Bhabha asks, "What tensions and ambivalences mark this enigmatic place from which theory speaks?" (Bhabha 1994:22). One of them is obviously a politics of scarcity in the support of professional critique—a reminder that the "interstices" and "borderlands" in which criticism gets done are not providential homelands for pure theory, but the particular points in the "nervous system" (Taussig 1992) where we're looking for meaning, friends, salaries, and health insurance.

Having found the first two of these but not the latter, I can report that criticism also finds sustenance outside the university. The Lower East Side is the place where I shop, push my children around in strollers, study Torah, go to shul—and practice ethnography. Though it was once, as is well known, the most densely crowded Jewish neighborhood in the world (Wasserman 1987), the decline of its Jewish population—inevitable given the demands for mobility of American capitalism—has left it more tolerant, and indeed more aged, than livelier centers of Orthodoxy. Both of these factors lead me to find it a more congenial point of entry into questions of Jewish community than the younger and more integral Orthodox and Hasidic areas of the New York region. These communities exercise an ambivalent centripetal force on me, composed of envy at their being fully *out* Jews on one hand, and rebellion at what seems the stultifying limitations of their world on the other. Such ambivalence indicates nothing so much as the still-unsettled articulation of my own attachment to the name "Jew."

After the Lubavitcher Rebbe's second stroke, however, he was at Beth Israel Hospital, a few blocks up from the Lower East Side, for several months, and his presence there occasioned a temporary shift in *gravity* of Lubavitch toward my neighborhood. Contingents of Lubavitchers were present at the hospital throughout the Rebbe's last illness. Many stayed over for the Sabbath, and small contingents began to attend the various synagogues on the Lower East Side, sharing the Rebbe's teachings when they were given the chance, urging prayer and action to favor the speedy revelation and arrival of the Messiah, and—following the Rebbe's death—somewhat more tentatively ending with expressions of faith in his imminent return. The Rebbe's "tenure" at Beth Israel Hospital has thus made Lubavitch less exotic to me in the shul context on the Lower East Side. His followers' visits to my synagogue, and their brief words of Torah delivered in the Lithuanian Yiddish to which I am nostalgically attached and that I rarely hear, along with the very pathos of the Rebbe's death, combine to make the predicament of Lubavitch a sympathetic one.

That sympathy is indeed new to me, and perhaps it would be to many "critical Jews." Until now, a habitual repulsion from the solution to contemporary Jewish identity proposed by Lubavitch has been one of the informal hallmarks of critical Jewish discourse.[11] Lubavitcher Hasidim are not content to let every Jew decide for herself what her identity should be. They are not content

11. Although not for Susan Handelman, who renders homage, in the preface to her recent volume *Fragments of Redemption*, "to Rabbi Menachem Mendel Schneerson, the Lubavitcher Rebbe, in honor of his life's work of dedication and devotion to the entire Jewish people and the sanctification of the world" (1991:xii). Significantly, however, I know this only because a colleague pointed it out to me as remarkable and odd.

I do not mean to suggest that this repulsion—which may extend to Orthodox Judaism more generally—is facile or ungrounded, especially since much of it has to do with serious questions about the retention of rigid gender distinctions in the name of tradition.

with Jewishness as marginality, nor (as it seems) would they understand why it is good for Jewish identities to be "split." They militantly espouse exclusive Jewish control of Greater Israel. They are involved in painful and embarrassing conflicts with neighboring ethnic others. As will be detailed below, they are aggressively "American" in their propaganda style; and they are unwilling to defer or allegorize Redemption.

If this is resistance—to homogenization, to the consumerism of postindustrial capitalism, to the secularization and atomization tied to the nation-statism I discussed at the very beginning of this essay—it is in many ways then a repugnant resistance. Following Susan Harding's recent articulation of the problem of ethnographic communication with "the repugnant other" (Harding 1991), I submit that considering sites of repugnant resistance is a powerful antidote to the inherent tendency of criticism to become stifled within its *own* marginality. This ethnographic sensibility suggests that, along with the articulation of various anti-essentialized "differences" for which academic space is currently being contested, criticism must also engage those "lumps" in the global web that are neither hegemonic nor progressive. To the extent that we remain committed to Enlightenment, it is primarily *our own* condition that we should intend to enlighten, and one of the ways to do so is by being open to the ways we might be cast as repugnant others in turn, from the "ethnographic" perspective of alternative social authorities such as the Lubavitcher community.

One salutary effect of such consideration is the realization that *reflection* is not limited to critical circles. There is a phrase sometimes used, by Lubavitchers, by other Hasidim, and by other Jews primarily engaged in intimate Orthodox communities, to describe themselves. They call themselves *yidishe yidn,* "Jewish Jews" (see Joselit 1990). This provides some purchase on the genealogical definition of Jewish identity—that a Jew is first of all one born of a Jewish mother. Of course this definition is valid in Jewish law, but it may well be that it is conventionally emphasized because the genealogical definition provides a strong diacritical contrast to the dynamics of Christian identity, provided by baptism or some other *assumption* of Christianity. The idea of the *yidisher yid* moves beyond the pole of givenness in identity, suggesting that on one hand there are Jews who are Jews because Jewishness is given to them, and on the other hand there are (doubled) Jews who make themselves as Jews: *Jewish* Jews. For a *yidisher yid,* the former are only once Jews. Becoming a Jew involves a self-making, a doubling, a supplement to the given of genealogy. Moreover, like circumcision, this constitutes a completion of the self, rather than a postmodern splitting, which would entail a reaction to a modernist presumption of wholeness and authenticity. Is this not an ironic "ethno"-twist back on the reflexivist discourse of modernity, which would claim that the *évolué,* ambivalently civilized Jew is really the doubled one (see Bhabha 1994, chap. 2)?

It would thus be tempting to call this essay "*Der yidisher yid* and the Non-Jewish Jew," except that I do not want to concede the diminution implied by the latter designation. The pairing nevertheless suggests intriguing juxtapositions (hypothetical "alliances" would be too strong a term) between various inflections of Jewishness[12]—inflections that provide an indispensable and sharp counterpoint to the self-styled "official Jewish community organizations'" stultifying slogan, "We are one, in Israel and around the world."

Such inflections are not total disengagements from the Jewish center, of course. In any case, the hegemony of the "major Jewish organizations" should not be exaggerated, and there is a certain disastrous irony inherent in the insistence on valorizing margins or interstitial spaces with regard to a group left in some sense with nothing *but* its margins. For a group of people whose collective cultural mission for a number of generations yet will consist largely in the finding of containers for fragments of a shattered world, there may be a common enterprise shared by those in the "core" and those at the "margins" of the group. For much of the past two decades or so, Lubavitch has received massive support from "less Jewish Jews" than they—people who implicitly regard them as the "real Jews," and who support the efforts of Lubavitch to rally the Jewish people to identification with, and practice centered on, "Torah." As suggested above, many academic Jews maintain overt ties with local Jewish communities, which may support their positions and which receive intellectual and social validation from the Jewish presence on campus. Still, the activist messianism of Lubavitch and the diffident, critical self-identification

12. On "multiply-inflected cultural objects," see Harding 1994.

of critical Jews places both, in different ways, outside the presumptive consensus of this slogan. To the limited extent to which that presumptive consensus implies theology, messianism is quite muted. Many synagogue liturgies continue to repeat passages expressing faith in the expected coming of the Messiah, but *fervent* expressions of desire for the advent are rare. While a strong strand of "religious" nationalist Zionism sees "events" such as the Nazi genocide and the establishment of the Zionist State of Israel as the beginning of an end, the birthpangs of the Messiah, the consensus tends to view such occurrences in terms of an *epochal* return to Hegelian history. Indeed we could speak of an apocalyptic tone recently rejected in Judaism, while it has been massively embraced in Lubavitch. Thus, after first becoming something of a collective "savior" of Jews, Lubavitch is now more like a scandal.

It seems therefore an apt moment to remember what it was that once made the Lubavitcher Hasidim seem so appealing and so unique in the Jewish world, or at least that which once appealed to me. I refer to their willingness to go and be with Jews wherever Jews might be found.

THIRD MILLENNIUM TIMESPACE

Trading nations, properly so called, exist in the ancient world
only in its interstices, like the gods of Epicurus in the Intermundia, or like Jews in the pores of Polish society.
—Karl Marx (1977:441)

Lubavitcher Hasidim are not "primitive," they are not "isolated," and they are in no sense "premodern." Lubavitcher messianism in 1994 is an instructive amalgam. On one hand Rabbi Schneerson's Hasidim went out on a limb in publicly proclaiming him the Messiah, and some of them at least have taken a further grave risk in proclaiming their faith in his resurrection. On the other hand they have not abrogated the Torah—a key to their legitimation of their messianism within the bounds of Orthodoxy—nor are they selling their houses and moving en masse to the Land of Israel. There is an effective *combination* of everyday and "dreamtime" temporalities here, through which Lubavitcher Hasidim insist on their own way of "narrat[ing] the present as a form of simultaneity that is neither punctual nor synchronous" (Bhabha 1994: 162). This was most evidently at work in the communications network the Lubavitchers prepared in order to be ready for the moment of the Messiah's announcement. A few weeks before the Rebbe died, I passed three young women, one with a baby carriage, at Second Avenue near 14th Street—three blocks from Beth Israel Hospital. There was a phone in the baby carriage, and I thought of saying to the women, "That's the first time I've seen a baby with a cellular phone!" I seem to remember thinking immediately of the boy in the bubble, and perhaps I wondered whether these might indeed be the days of miracles and wonders. . . . [13] After I passed them, saying nothing, one of them called to me, "Sir! In the beret? Are you Jewish?" and handed me a card advertising the Messiah and urging me to "do something nice today" to help bring him speedily.

A remarkably vague and general instruction, compared to those given by the Lubavitcher youth who used to roam in "mitzvah-tanks" importuning Jewish males to put on tefillin. The recent posters and handouts of Lubavitch, a group in many ways overtly chauvinistic about the specialness of Jews and of course insistent that the Torah is binding on all Jews, have indeed been pitched to non-Jews as well, and some of the texts bear only a few specific references to Jewish practice. [14] The message was that the

13. Though I certainly didn't think then of "the bomb in the baby carriage," another image in the spooky constellation assembled in Paul Simon's song (Paul Simon, "The Boy in the Bubble," on the *Graceland* album, 1986).

The beeper/cellular phone network features prominently in a lead article of the Chabad (Lubavitcher) magazine devoted to the Rebbe's death. Along with references to the Rebbe as a "father," the anonymous account suggests a collective *physical* crisis at the news: "The mind begins to work frenetically, but there is no focus, as there is nothing to think—it is fibrillating" ("Before, During and After the Funeral: Excerpts from a Chasid's Diary," *Chabad Magazine,* Tammuz 5754/June 1994, p. 11). After the Rebbe was ritually prepared for burial, his Hasidim paid their last respects: "The line outside 770 [Eastern Parkway] proceeds slowly—men, women and children, even tiny babies, hurriedly awakened in the middle of the night, hastily plucked out of cribs and brought in baby carriages to pass by the Rebbe one last time" (ibid.)—suggesting that perhaps the cellular phone I saw next to the baby in its carriage did not rest there only for the mother's convenience.

14. Large posters, which I saw placed in the area of the hospital but may have been distributed more widely, proclaimed March 23—the Rebbe's ninety-second birth-

Messiah was coming for everyone, even if the Jews have a special relationship to him. Lubavitcher Hasidim—the "real Jews"—turn out to preach an aggressively "universalistic" Judaism, famously using a variety of mass marketing media to cajole or charm Jews into following Torah.[15]

The remarkable spread of Lubavitcher mini-communities, of missions to the Jews throughout the world, is an odd echo of the global reach of American culture, not only in the marketing techniques, but also because the Rebbe's location in Brooklyn has sanctified fragments of culture couched in the American language. In Paris young Lubavitchers—the vast majority from North African family backgrounds—dance while singing ecstatically of their insistence that the Messiah arrive. The words are "We want Moshiach now."

The Rebbe sent his Hasidim out into the world, in a curious echo of Hebel's exhortation. Of course, he was not motivating them toward enlightenment, nor following the principle that travel broadens the mind; indeed, young Lubavitcher families who have gone on such missions over the years often complain of the loneliness and frustration of the work. Lubavitcher Hasidim were sent out into the world because 770 Eastern Parkway, their headquarters, was too small for the entire world to come in. Their global spread combined with localism, centered on the Rebbe and his insistence on staying in Crown Heights when all the non-Lubavitcher Jews, as so often happens, had already left. The Rebbe drew legions of visitors from around the world and a small number from far away came to live in Brooklyn. However, the thrust of the mission was aimed not at secular geographical cen-

---

day—as a "Global Day of Goodness." They stated in part, "If one of us can do it then ten of us can do it. If ten can, one hundred can . . . [ellipsis in original] a million can . . . [ellipsis in original] all six billion of us can. After all—six billion is made up of individuals like you and I making the decision to act responsibly." Further on they added, "[This] call must touch the intrinsic goodness and perfection innate in every human being. The Rebbe has sounded that call . . . [ellipsis added]. Will we seize the moment?"

15. Lubavitch has also ventured into cyberspace, a project with fascinating implications for the question of how and to what extent the *meanings* of founding texts can be reliably limited and controlled by a centralized communal authority. See the paper by Henry Goldschmidt cited above.

tralization, but implicitly at strengthening diaspora *in order to bring the Messiah* and thus the Divinely sponsored re-collection. Here the spectacular expectation and failure of the Messiah's arrival has the net result of dispersal. The Rebbe's distinctive enactment of the biblical injunction *ufaratsta*—literally "you shall spread out," originally referring to the conquest of the Land of Israel— thus brings us back to the question of literal, geographical Jewish global space. The difficulties and, doubtless, the rewards as well of Lubavitcher missions to the Jews reflect in a different key "the dilemma of projecting an international space on the trace of a decentred, fragmented subject" (Bhabha 1994:216).

Marx in the epigraph to this section was wrong, and in a way thoroughly characteristic of nineteenth-century Europe. He shares the assumptions that stable, nonoverlapping spatial nationalism is the everlasting normal state of humanity, and that it is natural for a nation to be likened to a body ("pores"). But "the ancient world" was hardly a set of mutually exclusive units linked by "interstices." Furthermore, while it is tempting to speak of the premodern world system in terms of transnationalism, such a designation is itself anachronistic, since it implies a standard nationalism that is then somehow transcended. Before the establishment of the modern world system, of course, even Western Europe was not organized into nation-states, and thus the question of links among collective identities, polities, and global spaces looked quite different. Amitav Ghosh has recently reimagined the personal experience of privileged Jewish traders in the Mediterranean–Indian Ocean world system of the twelfth century, working closely with documents from the Cairo Geniza, which also served as the basis for S. D. Goitein's earlier and monumental work (Ghosh 1993; Goitein 1967–73; see also Abu-Lughod 1989). Ghosh returns from oblivion intercultural, "interstitial" possibilities and contingencies hard to imagine in the exhaustion of nationalism at the end of the twentieth century, ranging from the sharing of saints by Jews and Muslims to the normativity of small states ruled by trade and not by military exclusion to the privileged status of at least some "slaves" active in that trade. But Ghosh also alludes to the end of that world, signaled by the violent advent of Portuguese war vessels on the Indian Coast, with consequences ultimately linked to the violent separation of

"Jews" and "Arabs." [16] Still, the structure of his book—alternating between a memoir of his years of ethnographic fieldwork in a contemporary Egyptian village, and the reconstruction of the interlocked identities of Jews and others in the Geniza world—leaves an overall impression of opening, a *re-vision*. Within a certain trajectory, it may be seen as a further extension of an imaginative timespace just barely maintained in between the alternating chapters of Perec's *W.*

Conjuring the vision of this premodern world system of trade and cultural exchanges tempts me to a highly *opportunistic* reading of Miyoshi's claim that the true meaning of "transnationalism" has to do with the workings of transnational capital. Might this not provide an important clue for the collective survival of a *mobile*, nonstate group, especially one whose collective memory is by no means limited to the time of modern, European-dominated capitalism? Of course, there is a tremendous *ideological* risk inherent in this opportunism. Homi Bhabha and Masao Miyoshi might understand the demands of "criticism" very differently, but the one still speaks about the cultural conditions of a possible socialism, while the other warns that we have first to be aware of the depredations of transnational capitalism. If I propose that awareness of the workings of capital is a strategic value to be "capitalized" on by Jews, rather than combatted, do I thereby turn away from my own insistence that nothing that is bad for the majority of the world can be "truly" good for Jews?

Generally speaking, Jewish collective self-interest is suspect per se. Never mind: I will ask the question: can transnationalism—I mean now the "real" kind, Miyoshi's TNC (for transnational corporation) kind—be made good for the Jews? I am not proposing a Jewish theory of globalization, nor asking how, on the ideological or ritual plane, the intertwining of Lubavitch and of critical post-Judaism might implicate the possibilities of Jewish cultural formation. What I'm trying to do is even harder, and again, I can only state the project. I'm trying *to make the Angel turn around*, to demand that we think of thinking the future, albeit without "progress" as our prop, without resort once again to the statism and unreflective individualism still endemic to main-

16. For elaborations on Ghosh's brief comments about the anamnestic values severed by the imposition of nationalism long after the breakup of that "Mediterranean world," see Alcalay 1993.

stream social theory. Indeed, it is not only in the Olympics that the state system is idealized, but also, for example, in the pages of the Social Science Research Council's house organ. There Professor Daniel Chirot reports on a Council-sponsored conference comparing the situation of the Jews in Central Europe with that of the Chinese in Southeast Asia. The conference participants were presumably not unsympathetic to the historical identity of these groups, yet Chirot's conclusion implicitly insists that they have no place exercising any collective power: "Something remains to the theory of modernization . . . includ[ing] the notion that the only way of navigating the transition to modern nationalism and powerful state structures without creating a high potential for ethnic warfare is to insist on the Enlightenment notion that it is individuals rather than hereditary communities that possess political rights" (Chirot 1994:94).[17] Lubavitch at any rate simultaneously subverts and exploits "modernization" in a direction totally opposite to that which Chirot has in mind, while critical post-Judaism is intensely aware of the ideological charge present in the way Chirot uses terms such as "modernization" and "the individual."

The comparison of Jews and overseas Chinese may be of more contemporary relevance than Chirot and his colleagues would suspect, and perhaps more than they would like. This possibility entails a prosaic question: Will/would there be a place for Jewish communities at the centers or peripheries of new world systems? Like the image of the Chinese investor who "can live anywhere, as long as it's near an airport," we may ponder whether such a suggestion is refreshingly diasporic or symptomatic of mobile exploitation of labor by transnational capital.[18] There is an answer: diasporas may be creative and peaceful, but they are not altruistic. They may perpetuate themselves through anamnesis, but they are open to chance as well.[19] Looking then toward China, one pole of

17. My thanks to Vassilis Lambropoulos for this reference.

18. The question is raised by James Clifford (1994:313), who borrows the image in turn from Aiwah Ong (1993:771–72).

19. Perhaps this is the spatial equivalent of that enculturated attention to temporal disjunctions through which, as Paul Gilroy cites Ralph Ellison, " 'Instead of the swift and imperceptible flowing of time, you are aware of its nodes, those points where time stands still or from which it leaps ahead. And you slip into the breaks and look around.' " *Invisible Man*, cited in Gilroy 1993:202.

the premodern world system, I cite a recent item in the *New York Times*, concerning a commemoration of "Shanghai's role as a safe haven for Jewish refugees fleeing the Holocaust." On that occasion, "city officials . . . were not shy about the economic implications. They conducted an investment seminar for the visitors." Meanwhile, delegation leader Rabbi Arthur Schneier of New York said, " 'Shanghai is going to become a major center of trade and finance in the future, so we have to dream and I firmly believe there will again be a Jewish community here' " (Tyler 1994:A12).

But I finish closer to home, and closer to the present, still at the end of *this* century. I happened to be in Brooklyn a few hours before Rabbi Schneerson's Sunday afternoon funeral. The subway trains were not running well that day, and I spent a good deal of time waiting to transfer at the Atlantic Avenue station. The 3 train and the 4 train both pass through the station, on different platforms each visible to the other. By this time hundreds of Hasidim—mostly young men, not Lubavitchers by the evidence of details of their clothing—waited and waited for the 3 train on the platform across from mine. As they stood, a 4 train heading toward Crown Heights came in on the platform where I stood, grumpy and tired in the heat. Seeing this, they began rushing en masse down the stairs, across to my platform, back up the stairs and into the 4, whose conductor waited several minutes until they all made it into his train. As he was finally getting ready to leave, a Hasidic woman in late middle age rushed up the stairs as fast as she could, calling out in Yiddish, *Halt di tir ofn!*—"Keep the door open."

ייִדישע וויסנשאפט
און די פּאסטמאדערן

מיהאָט עם שוין גענוג געלאָר און גענוג אָפֿט געזאָגט: אײדער מצ׳יט רעדן פֿון דער נײַער
רמיונס־באשאַפֿונג ״פּאָסט־מאָדערנקייט״ ווי זי וואָלט געוועזן אן אומאפהענגיק יש וואָס
מ'האָט נאָר וואָס אַנטדעקט, דאַרף מען שטעלן פֿריערדיקע פֿראַגעם. דהײנו, מיט וואָס איז
מען ״נאָך?״ און וואָס הייסט אײגענטלעך ״מאָדערנקייט?״

און מיר זײַנען שאַקע שוין צוגעוויינט צו ענטפֿערן אױף אַ פֿראַגע. אין דער נוסח. ״וואָס
הייסט $x?$״ מיט אַ תירוץ אין דער נוסח. ״x איז. . .״ מיר וֶועלן משלים זיין. אױף דער לינקער
זייט פֿון דעם קלײנעם (אבער ניט אומשולדיקן) וואָרט ״איז.״ דעם תוכן פֿון דעם סימבאָל x.
מיר באשרייבן x. די פֿראַגע וואָס מיר ענטפֿערן אַזוי איז ״וואָס לאָזט x שרײַבן?״

וואָס ״מאָדערנקייט״ לאָזט שרײַבן איז אַבער אָן אַ שיעור. און מיר זענען נאָך צו נאָענט
צו אַ אַ דער מאָדערנער וועלט. נאָך צו פֿיל אין איר. מיר זאָלן קענען מסכים זיין אױף אָן
ענטפֿער על רגל אחת. (דערפֿאַר פֿאַרנעמט דער ״מאָדערן״ צוויי טראַפֿן און דער ״פּאָסט״
נאָר איינם.) ״מאָדערן״ קלעקט ניט מער פֿאַר אונדז, אָבער דאָס הייסט נאָך ניט אַז מיר קענען
זיך באַגיין אָן אים.

וויל איך דערפֿאַר צוקומען מיט אָן אַנדער שיטה צו דער פֿריערדיקער פֿראַגע פֿון
מאָדערנקייט. איך וויל בעסער פֿאַרליידן פֿאַר אײַך (פֿאַר דיר. מײַן חבר וואָס איז מטריח צו
האַלטן ייִדיש אין קאָפּ) ענטפֿערס לויט דער מוסטער. ״x הייסט מאָדערנקייט!״ אײַ. אַ שלל
אײנצעלנע טערמינען קענען פֿאַרנעמען דעם פּלאַץ פֿון דעם דאָזיקן x? דער אונטערשייד
איז. אַז אַזױ קענען מיר מסכים זײַן. (אָדער ניט: אַבי דו פֿאַרשטייסט מיך) אַז x-יאַ איז אײן
זאַך וואָס הייסט מאָדערנקייט.

שוין. מײַן ערשטער תירוץ. הייסט עם. איז *Wissenschaft des Judentums* הייסט
מאָדערנקייט.״ לעולם דאַכט זיך. אַז *Wissenschaft des Judentums* שטיט אין אַן
ענליכער צוזאַמענהאַנג מיט ייִדישקייט ווי ״פּאַסטמאָדערנקייט״ מיט ״מאָדערנקייט.״ דאָס
הייסט. אַז מע טראַכט אוים אַ וואָרט וואָס מ'קאַן זיך קלײַבן אַרום אים–אָדער אים. דער
אַרויפֿקלעטערן אױף אים–און קוקן אַראָפּ. צורריק אױף וואָס איז שױן אױסגעלעבט אין דער
מענטשהייט. אָבער די אַנאלאָגיע איז מער אינטערעסאַנט וואָו זי האַלט ניט. ווו זי די
פֿלאַצט *Wissenschaft des Judentums* וויל באהאַרשן ייִדישקייט. ווייל זי אַרומזען.
באשרײַבן. און–די פֿיּאָנערן האָבן עם אָפֿט געזאָגט–באַגראָבן. די פּאַסטמאָדערן פֿאַרשטיט

זיך אַלײן װי אָן אױסװוּקס פֿון מאָדערנקײט. און װיל די מאָדערנקײט ניט באַגראָבן – ניערט –
אפֿשר פּאַסט צו נוצן דאָס װאָרט-הײלן.

אָן אַנדער תירוץ גיב איך אַזױ: המשך הײסט מאָדערנקײט. מ'זעט די אידעאָלאָגיע פֿון
המשך סײַ אין ײדישיזם – געוען אַמאָל אַ קעמפּ המשך – סײַ אין דזשודעיזם – גראָד הײַנט איז
פֿאַראַן אַ צוזאַמענטרעף אין ײדישן טעאָלאָגישן סעמינאַר אױף דער טעמע, "ײדישער המשך
זינט דער אױפֿקלערונג" דאַכט זיך אפֿשר. אַז מיט אידענטיפֿיצירן המשך מיט
מאָדערנקײט בין איך אַ ביסל דוחק. לעולם װאָלט המשך הײסן ניט דאָס מאָדערנע,
געהאַלטיק ברעכן מיט סתם-חי-געװען-בײ-איצט: המשך װאָלט געהײסן דער היפוך
מרידה קעגן שטײגער. נאָר איך האַלט בײַ מײַנס: אַז מע מח שױן מודה זײַן אַ קאַמף פֿאַר
"המשך." אַז מ'מח לעגן דעם טראָף אױף "המשך" (אײדער. למשל. אבֿידה צי פֿאַרגעסענהײט)
איז מען שױן אין אַ מאָדערנעם מעמד. און ניט. אנב. אין א פאָסטמאָדערנעם מעמד. װײל די
חכמת הפאָסטמאָדערן האָלט ניט צו פֿון המשך. זי האַלט גאָר אַז "טראַדיציע" איז קײנמאָל
גאָניק. אַז ס'איז קײנמאָל ניט קײן שלימותדיקע איבערגאַנג פֿון דור צו דור. אַז דעם זכרון
מאַכט מען חרוב אָדער מ'איז מחדש בכל יום תמיד.

איצט מעג מען איך צוקומען אַ ביסל נעענטער – כאַטש נאָך אַלץ אומדירעקט – צו דער
צוזאַמענהאַנג צװישן ײדישע װיסנשאַפֿט און די פאָסטמאָדערן. דעם חעג פֿון ײדישער
װיסנשאַפֿט דערזע איך ערשט קלאָר װען איך גײ אַ ביסל אױפֿן חעג פֿון דער
שפּראָך און פֿאַלק-שפּראָך. *Wissenschaft des Judentums*. דאַן קען מען זען דעם אונטערשײד צװישן העלט-
היסט זיך שרײַבן מיט לאָטײנישע אותיות און ײדישע װיסנשאַפֿט אין דער העברעישער
אלף-בית זאָגט זאָגט עדות אױף דעם. דאָס חאָס דער דײטשער טערמין איז אַ ביסל צװידײַטיק –
סידהאַלט אַ רמז כאַטש פֿון דעם חאָס ייִדן חײסן – באַאװדיטעט אַ געװיסע נאָסטאַלגיע אין אַן די
מאַטעריִרונגען פֿון אירע גרינדער. אָבער דער עיקר איז דאָך דער דרױסנדיקער. דער
קאָנטראָלירנדיקער.[1]

ײדישע װיסנשאַפֿט איז אַנדערש. גאָר אַנדערש. ײדישע װיסנשאַפֿט איז צװידײַטיק
ביזן סוף. ס'איז פֿאָרט װיסנשאַפֿט. הײַנטיק, חעלטלעך. אָבער ס'איז ניט אַ געביט פֿון
װיסנשאַפֿט. ס'איז אַ מין װיסנשאַפֿט. ס'איז אױך ניט ײדישקײט נופֿא. ס'איז אַ שעפֿערישע
מישלינג. אַזױ חאַרפֿט דער באַגריף פֿון ײדישער װיסנשאַפֿע אַ פֿראַנע-צײכן אין די אױגן פֿון
די חאָס חילן באַטראַכטן Western discourse חי אָן איינס. ס'איז נאָך דאָ דאָ פֿאַראַן
אדעלעכע חאָס האַלטן זיך פֿאַר אינעװײניקע אין דעם (אל)חעלטלעכן אױפֿגעקלערטן שמועז.
זײ גלױבן נאָך אַלץ אַז זײער חעג איז דער חעג. אַז דער גיהנום פֿון אימפּעריאַליזם און די
נאַציִשע טריט-חאָקאַנאַליע האָבן ניט מבטל געמאַכט זײערע טעגות אַז דורך זײ חערט
די חעלט באַפֿרײַט.

1. פ"ז די באַשרײבונג פֿון ענגלישער אריענטאַליזם אין אינדיע:

"One effect of establishing a version of the British system [of education in India] was the development of an uneasy separation between disciplinary formation in Sanskrit studies and the native, now alternative tradition of Sanskrit 'high culture.'" Spivak 1988:282.

אָבער יידישע ויסנשאַפֿט וואַרפֿט דיזעלבע פֿראַגע-צײכן אין די אויגן פֿון די וואָס
האַלטן זיך פֿאַר דרויסנדיקע אין דעם מערבדיקן שמועז. זיי קוקן אויף דער קאַרטע וואָס
האָט נאָר איין קאָליר פֿאַר גאַנץ אייראָפע. און געוויינטלעך האַלטן זיי אַלע וואָס שטאַמען פֿון
דאָנעם ווי מיטאַרבעטערס אין אימפעריאַליזם. זיי הערן ניט דעם שמועז וואָס גייט אָן אַרום און
קעגן און אונטער דעם מערבדיקן שמועז–דעם שמועז פֿון יידישער וויסנשאַפֿט. און דאָס איז
טאַקע אַ שאָד פֿאַר זייערע צילן אויך. ווײַל אין אַ גרויסן מאָס איז עס דוקא אָט דער
דערשטיקטער יידישער שמועז וואָס האָט צוגעגרייט אייראָפע אויסצוהערן זייערע טענות.

אָט דאָס וואָלט געדאַרפֿט קלאָר באַנעמען. למשל. אַזוי פֿיקחישע קריטיקער ווי
גאַיאַטרי טשאַקראָוואַרטי שפיוואַק, וועמען כ'האָב ציטירט אויבן. אין איר קריטישער
אַרבעט באַחײַזט זי קלאָר אַז זי פֿאַרשטייט ווי זי אַליין איז אַן 'אינעווייניקע'–זי לערנט, זעצט
איבער און שרײַבט וועגן אייראָפעישער פֿילאָזאָפֿיע–און אויך אַ דרויסנדיקע–איר נאָמען
און איר אויסזען זאָגן עדות אַז זי איז פֿון אינדיע, זי איז אַ קרובֿה פֿון די געוועזענע
קאָלאָניזירטע. אָפֿנים איז זי ניט קיין יידישע. און דער נאָמען שפיוואַק איז גאָר אַ פּוילישער.
נאָר זי ליגט עס אויס ענגליש. ניט פּויליש . . . אַ סימן אַז אָט דעם נאָמען האָט געטראָגן אַ
יידישער אימיגראַנט. געוויינטלעך איז די פֿרוי פֿון אַ באַקאַנטן מאַן די וואָס זי אינגאַריערט.
אָבער אין דעם פֿאַל ווייסן מיר ניט און הערן מיר ניט וועגן שפיוואַקס יידישן מאַן. בלײַבט נאָר
דער סימן פֿון יידישקייט. און וואָלט מען נאָר דערמאַנט 'שפיוואַק,' וואָלט איך אפֿילו אַ בעלן
געווען צו חײַזן אויף איר מין סובעיקטיוון אָבער דורכגעטראַכטן קריטיק ווי אַ מוסטער פֿאַר
יידישע וויסנשאַפֿט. דאָס וואָלט טאַקע געהייסן יידיש אַרויס פֿון די כלים.

אָבער ניין. אפֿילו אַזאַ קלאָר–זעענדיקע ווי ג. טש. שפיוואַק, וואָס הייסט אַז איר אינדיע
איז ניט דער מוסטער פֿאַר אַלע אייראָפעס 'אַנדערע.' צעטיילט נאָך די וועלט אין
געאָגראַפֿישע וועלטעלעך. דער אַלגעמיינער פּרינציפ בלײַבט: אייראָפע אויף איין זײַט קעגן
דער דריטער וועלט אויף דער אַנדער זײַט. אַ ראיה האָט איר פֿון דעם, וואָס איר בוך הייסט
"אין אַנדערע וועלטן." אַז אייראָפע זעט מען ווי אַין אימפיריאַלער אינעס. מוז יידיש בלײַבן
ניט געזען און ניט געהערט.

שפיוואָקס פֿראַגע אין אָט דעם ציטירטן עסיי איז. "צי קען דער אונטערטעעניק–
אַנדערער רעדן?" מיט דער אונטערטעעניק–אַנדערער ("subaltern" אויף ענגליש) מיינט זי
די פֿון די קאָלאָניזירטע פֿעלקער וואָס קענען זיך ניט דערשלאָגן צו עפעס אַן אָרט אין דער
הערנשדיקער סֿערע. די נאָענסטע אַנאַלאָגיע וואָס איך געפֿין אין אונדזער וועלט איז די
קדושים פֿון דעם לעצטן חורבן. און די מאָסן יידן וואָס זיינען געווען פֿאַר זיי. וואָס ווערן
פֿאַרגעסן מיט זייער אומקום. און איך האַלט טאַקע ווי דער נאָציזם האָט מיט זיך
פֿאַרגעשטעלט אין אַ גרויסן מאָס דאָס אַ אימפיריאַליסטישע מאַטיווירונג "אײַנצושטילן דעם
אַנדערן."

אינטערעסאַנט איז פֿאַר שפיוואַק פֿאַסט דער אימאַזש פֿון אייראָפע ווי אַ שטאָלצע.
אַליין–אויפֿקומענדיקע זון.[2] וואָס וואַרפֿט אַ שיין אויף אַלע אַנדערע. און זיי קענען אין איר גליץ
ניט קוקן. יידיש איז ניט ווי די זון. אין יידיש חיל מען ניקער זינגען "שיין ווי די לבֿנה. ליכטיק
ווי די שטערן." . . ." יידיש שפילט אָפ אַן אַנדער ליכט. יידיש האָט ניט מורא אָפצושפיגלען
אין זיך די מענטשהייט–דאָס לשון. דעם גוף–פֿונעם אַנדערן.

מיר פֿאַראַנדערן זיך אין ידיש. נעמען איבער שטיקער פֿון יענעמס שפּראַך און מיר
מאַכן זיי אייגענע. מיר באַשאַנען ניט נאָר אונדזער פֿאַרבינדונג מיט די פֿריערדיקע דורות
נאָר אונדזער וויַיטיקייט פֿון זיי. אין דעם וואָס אונדזער ידיש איז אַנדערש ווי זייערע. אָבער
דאָס וויכטיקסטע איז דאָס וואָס אַ פֿריַיוויליק שפֿראַכלעך אַנדערשקייט קען זיַין אַן
אַנדערשקייט אָן געוואַלט. און אַן שאָהינגיסטישע מיטאָס. קען זיַין: חיַיל ס׳חאַרט לשון
פֿאַרבינדערט אין זיך פֿײִשן וועזן און קולטורעלן אויסדרוק. פֿאַראַן דאָס לשון וואָס איז דער
צונג און פֿאַראַן דאָס לשון וואָס איז די שפֿראַך. אָט דאָס איז דער גרויסער כח פֿון לשון. איז
דאָס געפֿערליך אָדער ניטיק? אחדאי איז עס געפֿערליך און ניטיק. ווייל איך האַלטן ביַי די
צחיי לעצטע זאַצן מיט אַ מאָל.
שרײַב איך אַזוי: אגע דאָס אַ^ געפֿערליך אָדבע אַ^ ניטיק?.

דאָס איז גאָר אַ כאַראַקטעריסטישע פֿאַסטמאַדערנע שטיק, דאָס אויסגענעמקסט-וואָס-
מע-זעט-נאָך-אַליף. דאַכט זיך מיר. אָז דאָס איז גאָר אַ ידישע שטיק אויך. ס׳איז אַ גריכיש
אײַנפֿאַל אַז דער צחישנפֿלאַץ איז אויסגעשלאָסן. אַז ס׳איז ניט מעגליעך אַ זאַך זיַין און
ניט זיַין מיט אַין מאָל. קען זיַין. למשל. אַז דאָס וואָס אַ יד שרײַבט – איבערהויבט אויף גויִיש –
איז ידישלעך און ניט ידישלעך מיט אַין מאָל.

פֿאַראַן דריַי גרויסע ידישע מענער-דענקערס פֿון אונדזער יאָרהונדערט וואָס אַ סך
פֿון זייערע געדאַנקן זיַינען אַנויַיזוונגען אויף אַ פֿאָסטמאַדערנער ידישער וויסנשאַפֿט. כ׳וועל
ברענגען פֿון יעדן איינעם פֿון זיי אַ ציטאַט וואָס שוועמט אויף אין מיַין זכרון.

דער ערשטער איז דער אַלדזשעריע-געבוירענער פֿאַריזער פֿילאַזאָף. זשאַק דערידאַ.
ס׳רוב זיַינע ווערק געפֿינט זיך אין דער מסורה פֿון אײַראָפֿעיש-העגעליש חקירה. דאַ און
דאָרט. אָבער. נעמט ער זיך אָפֿן צו ידישע טעמעס. און אין אַין עסיי געווידמעט דעם
פֿראַנצייזיש-ידישן דיכטער עדמאָנד זשאַבעז. שריַיבט דערידאַ. אַז ׳די ערשטע זאַך וואָס
הייבט אָן מיטן באַטראַכטן זיך איז די ידישע געשיכטע.׳ ³ ס׳שיַיטשש? ווי קען אַ זאַך זיך
באַטראַכטן און ניט פֿריער עקזיסטירן? דער תירוץ. דאַכט זיך. האַט צו טאָן מיט דער ידידאָס
אַלגעמיין פֿאַרשטאַנקייט אין טעקסטן. אין שריַיבן. געשריבענע לשון. דערידאַ וויל
אַרויסברענגען. אַז ס׳איז גאָר ניטאָ פֿאַראַן קיין ניט-באַטראַכטע געשיכטע: און אַז ס׳איז ניטאָ
קיין ידישע געשיכטע וואָס איז דאָס בוך וואָס איז זייער געשיכטע. אַזוי אַרום.
פֿאַראַראַקסיקאַליש ברענגט דערידאַ כל התורה כולה ווי אַ ראיה. אַז אַלץ וואָס איז
מענטשלעך ווערט באַשאַפֿן מענטשלעך. אַלץ וואָס מיר האַלטן פֿאַר אייביק איז עוצנטואַל.
דאָס הייסט ניט. אַז ניט ניטיק: וואָס זיַינען ידן אַן ידישע געשיכטע? דערידאַ לאָזט זען דאַ אַ
געוויסע ידישע שטאַלץ. ווי אַיינער זאָגט: די ידישע חכמה האָט פֿריער פֿון אַלע
פֿאַרשטאַנען. אַז מ׳קען נאָר לעבן דור אַין. דור אויס אין דעם אַרט צחישן מיטאָס און
אפֿיקורסות ׳אַנהייבן מיטן באַטראַכטן זיך׳ איז אַ מעכטיקע און סכנהדיקע עקזיסטענץ-
מיטל: אַז די ידישע געשיכטע הערט אויף זיך צו באַטראַכטן. וועלן נאָר אַנדערע באַשטימען
די ידישע געשיכטע. אָבער טאָמער חלילה טוט די גישיכטע נאָר באַטראַכטן זיך. און
ס׳לעבט זיך גאָרניט אויס – שטאַרבט עס אוועק.

אַ צחישן ציטשאַט ברענג איך פֿון דעם דיטש–ידישן קריטיקער חאַלטער בעניאַמין.
וואָס ער איז אומגעקומען אין 1940 אַ קרבן פֿון די נאַציס און פֿון זיך אַליין. אין זיַין בעסט-

3. Jacques Derrida, "Edmond Jabès and the Question of the Book," in *Writing and Difference* (Chicago: University of Chicago Press, 1978), pp.64–78, at 65.

באקאנטן מאמר. "טעזעס וועגן דער פילאזאפיע פֿון דער געשיכטע." שרייבט בעניאמין אז
דער היסטאריקער דארף פֿארשטיין די געשיכטע ווי א פֿעלד פֿון קאמף. פֿאראן א פֿיַנט וואס
וויל אויסגלעטן די געשיכטע, פֿארשטאפֿן די מיילער פֿון די טויטע, צעמאלן זייער לעבנס אין
א טריאמפֿאלן שטראם וואס פֿירט גלייַך צו אין לעגיטימירטע איצטיקע אומגערעכטיקייט.
דערפֿאר

מח מען פֿרווהן. אין יעדע עפאכע, נאך א מאל אויסצוליידן די מסורה פֿון א קאנפֿארמיזם
וואס אָט-אָט פֿריטשמעליעט זיך . . . נאר דער היסטאריקער וואס האט זיך
איינגערעדט אז אפֿילו די טויטע וועלן ניט זיין זיכער נאך דעם שונאס נצחון. וועט
קענען אויספֿפֿלאקערן דעם ניצוץ פֿון האפֿנונג וואס ליגט אינעם עבר.[4]

אפֿילו די טויטע: בעניאמין אליין הייבט ארויס די דרייַ ווערטער. מיר אלע וואס לעבן מיט
און אין דער געשיכטע טראגן א מין אחריות פֿאר די אבות און אמהות. איז די געשיכטע
שאקע א מין קדיש–זאגן. נאר קדיש איז א א טרייסט, און די געשיכטע דארף וועקן . . . דאס
יאנדעס.

דער לעצטער אין מיַן טריא איז עמנואל לעווינאס. א ליטוואק וואס איז געווארן
דירעקטאר פֿון דער גימנאזיע פֿון אליאנס איזראעליט אוניווערסעל אין פֿאריז. און
וואס אין זיַן טיפֿן עלטער גיט זיַן שטערן אלץ אויף אין דעם היטל פֿון פֿילאזאפֿיע. לעווינאס
שרייבט א סך בפֿירוש אויף ייִדישע טעמעס. אין איינעם אזא עסיי הייבט לעווינאס אן מיט
א הארט. וואס קלינגט ווי אן ענטספֿער אויף דערידאס ווארט אויבן. אט שרייבט ער:

זיך פֿרעגן וועגן ייִדישער אידענטיטעט הייסט אז מ'האט זי שוין פֿארלוירן. דאך הייסט עס אויך
האלטן בייַ איר–אָנ'ט וואלט ניט געווען וואס צו פֿרעגן. צווישן שוין און דאך שיילט זיך ארויס
דער גבֿול. אָנגעצויגן ווי א שטריק אויף וועלכן די מערבֿדיקע ייִדן רייזיקירן זייער ייִדישקייט.[5]

צווישן שוין און דאך: סיוואלט געפֿאסט גאר פֿארן טיטל פֿון א קאלעקטיווער ייִדישער
אויטאביאגראפֿיע אין אונדזער צייַט. נאר איך האלט. אויף אזוי ווייַט ווי דער פראבלעם פֿון
ייִדישן קיום באשטייט אין אָנגיי נאך א בראך. איז דער אלגעמיינער פֿראבלעמאטיק פֿון
פאסטמאדערנקייט אן ענליכע: לעבן אין דער געשיכטע, בייַקומען די געשיכטע . . . לעבן דורך
אָט די סתירה.

אין א גרויסן מאס. קען מען זאגן אז די חכמת-הפאסטמאדערן ליגט אין איר
אנערקענונג, אז איינגעלעד איז דאס ניט קיין סתירה. אויב דאס מאדערנע גלויבן אין
פראגרעס זעט די געשיכטע ווי אן אויטאנאם וואס שלעפט די מענטשהייט מיט. קען מען זי
ניט בייַקומען: מ'דארף נאר מיטשווימען אין דער ריכטונג פֿון היסטארישן פראגרעס.
פאלנדריק דעם אויפֿגעקלערטן וועגווייַזער. פאסטמאדערן דענקען אבער פֿארשטייט די
מענטשעלעכע געשיכטע ווי א מענטשעלעכע באשאפֿונג. און ניט באשאפֿן איין מאל פֿאר אלע
מאל: תמיד האלט מען אין שאפֿן דעם עבר לויט די נויטן פֿון היַנט.

4. Walter Benjamin, "Theses on the Philosophy of History," in *Illuminations* (New York: Schocken Books, 1969), pp. 253–64, at 255.

5. Emmanuel Levinas, "Pièces d'Identité," in *Difficile Liberté* (Paris: Albin Michel, 1976, pp. 64–78, at 74.

אחדאי איז אן דאָס אַ געפֿערלעכע אײַנפֿאַל. אַ משל צו װאָס עס קען פֿירן האָט אונדז
געבראַכט דזשאַרדזש אָרװעל אין זײן ראָמאַן 1984. אין דער װעלט פֿון 1984 בײַט מען
די נעכטיקע צײַטונגען. זײ זאָלן גוט פּאַסן צו דער װאָר װאָס פּאַסט פֿאַר די רעגירונג. נאָר
מ׳קען װענדן דעם פּאָסטמאָדערנעם ׳פּרינציפּ׳ פֿון היסטאַרישער ניט-באַשטימקײט׳
אַנדערש, װען מ׳האַלט אין זינען בעניאַמינס זאָרג פֿאַר די לעבנס פֿון די געשטאָרבענע. אַזױ
קען מען אַריבערשטײַגן די מאָדערנע זאָבאַבאַנע, אַז די פֿריערדיקע דורות זײַנען ניט געװען
אַזױ קלוג װי אונדז הײַנטיקע. און אַזױ שטײַגט מען אַריבער די קעגנװײַטיקע ראָמאַנטישע
זאָבאַבאַנע, אַז די פֿריערדיקע דורות האָבן געהאַט אַ רײַכן כּוח צו פֿאַרכּישופֿן די װעלט.
בשעת מיר נעבעך זײַנען פֿאַראָרעמט. גיטסטלעד-נאָקעטע. מ׳זעט אַמאָל אַ מין פֿאַרקער
צװישן עלעמענטן פֿון די דרײַ אַזױ-באַטראַכטע ׳תּקופֿות׳ פֿון פֿאַר-מאָדערן. מאָדערן. און
נאָך-מאָדערן.

אַזױ. פֿון דעם שטאַנדפּונקט פֿון אַן עיקרדיקן פּאָסטמאָדערנעם פּרינציפּ – די
פֿילפֿאַכיקײט און צעפֿיצלטקײט פֿון שפּראַך-באַטײַט – קומען צונױף רש״י מיט פּרץ
מאַרקיש. רש״י. דאַכט זיך מער װי אײן מאָל אין זײַן חומש-פּירוש. גיט צו פֿאַרשטײן װי
ס׳קען זײַן אַן אַ שיעור מדרשים אױף אַן אינציק פּסוק. ער ברענגט דעם אימאַזש פֿון אַ
האַמער אױף אַ שטײן. װאָס לאָזט פֿליען צאַלרײַכע פֿונקן אין פֿאַרשײדענע ריכטונגען. אַזױ
פֿיל מעגולעכקײטן ליגן אין דעם שטײן און אַז מ׳ברענגט אַראָף דעם האַמער. דעם מכשיר פֿון
רבנישן דרוש. ערשט דאַן קען מען זען װאָס ליגט דערין. מאַרקישעס מעטאָפֿאָר שפּיגלט
אָפּ . . . שפּיגלט אַראָפּ רש״ין. בײַ אים איז שױן אַ שפּיגל װאָס צעברעכט אױף אַ שטײן. ניט אַ
האַמער װאָס שלאָגט און װערט ניט געשלאָגן. און דער שפּיגל איז אַ דער אָפּגעװאָרטער מענטש
אַלײן. טראַגישע אַקעגן רש״יס זיכערקײט בײַ זיך. אָבער מאַרקיש דער מענטש. דער
מאָדערנער ייד. איז געװאָרן אַ שפּיגל פֿון אַ װעלט-באַנעם װאָס האָט בכלל ניט מודה
געװעזן אין קײן פֿילפֿאַכיקײט פֿון טײַטש. פֿון באַטײַט. אַזױ איז די צעשפּאַלטונג פֿון דעם
שפּיגל אַ מין ניי-געװוינען פֿרײהייט. און די בראָכשטיקער[6] זײַנען אַזױ פֿיל
יאָדערן פֿאַר אַ באַנײַע ייִדישלעך שאַפֿונג. אַזױ װי רש״יס דעם האַמער װערט אַ מענטש-שפּיגל.
װערט רש״יס שטײן פֿון תּורה מאַרקישעס אומרחמנותדיק שטיין פֿון דער געשיכטע.

ייִדיש איז די כּלי. װאָס ברענגט צוזאַמען רש״י מיט מאַרקישן. נאָר כ׳װיל ניט נאָך
אַמאָל אַרײַנטײַטשן אין דעם אַ מין ניטראַלן המשך. בײַ רש״י. בײַ רש״י. װאָס האָט געלעבט אין דער
שעפֿערישער צײַט פֿון די מפֿרשים ראשונים. האָט פֿילפֿאַכיקע באַטײַט דעם מיטבאַטײַט פֿון
שפע. בײַ מאַרקישן נעמט אָן די צעברעכונג פֿון אײנפֿאַכיקע באַטײַט דעם כאַראַקטער פֿון אַ
קאַטאַסטראָף.

דאַכט זיך. אַז אונדזער ייִדיש פּאַסט זיך גיכער צום מעטאָפֿאָר פֿון אַ שפּיגל אױף אַ
שטײן. מיר פֿאַרשטײן זי ניט װי אַ מיטל. נאָר װי אַ טײל פֿון אונדזער עצם װעזן. און דאָך

---

6. מאַרקישעס ליד געפֿינט זיך אונטערן טיטל בראַכשטיקער אין דער אַנטאָלאָגיע **שפּיגל אױף אַ שטײן.**
רעדאַקציע. אַרינפֿיר און הערות פֿון חנא שמערוק . תּל-אָביב: פֿאַרלאַג די װאָלדענע קײט און י.ל. פּרץ פֿאַרלאַג.
1964. ז׳ 489. אינטערעסאַנט. אַז אױך רש״יס פֿאַרענגליכונג דינט װי דער טיטל פֿון אַן אַנטאָלאָגיע: *Hammer
on the Rock: A Midrash Reader,* ed. Nahum Glatzer (New York: Schocken Books,
1962).

איז פֿאַראַן אַ סתירה אין דער ידישיסטישער באַגריף פֿון דער שפּראַך. הײַ חיל זי האַלטן
גאַנץ. אָדער ווידער מאַכן גאַנץ. הײַ דער "שפּיגל פֿון אַ פֿאָלק."[7] האַלט. אַז מ׳דאַרף אַנהייבן
פֿון דער צעפּיצלטקײַט פֿון אונדזער שפּראַך. און אָנמוטיקן די מעגלעכקײַטן פֿון די
פֿאַרשיידענע פּיצלעך. אַזוי. למשל. וועט מען רעדן ידיש הײַ מ׳שרײַבט זי. ניט שרײַבן הײַ
מ׳רעדט. הײַל דער עיקר קאָמוניקאַצֿיע-מיטל פֿון הײַנטיקן העלטשלעכן ידיש איז שרײַבן און
ניט רעדן. אַזוי אויך. דאַכט זיך. איז בעסער צו זען מײַן ידיש אָדער דײַן ידיש ניט הײַ
פֿאַרשיידענע ערכדיקײַטן פֿון אַן אוממעגלעכן. פֿלאַטאַניש אידעאַל פֿון ידיש. נירערט הײַ אַזוי
פֿיל צעפּיצלטע תורות-היידיש הײַ מ׳לערנט זיך און אָנדערע הײַ כ׳בֿין. הײַסט עס. קעגן אַ
געקניצלטן שלמות: כ׳האַלט. אַז ס׳איז בעסער ניט צו יאָגן נאָך משיחן אין עבר.

אָבער ידיש פֿאַרגלײַכט זיך ניט נאָר מיט תורה. מ׳פֿאַרשטײַט דאָס לשון אויך הײַ אַ
מיניאַטור פֿונעם פֿאָלקס-לעבן. דערפֿאַר איז שווער פֿאַר ידן אַן עלטערן דור-האָס
פֿאַר זײ איז ידיש מאַמע-לשון ממש-צו באַנעמען אַפֿילו אַז ס׳זענען דאָ פֿאַראַן יונגע לײַט
הײַ קענען גוט די שפּראַך. אויסער דער גאָר-פֿרומער העלט (הײַס אין איר אַנטהיקלט זיך
ידיש גאַנץ אַנדערש) בלײַבט ידיש אַלץ מער אין רשות פֿון אַ מבֿינישן עליט. מ׳דאַרף
אָננעמען דעם פֿאַקט. אָבער מ׳טאָר אויך ניט פֿאַרגעסן אַז דער יאָדער-כוח פֿון ידיש
נעמט זיך פֿון דעם. הײַס ידן פֿון אַלע שיכטן האָבן זי גערעדט. האָבן זי גענוצט טאָג-
טעגלעך. איצט. וען בײַ אונדז אין ידיש ניט קײַן גאַסן-שפּראַך. ניט קײַן קיך-שפּראַך. שטײַט
פֿאַר אונדז דער פּראָבלעם הײַ אַזוי אויפֿצונעמען די ירושה פֿון אַ לעבעדיקן ידיש.

כ׳חיל ניט פֿרוון ברענגען אַ תירוץ על רגל אחת. כ׳חיל נאָר מרמז זײַן. אַז צוזאַמען
מיטן מסתריח זײַן זיך פּשוט אויפֿצוהאַלטן די לעבעדיקע שפּראַך. מוז מען אויך
אָפּלערנען פֿון איר אונטערגאַנג. דאַכט זיך. ס׳האָט צו טאָן מיט דעם. הײַס ידן הײַ גנבֿים זענען זענען
דרויסענדיקע לגבי די בירגערליכע געזעלשאַפֿט: ידן. הײַ גנבֿים. האָבן פֿאַרמאַנט אַ
"סודותדיקן" זשאַרגאָן:[8] טײַל ידן האָבן געלעבט אין אַן "אונטערוועלט" מיט ניט-ידישע
פֿאַרברעכערס. נאָר כ׳מײַן אַז די פֿאַרבינדונג גײַט אַפֿילו טיפֿער. פֿון דער שטאַנדפֿונקט פֿון
דער אײַראָפּעיש-ראָמאַנטישער נאַצֿיאָנאַליזם. איז נאָרמאַל אַז יעדער פֿאָלק זאָל זײַן
אומאָפּהענגיק אויף זײַן אײַגן לאַנד און רעדן זײַן אײַגן לשון. ידיש פּאַסט ניט אַרײַן אין די
ראַמען. ידיש נעמט פֿרײַ דאָ און דאָרט פֿון די שפּראַך-ירושות פֿון אָנדערע פֿעלקער. ידיש
איז אינטערנאַצֿיאָנאַל. ידיש איז משיג-גבֿול: ס׳איז טאַקע אַ פֿאַרברעך-שפּראַך: און
דערפֿאַר האָט מען עס ניט געלאָזט לעבן. מ׳האָט געוואָלט אין באַשטראָפֿן ידיש מיט דער טויט.

כ׳שרײַב דאָס אַקעגן דעם. הײַס מ׳רעדט אירֿאַניש און נאָסטאַלגֿיש פֿון אַ
פֿאַרלוירענעם. אָדער אַ געחלומט ידישלאַנד. בעסער צו האַלטן אין זינען דחוקא דאָס ידיש
ניט-לאַנד. ממה לעבן אויף דער ערד. אמת: אָבער אין גאַנצן ערדיש זײַן איז אויך ניט געזונט.
דאָס הײַס כ׳חיל זיך קעגנשטעלן קעגן דער אַסאַסֿיאַצֿיע פֿון לאַנד. פֿאָלק. און שפּראַך
שטמט מיט דעם הײַס דער טעמאַטיק פֿון גלות האַלט אַ בכבֿודיקן. אַפֿילו עיקרדיקן. פּלאַץ

7. אַזוי הײַסט די אַנטאָלאָגֿיע פֿון דער ידישער פּאָעזֿיע אויף פֿראַנצֿייזיש: Charles Dobzynski,
ed., *Le Miroir d'un peuple* (Paris: Gallimard, 1971).

8. ז׳ פ׳ Sander Gilman, *Jewish Self-Hatred: Anti-Semitism and the Hidden
Language of the Jews* (Baltimore: Johns Hopkins University Press, 1986).

אין דער פֿאַסטמאָדערנער המיון-וועלט. אַזוי. למשל. שרײַבן די רעדאַקטאָרן פֿון אַ נײַער
חיסנשאַפֿטלעכער אויסגאַבע: "הײַנט דאַכט זיך עפּעס אַז גלות איז דער כּלל. גלותן פֿאַלן
אַרײַן אין אַ פֿאַרעם פֿון מענטשלעכער באַוועגונג און אומסטאַביליקײט. און אַנטקעגן זײ חידזן
זיך געאָגראַפֿישע און טעריטאָריאַלע זיכערקײטן ווי אַלץ מער ברעכעוודיק."[9] דאָס וואָס
מדהאָט פֿריער באַטראַכט פֿאַר אַן אויסנאַם-שטריך בײַ ייִדן ווערט אַלץ מער באַטראַכט
ווי אַ מענטשלעכע נאָרמע. און דאָס אין די גײסט-חיסנשאַפֿטן ווי אין דער געשיכטע גופֿא.
אַזוי. אַ שטייגער. איז חיכטיק אין זשאַק דערידאָס שרײַבן דאָס וואָרט trace. ס'פּאַסט צו
טײַטשן דאָס וואָרט ווי זכר. דערידאַ חיל מיט דעם באַטאָנען עפּעס ענגליכס צום אויבן-
דערמאַנטן אויסנעמעקסט-וואָס-מע-זעט-נאָך-אַלץ. דער זכר איז דאָס וואָס דיערט פֿון אַ
יש וואָס ווערט פֿאַרגעסן. עס לאָזט נ ניט "חיטשער" שאַפֿן פֿון זיך אַ פֿאַלשע. באַנײַטע גאַנצקײט.
נאָר פֿון דער אַנדער זײַט איז עס געגן שטאַרק. געגנ דאָיק. עס זאָל קענען דעסטאַביליזירן
דאָס פּאַזיטיוווע טראַכטן פֿון אַ הײַנט-מאַרגן וואָס חיל זיך מאַכן אומבאַחוסטזיניק. ס'איז ניט
צופֿעליק. דאַכט זיך. אַז דער יד פֿון אַלדושערריע איז געוואָרן דער פֿראַנצײזישער
פֿילאָזאָף פֿון trace. פֿון זכר. ייִדישע לעבן-מיט-אַבֿיחה. דער ייִדישער אופֿן פֿון זײַן בײַ זיך
אין דער פֿרעמד. איז אַ מוסטער פֿאַר נאָך-מלחמהדיקן. נאָך-חורבנדיקן שרײַבן און
דענקען.[10]

נאָר אויב דאָס ייִדישע ווערט אַזוי לײַכט פֿאַראַלוועלטלעכט מיט פֿאַסטמאָדערנעם
כישוף. איז וואָס בלײַבט אין דעם ייִדישלעך?
לאָמיר ניט אוועקמעקן דעם פֿראַגע-צײכן.
לאָמיר בעסער זיך קלײַבן ארום אים. און לאָמיר נאָך פֿרעגן. נאָך חײַטער.

---

9. "Editors' Comment," *Public Culture* 2, no. 1 (Fall 1989): i.

10. פֿ'ג Maurice Blanchot, *The Writing of the Disaster* (Lincoln: University of Nebraska Press, 1986).

Yiddish Science
and the Postmodern

It's been said clearly and often enough: before we begin speaking of the new concept of "postmodernity" as if it were an autonomous entity that had just been discovered, we must pose a few preliminary questions. That is, what is it that the postmodern comes "after?" And what, for that matter, do we mean by "modernity?"

And indeed we're accustomed to answering a question in the form of "What does x mean?" with a solution in the form of "x is . . ." We would like to fill in, on the right side of the small (but not innocent) word "is," the value of the symbol x. We describe x. The question we answer in this way is "What writing does x allow?"

What "modernity" allows us to write, however, is limitless. And we are still too close to the modern world, too much in it, to be able to come up with an answer on one foot. (That's why "modern" has two syllables, while "post" has only one.) "Modern" is no longer sufficient for us, but that doesn't mean we can do without it altogether.

For that reason I'd like to try another approach to the previous question of modernity. I would, rather, like to propose to you (to you, my friend who troubles to keep Yiddish in your head) answers in the form of "x means modernity!" But aren't there dozens of discrete terms could take the place of that *x*? The difference is that this way we can agree (or not: as long as you understand me) that yes—*x* is one thing that modernity means.

So. My first solution, in that case, is "*Wissenschaft des Judentums* means modernity." In a way, *Wissenschaft des Judentums* seems to stand in a similar relation to Yiddishkeit as "postmodernity" does to "modernity." That is, we devise a word around which we can gather—or better yet, atop which we can climb, in order to see down, look back at what we, as humanity, have already experienced. But the analogy is more interesting where it doesn't hold, where it falls apart. *Wissenschaft des Judentums* wants to control Yiddishkeit, wants to consider it, describe it, and—the pioneers said so openly—bury it. The postmodern understands itself as an outgrowth of modernity, and doesn't want to bury it, but rather to— maybe the proper word would be—*heal* it.

Another solution I would propose is this one: Continuity [*hemshikh*] means modernity. One can see the ideology of continuity both in Yiddishism—there was once a summer camp named Hemshikh—and in Judaism—just today there is a conference at the Jewish Theological Seminary on the theme "Jewish Continuity since the Enlightenment." It might seem that by identifying continuity with modernity I may be stretching the point a little. In a way continuity would mean *not* the modern, the violent break with things-just-as-they-have-been-until-now; continuity would mean the opposite of a revolt against convention. But I insist: If one already admits a struggle for "continuity," if one must put the stress on continuity (rather than, say, loss or forgetting), one is already in a modern stance. And not, by the way, in a postmodern stance, since postmodern thought doesn't subscribe to the idea of continuity. It insists, rather, that "tradition" is never whole, that it's never a perfect transfer from generation to generation, that we annihilate memory or renew it at every moment in time.

Now I can approach a little more closely—although still indirectly—the relationship between Yiddish science [*yidishe visnshaft*] and the postmodern. I can see the way to Yiddish science clearly only when I go down the road of *Wissenschaft des Judentums* a stretch. This brings into focus the difference between a world-language and a folk-language. The very fact that *Wissenschaft des Judentums* demands to be written in the Latin alphabet and Yiddish science is written in Hebrew letters testifies to this. The fact that the German term is somewhat ambiguous—it implies at least a hint of that which Jews know—demonstrates a certain nostalgia in the motivations of its founders. But the principle factor is still the external, the controlling one.[1]

Yiddish science is different. Utterly different. Yiddish science is ambiguous through and through. It is indeed a science, contemporary, secular. But it isn't a field of science. It's a kind of science. It also isn't Yiddishkeit itself. It's a creative hybrid. In that way the concept of Yiddish science throws a question mark into the eyes of those who would like to see Western discourse as a unit. There are still some people who consider themselves insiders in that universal, enlightened conversation. They still believe that their way is *the* way, that the hell of imperialism and the Nazi death-orgy haven't canceled their claims, that through them the world will be set free.

But Yiddish science throws the same question to the humanities as it does to those who consider themselves outsiders in this Western conversation. They look at the map that has only one color for all of Europe, and usually consider all of those who come from there fellow-travelers to imperialism. They don't hear the conversation that goes on around and against and under the Western conversation—the conversation of Yiddish science. And it's truly a loss for their own purposes too, since to a great extent it was just that silenced Yiddish conversation that prepared Europe to hear their claims.

It is just this that should have been readily grasped by such an astute critic as Gayatri Chakravorty Spivak, for example, whom I cited above. In her critical work she clearly shows that she understands how she herself is both an "insider"—she teaches, translates, and writes about European philosophy—and an outsider—her name and her appearance attest to her Indian origin, to her connection with the formerly colonized. Apparently she is not Jewish. And the name Spivak is actually a Polish one. But she

---

1. Cf. the description of English Orientalism in India: "One effect of establishing a version of the British system [of education in India] was the development of an uneasy separation between disciplinary formation in Sanskrit studies and the native, now alternative tradition of Sanskrit 'high culture.' " Gayatri Chakravorty Spivak, "Can the Subaltern Speak?" in *Marxism and the Interpretation of Culture*, ed. Cary Nelson and Lawrence Grossberg (Urbana and Chicago: University of Illinois Press, 1988), pp. 271–313, at 282.

spells it in the English way, not as it's spelled in Polish . . . a sign
that it was a Jewish immigrant that carried this name. Usually it's
the wife of a famous person who is overlooked, but in this case we
don't know or hear anything about Spivak's Jewish husband. All
that's left is the mark of Yiddishkeit. And if only "Spivak" were
mentioned, I might even have felt the urge to demonstrate how
her subjective but carefully thought-out criticism is a model for
Yiddish science. That would certainly have constituted Yiddish beyond a boundary.

But no. Even so insightful a person as G. Ch. Spivak, who
knows that her India is not the model of all Europe's "Others,"
still divides the world into smaller geographical worlds. The universal principle remains: Europe on one side against the third
world on the other. Proof of this lies in the fact that her book is
called *In Other Worlds* (*In Other Worlds: Essays in Cultural Politics*
[New York: Methuen, 1987]). When Europe is seen as one imperial unit, Yiddish must remain unseen and unheard.

Spivak's question in the essay I cited is: "Can the subaltern
speak?" By subalterns she means those colonized people who
cannot attain a foothold in the hegemonic sphere. The closest
analogy I find in our world is with the victims of the last catastrophe, and the masses of Jews that came before them, who were
forgotten with their murder. And indeed I believe that Nazism
presented itself, to a great degree, with the same imperialistic motivation of "silencing the Other."

It's interesting that Spivak finds a fitting image for Europe as
a proud, self-originating sun,[2] throwing its intense light on others
so that they cannot gaze upon it directly. Yiddish is nothing like
the sun. In Yiddish we would sooner sing the song "Beautiful as
the moon, shining like the stars. . . ." Yiddish reflects a different
light. Yiddish is not afraid to reflect in itself the humanity—the
language, the body—of the Other.

We make ourselves different in Yiddish. We take over pieces
of someone else's language and make them our own. We lay the
stress not only on our connection with earlier generations, but
also on our distance from them, in that our Yiddish is different
from theirs. But the most important thing is that a freely chosen

2. Spivak, p. 274.

linguistic alterity can be an alterity without violence. And without chauvinistic myths. Maybe that's because the word "tongue" connects in itself physical substance and cultural expression. There is the tongue that is part of the body and the tongue that is one's language. And that is its great power. Is that dangerous or necessary? Certainly it is both dangerous and necessary. I want to stand by these two sentences simultaneously, so I write them in this way:

$$\underbrace{\text{That is}}_{\text{Is that}} \wedge \quad \text{dangerous} \underset{\text{or}}{\wedge} \quad \underbrace{\text{and}}_{\text{necessary}}$$

That is an altogether characteristic postmodern trick, the erased-that-one-can-still-read. It seems to me that it's also an altogether characteristic Jewish trick, as well. It's a Greek notion that the space in between is ruled out, that it's impossible for something to be and not be at the same time. It could be, for example, that what a Jew writes—particularly in a non-Jewish language—is Jewish and not Jewish at the same time.

There are three great Jewish thinkers of our century much of whose work can be seen as signposts leading toward a postmodern Jewish science. I want to bring in a quote from each of them that swims up in my memory.

The first is the Algerian-born philosopher Jacques Derrida. Most of his work is in the tradition of European-Hegelian speculation. Here and there, though, he explicitly deals with Jewish themes. And in one essay dedicated to the French-Jewish poet Edmond Jabès, Derrida writes that "the first thing that begins by describing itself is Jewish history."[3] What does that mean? How can something describe itself and not exist first? The solution, it seems to me, has to do with Derrida's general engagement with texts, with writing, with written language. Derrida wants to bring out that there is no such thing as unexamined history; and that there is no Jewish history to describe without the book that is this history. In this way, Derrida paradoxically brings the entire Torah as evidence that everything that is human is a human creation. Everything we consider eternal is contingent. That doesn't mean

3. Jacques Derrida, "Edmond Jabès and the Question of the Book," in *Writing and Difference* (Chicago: University of Chicago Press, 1978), pp. 64–78, at 65.

that it isn't necessary; what are Jews without Jewish history? Derrida reveals here a certain Jewish pride, as if to say: Jewish thought understood before any other that we can only live, from generation to generation, in the space between myth and heresy. "To begin by thinking oneself" is a powerful and dangerous means of existence: When Jewish history stops considering itself, only others will define Jewish history. But if history only considers itself, God forbid, and it doesn't live itself at all—it will cease to exist.

My second citation is from the German-Jewish critic Walter Benjamin, who died in 1940, a victim of the Nazis and of his own hand. In his best-known work, "Theses on the Philosophy of History," Benjamin writes that the historian must understand history as a battlefield. There is an enemy who wishes to smooth over history, stopping the mouths of the dead, grinding their lives beneath the triumphant stream that leads directly to a single legitimated present injustice. Therefore

> in every era the attempt must be made anew to wrest tradition away
> from a conformism that is about to overpower it. . . . Only that
> historian will have the gift of fanning the spark of hope in the past
> who is firmly convinced that *even the dead* will not be safe from the
> enemy if he wins.[4]

Even the dead: Benjamin himself emphasizes those three words. All of us who live with and in history carry a kind of responsibility for the ancestors. History is truly a way of saying Kaddish for the dead. Only the Kaddish prayer is a consolation, and history must awaken . . . one's *yandes*.[5]

The last in my trio is Emmanuel Levinas, a Lithuanian-born Jew who was appointed director of the Alliance Israelite Universelle High School in Paris, and whose star, in his advanced age, has climbed higher and higher in the skies of philosophy. Levinas often writes explicitly on Jewish themes. In one such essay Levinas begins with an insight that sounds like an answer to Derrida's above. He writes as follows:

4. Walter Benjamin, "Theses on the Philosophy of History," in *Illuminations* (New York: Schocken Books, 1969), pp. 253–64, at 255.

5. The untranslatable term *yandes* signifies not only a sense of one's ethnic identity but also an active and ethical engagement in the world in conformity with one's awareness of Jewish experience. See Mordkhe Schaechter, "*S'yandes*," *Laytish mame-loshn* (New York: League for Yiddish, 1986), pp. 148–49.

The very fact of questioning one's Jewish identity means it is already lost. But by the same token, it is precisely through this kind of cross-examination that one still hangs on to it. Between *already* and *still* Western Judaism walks a tightrope.[6]

Between *already* and *still:* That would work well as the title of a collective Jewish autobiography of our time. But I believe that, to the extent that the problem of Jewish existence consists in the question of how to go on after a break, the general problematic of postmodernity resembles it: living in history, overcoming history . . . living through just this contradiction.

To a great extent, one can say that postmodern thought takes shape in the recognition that, actually, this is no contradiction. If the modern belief in progress sees history as an automaton that pulls humanity along, then we cannot overcome it; we can only swim along in the direction of historical progress, in obedience to the enlightened guides. Postmodern thought, though, understands human history as a human creation. And not created once and for all; the past is always being created anew according to the needs of the present.

Certainly this is a frightening notion. George Orwell gave us a parable of where this might lead in his novel *1984*. In the world of *1984* the nightly newspapers are changed, to make them fit the truths the government asserts. But we can turn the postmodern "principle of historical uncertainty" differently, if we keep in mind Benjamin's concern for the lives of the dead. In that way we can get beyond the modern superstition that previous generations were not as wise as we are. And that is how we get beyond the opposite Romantic superstition, that previous generations had the bountiful powers of enchanting the world, while we are pathetically impoverished, spiritually naked. Sometimes one can see a kind of reversal among elements of the three so-called "eras" of the premodern, the modern, and the postmodern.

In this way, from the perspective of a basic postmodern principle—the multiplicity and fragmentation of linguistic meaning—Rashi and Peretz Markish come together. Rashi, more than once, I think, in his Torah commentary, provides an explanation for

6. Emmanuel Levinas, "Means of Identification," *Difficult Liberty: Essays on Judaism*, trans. Sean Hand (Baltimore: Johns Hopkins University Press, 1990 [1963]), p. 50.

how there can be a limitless number of commentaries on a single verse. He introduces the image of a hammer on a rock, which shoots forth an infinite spray of sparks in all directions. That is how many potentialities rest in the rock, and only as the hammer—the tool of rabbinic homiletics—strikes does one see what lies within. Markish's metaphor reflects . . . refracts Rashi's. He writes of a mirror that breaks against a rock, not a hammer that strikes and is not stricken. And the mirror is the deluded human being himself. Tragic in contrast with Rashi's self-assurance. But Markish the man, the modern Jew, became the mirror of a worldview that was utterly incapable of admitting the multiplicity of meaning, of significance. So the smashing of the mirror is a kind of newly won freedom, and the slivers[7] so many kernels of a renewed Jewish creativity. Just as Rashi's hammer becomes a humanmirror, Rashi's rock of Torah becomes Markish's pitiless rock of history.

Yiddish is the vessel that brings Rashi together with Markish. But I don't want to once again invest the connection with a kind of neutral continuity. For Rashi, who lived in the creative era of the Early Commentators, multiplicity had the connotation of abundance. For Markish, the shattering of univocal meaning took on the character of a nightmare.

It would seem that, for our Yiddish, the metaphor of a mirror on a rock is more appropriate. We understand Yiddish not as a medium, but rather as a part of our fundamental being. And yet there is a contradiction within the Yiddishist conception of the language, which wants to keep it whole, or make it whole again, as the "mirror of a people."[8] I maintain that we must begin with the fragmentation of our language and encourage the possibilities of the various fragments. Thus, for example, Yiddish will be spoken the way it is written, not written as it is spoken, because the basic means of communication of today's secular Yiddish is writing, not speech. In the same way, I suppose, it is better to view

7. Markish's poem "Slivers" is included in the anthology *Mirror on the Rock*, edited and with an introduction and notes by Chone Shmeruk (Tel Aviv: Goldene Kayt and Y. L. Peretz Press, 1964), p. 489. Interestingly, Rashi's metaphor also serves as the title of another anthology: *Hammer on the Rock: A Midrash Reader*, ed. Nahum Glatzer (New York: Schocken Books, 1962).

8. That is the title of an anthology of Jewish poetry in French: Charles Dobzynski, ed., *Le Miroir d'un peuple* (Paris: Gallimard, 1971).

my Yiddish or your Yiddish not as various approximations of an impossible Platonic ideal of Yiddish, but rather as so many fragmented Torah-sparks of Yiddish that we study among others. I am against an artificial wholeness, that is; I believe that it's better not to chase after the Messiah in the past.

But Yiddish can be compared not only with Torah. We also understand the language as a microcosm of folklife. For that reason it's hard for Jews of an older generation—for whom Yiddish really is the mother-tongue—even to grasp that there are young people who know the language well. Outside the "traditional" Orthodox world, where Yiddish is developing in an entirely different way, Yiddish is becoming more and more the province of a learned elite. We must embrace that reality. But we must also not forget that the core strength of Yiddish derives from the fact that Jews of all classes spoke it, used it daily. Now, when Yiddish is no longer a street-language for us, no longer a kitchen-language, the problem arises of how to take up the inheritance of a living language.

I don't want to try to provide a solution on one foot. I only want to intimate that, along with working hard at simply maintaining the living language, we must also learn something from its decline. It seems to me, for instance, that we can draw a moral from the association between Yiddish and the language of thieves. It involves the fact that Jews, like thieves, were outsiders in relation to bourgeois society; Jews, like thieves, possessed a "hidden" jargon;[9] some Jews lived in an "underworld" along with non-Jewish criminals. But I think that the connection goes even deeper. From the perspective of European Romantic nationalism, each nationality would normally be an independent entity on its own land and speaking its own language. Yiddish doesn't fit into this fairytale. Yiddish freely takes here and there from the linguistic heritage of other peoples. Yiddish is international. Yiddish is a border-smuggler; it really is a language for transgressors; and that's why they didn't let it live. They wanted to sentence Yiddish to death.

I write this in opposition to the ironic or nostalgic discourse of a lost or dreamed Yiddishland. It's better to keep in mind the

9. See Sander Gilman, *Jewish Self-Hatred: Anti-Semitism and the Hidden Language of the Jews* (Baltimore: Johns Hopkins University Press, 1986).

Yiddish nowhere-land. One must live on this earth, true; but to be entirely earthbound is also unhealthy. What I would like to oppose to the association between land, folk, and language derives from the thematic of Diaspora, which has an honorable, even primary place in the postmodern worldview. Thus, for example, the editor of a new academic journal writes: "Today's diasporas seem somehow normative, creating a pattern of human movement and instability, against which geographical and territorial certainties seem increasingly fragile." [10] That which once seemed an exceptional trait of the Jewish people seems more and more a human norm. And this is as true for the humanities as it is for history itself. Thus, for example, the word *trace* is important in Jacques Derrida's writing. By this, Derrida wants to allow for something similar to the previously discussed erased-that-one-can-still-read. A remnant is what endures of an entity that has been forgotten. It does not allow for any "further" creation from itself of a false, renewed wholeness, but, on the other hand, it is also strong enough, present enough, to be able to destabilize the positive designs of a here-and-now that wants to pretend ignorance. It's no coincidence, it would seem, that the Jew from Algeria became the French philosopher of the "trace," or the "remnant." Jewish living-with-loss, the Jewish mode of holding one's own in a foreign land, is a model for postwar, postcatastrophe writing and thinking. [11]

But if the Yiddish word so easily universalizes itself with postmodern magic, what in it remains, then, Jewish?

Let us not wipe away that question mark.

Let us rather gather around it, and let us ask more questions, and then some more.

10. "Editor's Comment," *Public Culture* 2, no. 1 (Fall 1989): i.

11. Cf. Maurice Blanchot, *The Writing of the Disaster* (Lincoln: University of Nebraska Press, 1986).

❧ REFERENCES ❧

Abu-Lughod, Janet. 1989. *Before European Hegemony*. New York: Oxford University Press.

Akenson, Donald Harmon. 1992. *God's Peoples: Covenant and Land in South Africa, Israel, and Ulster*. Ithaca: Cornell University Press.

Alcalay, Ammiel. 1993. *After Jews and Arabs: Remaking Levantine Culture*. Minneapolis: University of Minnesota Press.

Anderson, Benedict. 1991. *Imagined Communities: Reflections on the Spread of Nationalism*, second edition. London: Verso.

Anidjar, Gil. 1996. "On the (Under)Cutting Edge: Does Jewish Memory Need Sharpening?" In *Jews and Other Differences*, edited by Jonathan Boyarin and Daniel Boyarin. Minneapolis: University of Minnesota Press.

Arendt, Hannah. 1969. "Introduction: Walter Benjamin." In *Illuminations*. Pp. 1–55. New York: Schocken Books.

Asad, Talal. 1993. *Genealogies of Religion: Discipline and Reasons of Power in Christianity and Islam*. Baltimore: Johns Hopkins University Press.

Auerbach, Erich. 1953. *Mimesis: The Representation of Reality in Western Literature*, translated by Willard B. Trask. Princeton: Princeton University Press.

Bahloul, Joelle. 1992. *La Maison de la mémoire: ethnologie d'une demeur judeo-arabe en Algerie*. Paris: Editions Metailie.

Bakan, David. 1958. *Sigmund Freud and the Jewish Mystical Tradition*. Princeton, N.J.: Van Nostrand.

Balibar, Etienne. 1990. "Paradoxes of Universality." In *Anatomy of Racism*, edited by David Theo Goldberg. Pp. 283–94. Minneapolis: University of Minnesota Press.

Barth, Lewis M. 1991. "Circumcision and the Unity of God: A Comment on Stern." *S'vara* 2(2):49–51.

Baudrillard, Jean. 1983. *Simulations*. New York: Semiotext(e).

Belcove-Shalin, Janet. 1988. "Becoming More of an Eskimo." In *Between Two Worlds: Ethnographic Essays on American Jews*. Pp. 77–98. Ithaca, N.Y.: Cornell University Press.

Benjamin, Walter. 1969. "Theses on the Philosophy of History." In *Illuminations*, translated by Harry Zohn, edited by Hannah Arendt. New York: Schocken Books.

Beranek, Franz. 1965. *Westjiddischer Sprachatlas*. Marburg: N. G. Elwert Verlag.

Bhabha, Homi. 1993. "Call for Proposals: Frontlines/borderposts." *Critical Inquiry* 19(3):595–98.

———. 1994. *The Location of Culture*. New York: Routledge.

Blanchot, Maurice. 1957. *Le Dernier Homme*. Paris: Gallimard.

———. 1982. *The Unavowable Community*, translated and with a preface by Pierre Joris. Barrytown, N.Y.: Station Hill Press.

———. 1984. "Les Intellectuels en Question." *Le Débat*, May.

———. 1986. *The Writing of the Disaster*. Lincoln: University of Nebraska Press.

Boon, James A. 1994. "Circumscribing Circumcision/Uncircumcision: An Essay amidst the History of Difficult Description." In *Implicit Understandings*, edited by Stuart Schwartz. Pp. 556–85. New York: Cambridge University Press.

Bourdieu, Pierre. 1972. *Esquisse d'une théorie de la pratique. Précédée de trois études d'ethnologie kabyle*. Genève: Droz.

———. 1977. *Outline of a Theory of Practice*. Cambridge: Cambridge University Press.

Boyarin, Daniel. 1990a. "The Eye in the Torah: Ocular Desire in Midrashic Hermeneutic." *Critical Inquiry* 16(3):532–50.

———. 1990b. *Intertextuality and the Reading of Midrash*. Bloomington: Indiana University Press.

———. 1994. *A Radical Jew: Paul and the Politics of Identity*. Berkeley and Los Angeles: University of California Press.

———. 1997. *Judaism as a Gender*. Berkeley and Los Angeles: University of California Press.

Boyarin, Daniel, and Jonathan Boyarin. 1993. "Diaspora: Generation and the Ground of Jewish Identity." *Critical Inquiry* 19(4):693–725.

Boyarin, Jonathan. 1989. "Voices around the Text: The Ethnography of Reading at Mesivta Tifereth Jerusalem." *Cultural Anthropology* 4:399–421.

———. 1990. "Observant Participation: The Ethnography of Jews on the Lower East Side." *Yivo Annual* 19:233–54.

———. 1991. *Polish Jews in Paris: The Ethnography of Memory.* Bloomington: Indiana University Press.

———. 1992a. "Jews and Palestinians: From Margin to Center and Back Again?" Paper written for Social Science Research Council Research Group on the Security of Marginal Populations.

———. 1992b. *Storm from Paradise: The Politics of Jewish Memory.* Minneapolis: University of Minnesota Press.

———. 1993. *Jews, Indians and the Identity of Christian Europe.* Working Papers of the Center for Studies of Social Change, no. 161.

———. 1994a. "Hegel's Zionism?" In *Space, Time and the Politics of Memory,* edited by Jonathan Boyarin. Pp.137–60. Minneapolis: University of Minnesota Press.

———. 1994b. "Space, Time and the Politics of Memory." In *Remapping Memory: The Politics of TimeSpace,* edited by Jonathan Boyarin. Pp. 1–37. Minneapolis: University of Minnesota Press.

———. 1994c. *A Storyteller's Worlds: The Education of Shlomo Noble in Europe and America.* New York: Holmer and Meier.

Bradford, Phillips Verner, and Harvey Blume. 1992. *Ota Benga: The Pygmy in the Zoo.* New York: St. Martin's Press.

Butler, Judith. 1990. *Gender Trouble: Feminism and the Subversion of Identity.* New York: Routledge.

———. 1991. "Contingent Foundations: Feminism and the Question of 'Postmodernism.' " *Praxis International* 11(2):150–65.

———. 1993. *Bodies That Matter: On the Discursive Limits of "Sex."* New York: Routledge.

Chambers, Iain. 1994. *Migrancy, Culture, Identity.* New York and London: Routledge.

Chatterjee, Partha. 1990. "A Response to Taylor's 'Modes of Civil Society.' " *Public Culture* 3(1):119–34.

Chirot, Daniel. 1994. "Outsiders and Insiders: Entrepreneurial Minorities and Conflicting Ethnic Identities in the Modern Transformation of Southeast Asia and Central Europe." *Items* 48(4):90–94.

Clifford, James. 1986. "On Ethnographic Allegory." In *Writing Culture: The Poetics and Politics of Ethnography,* edited by James Clifford and George Marcus. Pp. 98–121. Berkeley and Los Angeles: University of California Press.

———. 1988. "Identity in Mashpee." In *The Predicament of Culture:*

Twentieth-Century Ethnography, Literature, and Art. Pp. 277–346. Cambridge, Mass.: Harvard University Press.

———. 1994. "Diasporas." *Cultural Anthropology* 9 (August):302–38. Paper presented to annual meeting of the Society for Cultural Anthropology.

Cohen, Jeremy. 1982. *The Friars and the Jews: The Evolution of Medieval Anti-Judaism.* Ithaca: Cornell University Press.

Collins, John J. 1985. "A Symbol of Otherness: Circumcision and Salvation in the First Century." In *"To See Ourselves as Others See Us": Christians, Jews, and "Others" in Late Antiquity.* Pp. 163–86. Chico, Calif.: Scholars Press.

———. 1987. *The Apocalyptic Imagination: An Introduction to the Jewish Matrix of Christianity.* New York: Crossroad.

Connolly, William E. 1991. *Identity difference: Democratic Negotiations of Political Paradox.* Ithaca: Cornell University Press.

———. 1993. *The Augustinian Imperative: A Reflection on the Politics of Morality.* Beverly Hills: Sage Publications.

Cowan, Paul. 1986. *Orphan in History.* New York: Bantam Books.

Cuddihy, John. 1974. *The Ordeal of Civility: Freud, Marx, Lévi-Strauss and the Jewish Struggle with Modernity.* New York: Basic Books.

Dahan, Gilbert. 1990. *Les Intellectuels chretiens et les juifs au moyen age.* Paris: Le Cerf.

de Certeau, Michel. 1984. *The Practice of Everyday Life.* Berkeley and Los Angeles: University of California Press.

Deleuze, Gilles, and Felix Guattari. 1986. *Kafka: Toward a Minor Literature.* Minneapolis: University of Minnesota Press.

DeLillo, Don. 1985. *White Noise.* New York: Viking.

Derrida, Jacques. 1976. "The Question of the Book." In *Writing and Difference.* Pp. 64–78. Chicago: University of Chicago Press.

———. 1978. "Structure, Sign and Play in the Human Sciences." In *Writing and Difference,* translated by Alan Bass. Chicago: University of Chicago Press.

———. 1984. "Of an Apocalyptic Tone Recently Adopted in Philosophy." *Oxford Literary Review* 6(2):1–37.

———. 1991. "Interpretations at War: Kant, the Jew, the German." *New Literary History* 22(1):39–96.

———. 1992. *The Other Heading: Reflections on Today's Europe.* Bloomington: Indiana University Press.

———. 1993. "Circumfession." In *Jacques Derrida*, edited by Geoff Bennington. Chicago: University of Chicago Press.

Dobzynski, Charles, ed. 1976. *Le Miroir d'un peuple*. Paris: Gallimard.

Dundes, Alan, ed. 1991. *The Blood Libel Legend: A Casebook in Anti-semitic Folklore*. Madison: University of Wisconsin Press.

Edwards, John. 1991. *The Jews in Christian Europe, 1400–1700*. New York: Routledge.

Eilberg-Schwartz, Howard. 1990. *The Savage in Judaism*. Bloomington: Indiana University Press.

El-Or, Tamar. 1994. *Educated and Ignorant: Ultraorthodox Jewish Women and Their World*. Boulder & London: Lynn Rienner.

Esonwanne, Uzo. 1990–91. "The Madness of Africa(ns); Or, Anthropology's Reason." *Cultural Critique* (17):107–26.

Fabian, Johannes. 1983. *Time and the Other*. New York: Columbia University Press.

Fabre-Vassas, Claudine. 1994. *La Bête Singulière: Les Juifs, les Chrétiens et le Cochon*. Paris: Gallimard.

Faur, José. 1986. *Golden Doves with Silver Dots*. Bloomington: Indiana University Press.

Fenves, Peter. 1993. *Raising the Tone of Philosophy: Late Essays by Immanuel Kant, Transformative Critique by Jacques Derrida*. Baltimore: Johns Hopkins University Press.

Fichte, Johann Gottlieb. 1979. *Addresses to the German Nation*, translated by R. F. Jones and G. H. Turnbull. Westport: Greenwood Press.

Fine, Jo Renée, and Gerard Wolfe. 1978. *The Synagogues of New York's Lower East Side*. New York: Washington Mews Books.

Fineman, Joel. 1989. "The History of the Anecdote: Fiction and Fiction." In *The New Historicism*, edited by H. Aram Veeser. Pp. 49–76. New York: Routledge.

Finkielkraut, Alain. 1982. *L'Avenir d'une negation*. Paris: Le Seuil.

———. 1987. *La Défaite de la pensée*. Paris: Gallimard.

———. 1994. *The Imaginary Jew*, edited by Kevin and David Suchoff O'Neill, with an introduction by David Suchoff. Lincoln: University of Nebraska Press.

———. 1995. *The Defeat of the Mind*, translated by Judith Friedlander. New York: Columbia University Press.

Friedlander, Judith. 1990. *Vilna on the Seine*. New Haven: Yale University Press.

Gallop, Jane. 1988. *Thinking Through the Body.* New York: Columbia University Press.

Geller, Jay. 1993. "A Paleontological View of Freud's Study of Religion: Unearthing the Leitfossil Circumcision." *Modern Judaism* 13:49–70.

Gerlitz, Menachem Mendel, ed. 1983. *Hagode Shel Pesakh Mibeys Levi.* Jerusalem: Oraysoh.

Ghosh, Amitav. 1993. *In an Antique Land.* New York: Vintage Books.

Gilman, Sander. 1986. *Jewish Self-hatred: Anti-Semitism and the Hidden Language of the Jews.* Baltimore: Johns Hopkins University Press.

———. 1992. *The Jew's Body.* New York: Routledge.

Gilroy, Paul. 1993. *The Black Atlantic: Modernity and Double Consciousness.* Cambridge: Harvard University Press.

Glatzer, Nahum, ed. 1962. *Hammer on the Rock: A Midrash Reader.* New York: Schocken Books.

Glueckel of Hameln. 1977. *The Memoirs of Glueckel of Hameln,* translated by Marvin Lowenthal. New York: Schocken Books.

Goitein, Shlomo Dov. 1967–73. *A Mediterranean Society: The Jews of the Arab World as Portrayed in the Cairo Geniza.* Four volumes. Berkeley and Los Angeles: University of California Press.

Goldman, Pierre. 1977. *Dim Memories of a Polish Jew Born in France,* translated by J. Pinkham. New York: Viking.

Goldsmith, Steven. 1993. *Unbuilding Jerusalem: Apocalypse and Romantic Representation.* Ithaca: Cornell University Press.

Gough, Kathleen. 1968. "Anthropology and Imperialism." *Monthly Review* 19:12–27.

Greenblatt, Stephen. 1993. "Kindly Visions." *New Yorker* (October 11), 112–20.

Hadarshan, Shimon. 1960. *Numbers Rabbah.* Tel Aviv: Moriah.

Halevi, Ilan. 1987. *A History of the Jews, Ancient and Modern.* London and Atlantic Highlands, N.J.: Zed Press.

Halpérin, Jean, and Georges Lévitte, eds. 1989. *Colloque des intellectuels juifs: La question de l'état.* Paris: Denoël.

Handelman, Susan A. 1991. *Fragments of Redemption: Jewish Thought and Literary Theory in Benjamin, Scholem, and Levinas.* Bloomington: Indiana University Press.

Hanson, Paul D. 1975. *The Dawn of Apocalyptic.* Philadelphia: Fortress Press.

Haraway, Donna J. 1991. *Simians, Cyborgs, and Women.* New York: Routledge.

Harding, Susan. 1991. "Representing Fundamentalism: The Problem of the Repugnant Cultural Other." *Social Research* 58(2):373–94.

———. 1994. "Further Reflections." *Cultural Anthropology* 9(3):276–79.

Hebel, Johann Peter. N.d. *Poetische werke.* Wiesbaden: Elmer Vollmer Verlag.

Holquist, Michael. 1989. "From Body-talk to Biography: The Chronobiological Bases of Narrative." *Yale Journal of Criticism* 3(1):1–35.

Horkheimer, Max, and Theodor Adorno. 1972. *Dialectic of Enlightenment.* New York: Seabury Press.

Husserl, Edmund. 1970. *The Crisis of the European Sciences and Transcendental Phenomenology*, edited and translated by David Carr. Evanston: Northwestern University Press.

Irigaray, Luce. 1985. *This Sex Which Is Not One*, translated by Catherine Porter with Carolyn Burke. Ithaca: Cornell University Press.

James, C. L. R. 1963. *The Black Jacobins.* New York: Random House.

Jankélévitch, Vladimir. 1974. *L'Irréversible et la nostalgie.* Paris: Flammarion.

Joselit, Jenna Weissman. 1990. *New York's Jewish Jews: The Orthodox Community in the Interwar Years.* Bloomington: Indiana University Press.

Joyce, James. 1968 (1916). *Portrait of the Artist as a Young Man.* New York: Viking Press.

Koshar, Rudy. 1991. "Altar, State and City: Historic Preservation and Urban Meaning in Nazi Germany." *History and Memory* 3(1):30–59.

Kroeber, Theodora. 1976. *Ishi in Two Worlds: A Biography of the Last Wild Indian in North America.* Berkeley: University of California Press.

Kronfeld, Chana. 1996. "Minor Modernisms: Beyond Deleuze and Guattari." In *Jews and Other Differences: The New Jewish Cultural Studies*, edited by Daniel Boyarin and Jonathan Boyarin. Pp. 137–60. Minneapolis: University of Minnesota Press.

Kronick, Joseph G. 1990. "Dr. Heidegger's Experiment." *boundary* 2, no. 17 (Fall): 116–53.

Kugelmass, Jack. 1986. *The Miracle of Intervale Avenue.* New York: Schocken Books.

Lacoue-Labarthe, Philippe, and Jean-Luc Nancy. 1990. "The Nazi Myth," translated by Brian Holmes. *Critical Inquiry* 16(2):291–312.

Lambropoulos, Vassilis. 1988. *Literature as National Institution: Studies in the Politics of Modern Greek Criticism.* Princeton: Princeton University Press.

————. 1992. *The Rise of Eurocentrism: Anatomy of Interpretation.* Princeton: Princeton University Press.

Levinas, Emmanuel. 1976. "Pièces d'identité." In *Difficile liberté.* Pp. 74–78. Paris: Albin Michel.

————. 1989. *The Levinas Reader,* edited by Sean Hand. Cambridge, Mass.: Basil Blackwell.

Low, Alfred. 1979. *Jews in the Eyes of the Germans.* Philadelphia: Institute for the Study of Human Issues.

Lustick, Ian. 1988. *For the Land and the Lord: Jewish Fundamentalism in Israel.* New York: Council on Foreign Relations.

Lyotard, Jean-François. 1988. *The Differend: Phrases in Dispute.* Minneapolis: University of Minnesota Press.

————. 1990. *Heidegger and "the Jews,"* translated by Andreas Michel and Mark Roberts, with an introduction by David Carroll. Minneapolis: University of Minnesota Press.

Marin, Louis. 1993. "Frontiers of Utopia: Past and Present." *Critical Inquiry* 19(3):397–420.

Marx, Karl. 1977. *Selected Writings,* edited by David McLellan. Oxford: Oxford University Press.

Mehlman, Jeffrey. 1983. *Legacies of Anti-semitism in France.* Minneapolis: University of Minnesota Press.

Memmi, Albert. 1992 (1955). *The Pillar of Salt.* Boston: Beacon Press.

Menocal, María Rosa. 1987. *The Arabic Role in Medieval Literary History.* Philadelphia: University of Pennsylvania Press.

Michaels, Walter Benn. 1992. "Race into Culture: A Critical Genealogy of Cultural Identity." *Critical Inquiry* 18 (Summer): 655–85.

Miller, Walter. 1959. *A Canticle for Leibowitz.* New York: J. B. Lippincott.

Miyoshi, Masao. 1993. "A Borderless World? From Colonialism to Transnationalism and the Decline of the Nation-state." *Critical Inquiry* 19(4):726–51.

Morrison, Karl F. 1988. *I Am You: The Hermeneutics of Empathy in Western Literature, Theology, and Art.* Princeton: Princeton University Press.

Naas, Michael B. 1992. "Introduction." In Jacques Derrida, *The Other Heading: Reflections on Today's Europe.* Pp. vii–lix. Bloomington: Indiana University Press.

Nancy, Jean-Luc. 1986. *La Communauté désouvrée.* Paris.

————. 1991. *The Inoperative Community.* Minneapolis: University of Minnesota Press.

Newfield, Christopher. 1993. "What Was Political Correctness? Race, the Right, and Managerial Democracy in the Humanities." *Critical Inquiry* 19(2):308–36.

Noakes, Susan. 1993. "Gracious Words: Luke's Jesus and the Reading of Sacred Poetry at the Beginning of the Sacred Era." In *The Ethnography of Reading*, edited by Jonathan Boyarin. Pp. 38–57. Berkeley and Los Angeles: University of California Press.

Olender, Maurice. 1992. *The Languages of Paradise: Race, Religion, and Philology in the Nineteenth Century*, translated by Arthur Goldhammer. Cambridge: Harvard University Press.

Ong, Aiwah. 1993. "On the Edge of Empires: Flexible Citizenship among Chinese in Diaspora." *Positions* 1:745–78.

Ortner, Sherry. 1984. "Theory in Anthropology Since the Sixties." *Comparative Studies in Society and History* 26 (January): 126–66.

Pagden, Anthony. 1986. *The Fall of Natural Man*. New York: Columbia University Press.

Paine, Robert. 1983. "Israeli and Totemic Time?" *Royal Anthropological Institute Newsletter (RAIN)* 59.

Patraka, Vivian. 1992. *Spectacles of Suffering: The Tropological Use of the Term Holocaust in Public Discourse*. New York: Modern Language Association.

Pensky, Max. 1993. *Melancholy Dialectics: Walter Benjamin and the Play of Mourning*. Amherst: University of Massachusetts Press.

Perec, Georges. 1989. *W or the Memory of Childhood*, translated by David Bellos. London: Collins Harvill.

Petrushka, Simkhe. 1949. *Yidishe folks-entsiklopedye*, vol. 2. New York and Montreal: Gilead.

Popkin, Richard H. 1990. "Medicine, Racism, Anti-semitism: A Dimension of Enlightenment Culture." In *The Languages of Psyche: Mind and Body in Enlightenment Thought*, edited by G. B. Rousseau. Pp. 405–42. Berkeley and Los Angeles: University of California Press.

Rabi, Wladimir. 1979. *Un Peuple de trop sur la terre?* Paris: Presses D'Aujourd'hui.

Ratzel, Friedrich. 1898. *The History of Mankind*, vol. 3. London and New York: MacMillan.

Renan, Ernest. 1943. *Le Judaisme comme race et comme religion*. New York: Rand School of Social Science.

———. 1990. "What Is a Nation?" In *Nation and Narration*, edited by Homi Bhabha. Pp. 8–22. New York: Routledge.

Sarris, Greg. 1993. *Keeping Slug Woman Alive: A Holistic Approach to Ameri-*

can Indian Texts. Berkeley and Los Angeles: University of California Press.

Schnapper, Dominique. 1983. *Jewish Identities in France: An Analysis of Contemporary French Jewry,* translated by Arthur Goldhammer. Chicago: University of Chicago Press.

Scholem, Gershom. 1971. *The Messianic Idea in Judaism.* New York: Schocken Books.

———. 1976. "Against the Myth of the German-Jewish Dialogue." In *On Jews and Judaism in Crisis.* Pp. 61–64. New York: Schocken.

Schwartz, Regina M. 1992. "Nations and Nationalism: Adultery in the House of David." *Critical Inquiry* 19 (Autumn): 131–50.

Schwarz-Bart, André. 1960. *The Last of the Just,* translated by Stephen Becker. New York: Atheneum.

"Sharon and Stephen." 1992. "A Considered Decision." *Jewish Socialist* (26):19.

Shell, Marc. 1988. *The End of Kinship: "Measure for Measure," Incest, and the Ideal of Universal Siblinghood.* Stanford: Stanford University Press.

Shmeruk, Khone, ed. 1964. *A shpigl oyf a shteyn.* Tel-Aviv: Farlag Di Goldene Keyt.

Shohat, Ella. 1992. "Notes on the 'Post-Colonial.' " *Social Text* (32–33): 99–113.

Simenon, Georges. 1963. *Maigret and the Enigmatic Lett,* edited by Daphne Woodward. New York: Penguin Books.

Singer, Linda. 1991. "Recalling a Community at Loose Ends." In *Community at Loose Ends,* edited by the Miami Theory Collective. Pp. 121–30. Minneapolis: University of Minnesota Press.

Spivak, Gayatri Chakravorti. 1988. "Can the Subaltern Speak?" In *Marxism and the Interpretation of Culture,* edited by Cary Nelson and Lawrence Grossberg. Pp. 271–313. Urbana and Chicago: University of Illinois Press.

Stendahl, Krister. 1976. "The Apostle Paul and the Introspective Conscience of the West." In *Paul among Jews and Gentiles.* Pp. 78–96. Philadelphia: Fortress Press.

Stern, Josef. 1991. "Maimonides' Parable of Circumcision." *S'vara* 2(2): 35–48.

Stock, Brian. 1990. *Listening for the Text: On the Uses of the Past.* Baltimore: Johns Hopkins University Press.

Szulsztein, Moshe. 1982. *Dort vu mayn vig iz geshtanen.* Paris: Published by a Committee.

Taussig, Michael. 1992. *The Nervous System*. New York: Routledge.

Taylor, Charles. 1989. *Sources of the Self: The Making of the Modern Identity*. Cambridge: Harvard University Press.

———. 1990. "Modes of Civil Society." *Public Culture* 3 (Fall): 95–118.

———. 1992. "The Politics of Recognition." In *Multiculturalism and "the Politics of Recognition,"* edited by Amy Gutmann. Pp. 25–73. Princeton: Princeton University Press.

Terdiman, Richard. 1991. "On the Dialectics of Postdialectical Thinking." In *Community at Loose Ends*, edited by the Miami Theory Collective. Pp. 111–20. Minneapolis: University of Minnesota Press.

Theodor, Jehuda, and Hanoch Albeck, eds. 1965. *Genesis Rabbah.* Jerusalem: Wahrmann.

Trumpener, Katie. 1992. "The Time of the Gypsies: A 'People without History' in the Narratives of the West." *Critical Inquiry* 18(4):843–84.

Turner, Terence. 1993. "Anthropology and Multiculturalism: What Is Anthropology That Multiculturalists Should Be Mindful of It?" *Cultural Anthropology* 8 (November): 411–29.

Tyler, Patrick E. 1994. "Jews Revisit Shanghai, Grateful Still That It Sheltered Them." *New York Times,* June 29, 1994, A12.

Van Den Abbeele, Georges. 1991. "Introduction." In *Community at Loose Ends*, edited by the Miami Theory Collective. Pp. ix–xxvi. Minneapolis: University of Minnesota Press.

Vizenor, Gerald. 1994. *Manifest Manners: Postindian Warriors of Survivance*. Hanover, N.H.: Wesleyan University Press/University Press of New England.

Von Rad, Gerhard. 1962. *Old Testament Theology*, vol. 1. New York: Harper and Row.

Wasserman, Suzanne. 1987. "Shvitzing, Shpritzing and Fressing: A Critical Look at Memories of the 'Good Old Days' on the Lower East Side." Paper presented at YIVO Conference on Authenticity and Nostalgia, New York City.

Weinreich, Max. 1980. *The History of the Yiddish Language*. Chicago: University of Chicago Press.

White, Luise. 1992. Review of Dundes 1991. *Times Literary Supplement,* May 15, p. 23.

Wolff, Kurt. 1970. "The Sociology of Knowledge and Sociological Theory." In *The Sociology of Sociology*, edited by Larry T. Reynolds and Janice M. Reynolds. Pp. 31–67. New York: David McKay.

Wolfson, Elliot R. 1987a. "Circumcision and the Divine Name: A Study in the Transmission of Esoteric Doctrine." *Jewish Quarterly Review* 78 (October): 77–112.

——. 1987b. "Circumcision, Vision of God, and Textual Interpretation: From Midrashic Trope to Mystical Symbol." *History of Religions* 27 (November): 189–215.

Woocher, Jonathan. 1985. "Sacred Survival." *Judaism* 34(2):151–62.

Yerushalmi, Yosef Haim. 1994. "A Critic as Solitary as Kafka." *New York Times Book Review,* July 31, 1994, 13–14.

Zukier, Henri. 1993. "The Uncertain Future of Anti-Semitism." *New School Commentator* 4(5):1–4.

✌ INDEX ✌

Adorno, Theodor, 133, 138, 169
Age of Reason (see also Enlight-
    enment), 48
Allen, Woody, 169
American (as ethnic group), 16,
    18, 39
American Anthropological Asso-
    ciation, 35
Anderson, Benedict, 165
Anidjar, Gil, 117n
anthropology, 131
anti-gay violence, 57
anti-Semitism, 14, 28, 40, 48, 53,
    111, 119, 124, 132, 161n
apocalypse, 140–59
Arabs, 180
    as excluded, 114
Arendt, Hannah, 144
Aristotle, 59n
Ashkenaz, 110
Auerbach, Erich, 133, 138
Augustine, 77, 95, 146
Auschwitz, 145, 161

Balibar, Etienne, 5, 114–15, 126
Barbie trial, 166
Barth, Lewis, 44
Bataille, Georges, 73, 83n
Battaglia, Debbora, 37
Baudrillard, Jean, 81

Bedouin, 58
Begin, Menachem, 51
Bengali, 89
Benjamin, Walter, 6, 35, 116,
    144, 163–82 passim, 196
Beranek, Franz, 121
Bereshit Rabbah, 44
Bergson, Henri, 121
Bet-Sahour, 52
Beth Israel Hospital, 173, 177
Bethlehem, 52
Bhabha, Homi, 163–64, 172
Bible, Christian, 140–59 passim
Bible, Jewish, 149, 151
black (as ethnic group), 9, 56
Blanchot, Maurice, 63, 67, 76,
    83n, 84, 85, 141–45, 156, 157
Bloom, Harold, 133
Boon, James, 37
Boro Park, 23
Bourdieu, Pierre, 8
Boyarin, Aaron, 12
Boyarin, Daniel, 2, 24, 51, 94,
    157, 164
Boyarin, Israel, 9
Boyarin, Jonah Sampson, 50
Boyarin, Jonathan, 89, 151
Breton, 130
Brooklyn, 167n, 168, 178, 182
Brown, Goldie, 26

Bruce, Lenny, 17, 93
Butler, Judith, 38n, 61, 82, 88–
107 passim

Canada, 91
capitalism, 38, 65, 117, 180
late, 171
Cartesian, 163
castration, 53n
Chambers, Iain, 4
Chatterjee, Partha, 96n, 117n
China, 181–82
Chinese (as ethnic group), 181
Chirot, Daniel, 181
Christianity (see also apocalypse;
Europe; post-Christianity; Pietism; Protestantism)
and the body, 61
and time, 162–63, 167
churches, 18
and circumcision, 40
and community, 81–82
and Fascism, 82
and God, 78
and identity, 39, 96, 174
Puritan, 97
circumcision, 2, 34–63 passim,
145, 175
Clifford, James, 34
clitoridectomy, 37
Cohen, Hermann, 121, 128
Columbus, Christopher, 109
community
nostalgia for, 8, 32, 76, 81, 86
intentional, 32
fragmented, 73–86
Connolly, William, 48–62 passim,
77
Coser, Lewis, 71
Cowan, Paul, 74n
Critical Inquiry (journal), 163
critical theory, 88, 170
as always situated, 3–4, 63
cultural studies, 172

deafness, 73
de Certeau, Michel, 65n
Deleuze, Gilles, 126
DeLillo, Don, 147–48
Derrida, Jacques, 5, 92, 100,
113–39 passim, 145–46, 148,
151–54, 195–96, 200
diaspora, 161–82 passim
Djerba, 58
Durkheim, Emile, 59

Eastern Europe, 1, 12
Eighth Street Shul, 21–33
El-Or, Tamar, 104
Elkin, Stanley, 146
English language, 2–4, 10, 15,
105
prayerbook, 72
and theory, 89
Enlightenment, 96, 105, 110,
112, 118–19, 121, 123, 128,
137, 143, 152, 154, 174, 181,
192
Enterprise, the. *See* minyan
Eskimos, 144
ethnography
as cultural resource, 18
criticism of, 8, 17, 35
of Europe, 113
Jewish, 1, 4, 16, 17, 23, 31, 79
and landscape, 12
and reflexivity, 174
and social theory, 63, 65
Europa, Europa (film), 41
Europe, 42, 51, 108–33, 179,
193–94
as Christian, 85, 91, 108, 115
Eurocentrism, 163

Fabian, Johannes, 8
Farmingdale, New Jersey, 8 ff.
Fascism, 66, 82
Faurisson affair, 166
female body, 91

feminist theory, 2, 92, 93
Fichte, Johann Gottlieb, 113–33
   passim
Fineman, Joel, 68n
Finkielkraut, Alain, 165–66
Flying Eagle, Chief, 34
Fogel, Moshe, 22–24, 27
Foucault, Michel, 77, 90, 92, 98,
   103, 132
Freud, Sigmund, 14, 16
Friedlander, Judith, 160

Gallop, Jane, 2
gay studies, 172
Gebert, Konstanty, 112
Geller, Jay, 160
genealogy, 152, 174
gender, 89
   and law, 100, 102
Geniza, 179–80
Germany, 109
Ghosh, Amitav, 179
Gilroy, Paul, 181n
Glueckel of Hameln, 110
God, 72, 73, 78, 101, 141, 150
Goffman, Erving, 71
Goitein, S. D., 179
Goldschmidt, Henry, 167
Goldsmith, Steven, 157
Gospel of John, 148, 151, 152
Greeks, 131–39
Greenblatt, Stephen, 139
Guattari, Felix, 126
Gush Emunim, 36, 156
"Gypsies," 111, 126

Haar, Michel, 94
Habermas, Jürgen, 97n
Haitian (ethnicity), 163
Halloween, 14
Handelman, Susan, 173n
Hanson, Paul, 155
Harding, Susan, 174
Harvard, 116

Hasidim
   in Israel, 51, 122
   as litigants, 56
   Lubavitch, 3, 10, 19, 156, 167–
      82 passim
   and messianism, 167–82
      passim
   in Paris, 28
   and Yiddish, 122
Hasidism, 96
Hebel, Johann Peter, 122n, 160,
   178
Hebraism, 131–39 passim
Hebrew, 58, 69
   alphabet, 11, 192
   biblical, 49
   prayer, 72
Hegel, 59n, 91, 94, 101, 156
Hellenism, 132
hermaphrodites, 91
Herzfeld, Michael, 109, 137
heterosexuality, 90
Hillerman, Tony, 57
Hobbes, Thomas, 84
Holland, Agnieszka, 41
Holquist, Michael, 54
Horkheimer, Max, 133, 138
Husserl, Edmund, 115, 127,
   129n, 139

identity politics, 4–5
India, 194
Indian Ocean, 179
Indians, 129, 134, 144
Irigaray, Luce, 94
Islam, 56. See also Muslims
Israel, 42, 85, 176
   and male Jewish headcovering,
      51, 55
   Rabbi Singer in, 74

Jabès, Edmond, 137, 194
Japanese (as ethnicity), 9
Jerusalem, 30, 52

Jewish
    as synonym for Yiddish, 1, 95
    civil law, 87
    history, 195–96
    studies, 170, 172
Jewish Theological Seminary, 192
Jews
    American, 116, 121
    Christian, 41
    Conservative, 14–15
    English, 42
    for example, 125–28
    female, 40, 68n, 83, 103
    as fossils, 102
    French, 19–20, 28, 51n, 111,
        127, 161, 165
    German, 121
    Lithuanian, 10, 24
    male, 34–62, 83
    Native American, 57
    North African, 29, 58, 116,
        178, 179
    not-for-Jesus, 162
    and pigs, 161n
    Polish, 19–20, 27, 41, 112,
        161, 165, 194
    Reform, 68n, 122n
    "real" 158, 166
    religious vis-à-vis secular, 102
    Russian, 74, 110
    Spanish, 109, 110
    and thieves, 199
    and transnationalism, 109–10
    Western, 197
    See also post-Judaism
Joyce, James, 13n

Kaddish, 69, 73, 78, 196
Kafka, Franz, 158
Kant, Immanuel, 85n, 127, 153
Koheleth, 95
Koshar, Rudy, 169
Kristeva, Julia, 98, 17

Kugelmass, Jack, 32, 78

Lacan, Jacques, 100
Lacoue-Labarthe, Philippe, 50
Lambropoulos, Vassilis, 117–19,
    131–39, 181n
late modernity, 46, 48
Latin alphabet, 192
Law, 88, 105
    and gender, 100
    and salvation, 96
    Old Testament, 100
Lemberger Gaon, 87–88, 105
lesbian studies, 172
lesbianism, 98
Levinas, Emmanuel, 106, 129,
    136, 196
Locke, John, 4, 84
Lower East Side, 1, 20–33, 56,
    64–86, 88, 172–82
Lyotard, Jean-François, 85, 127

Maimonides, 44, 46, 78
Malamud, Bernard, 146
Marin, Louis, 170
Markish, Peretz, 197–98
Martini, Raymond, 1, 6
Marx, Karl, 16, 171, 176, 179
Massada, 83n
Mediterranean, 179n, 180
Memmi, Albert, 58–59
midrash, 84
Miller, Walter, 146–47
minyan, 64–86 passim
    on the Enterprise, 161
mis-Hellenism, 132
Miss Piggy, 161
Miyoshi, Masao, 170n, 180
Morrison, Karl, 118n
multiculturalism, 92–93, 119
Muppet Show, 161
Muslims, 51n, 58, 129, 134, 179
myth, 73, 84, 133
    Jewish freedom from, 84

Naas, Michael, 125, 129n
Nancy, Jean-Luc, 2, 49, 63–86
    passim, 157
nation-state form, 4
Native Americans, 57
Nazism, 40, 42, 63, 67, 109, 120,
    126, 143, 147, 155, 176, 193
    as myth, 84–85
Newfield, Christopher, 171
New York Jewish (as cultural iden-
    tity), 18
Nietzsche, 92, 100–101, 132
Noakes, Susan, 142
Noble, Dr. Shlomo, 56
normality, 53–55
nostalgia, 80–81, 86

Offenback, Jules, 28
Olympics, 160, 181
Orientalism, 193n
Orthodoxy, Jewish
    damned as immovable, 102
    geography of in America, 10,
        23, 172–73
Ortner, Sherry, 75
Orwell, George, 197
otherness, 55–60
Ozick, Cynthia, 133

Palestinians, 51–52, 161n
Paris, 19–20, 24, 27 ff., 178
    Clignoncourt, 19
    Sacré Coeur, 25
    Montmartre, 25
Passover. See seder
Paul, 40–41, 96, 97n, 101, 151,
    157
Pensky, Max, 166, 169
Perec, Georges, 160–61
Perel, Salomon, 41–42, 49, 59
Perot, Ross, 49
Petronius, 55
Pietism, 96

Philo, 128
Platonism, 46
politics of identity, 4–5
post-Christianity, 64, 91, 163
post-Judaism, 158, 163–82
    passim
    defined, 170
postmodernism, 48, 175, 191–
    200
    and apocalypse, 142
    and self-fashioning, 36
Protestantism, 101
    and Hebraism, 118, 131–39
    and Kant, 85n
    and self-making, 38
Pugio Fidei, 1
Purim, 12
Pygmies, 144

Rabbi Singer, 50, 64–86 passim,
    105
Rabi, Wladimir, 161n
Rashi, 197–98
Renan, Ernest, 1, 6, 110
Renaissance, 48
resistance, 174
Revelation, 140–41, 153, 158
Rosh Hashanah, 12, 28
Romans, 1, 55
Romanticism, 128, 158, 197, 199

Sabbath, 1, 3, 10, 24, 27, 30, 102,
    164, 173
Said, Edward, 137
Sampson, Elissa, 24, 27
Sartre, Jean-Paul, 60
Schaechter, Mordkhe, 196n
Schnapper, Dominique, 18
Schneebalg, Rabbi Shimon, 168n
Schneerson, Rabbi Menachem
    Mendl, 167–82 passim
Schneier, Rabbi Arthur, 182
Scholem, Gershom, 121n, 169

Schwarz-Bart, André, 143
seder, 83n, 149–50
Sephardim, 110
Shavuot, 31
Shelley, Mary, 157
Shohat, Ella, 167
Simchas Torah, 12, 29
Simenon, Georges, 25
Social Science Research Council,
    181
Soloveitchik, Reb Chaim, 150
South Bronx, 78
Spinoza, 53
Spivak, Gayatri Chakravorty,
    193–94
State, 50–53, 84
Stendahl, Krister, 95, 101
Stern, Josef, 44
subaltern, 194
Szulsztein, Moshe, 13

Talmud, 50, 69, 103
Taylor, Charles, 88–107 passim
Telshe Yeshiva (Cleveland), 31
Temple (in Jerusalem), 1, 6, 14,
    27, 68, 84, 150, 155
Terdiman, Richard, 66
transnationalism, 180
Trumpener, Katie, 126
Tunis, 58
Turner, Terence, 93n, 97n

United States, 116

Valéry, Paul, 116, 131
Van Den Abbeele, Georges, 79,
    81, 84

Weber, Max, 132
white (as ethnic group), 9, 17, 39
Williamsburg, 18

Wissenschaft des Judentums, 192
Wittig, Monique, 103
women, 158
    as category, 99
    exclusion of, 40, 83
    and self-making, 49
    in Reform and Conservative
        Jewish congregations, 68n
    See also female body; Jews,
        female
Woocher, Jonathan, 12

yandes, 196
yarmulke, 19, 34–62 passim
Yerushalmi, Yosef Haim, 164n,
    169n
Yiddish language, 1–4, 11, 17–
    19, 24–26, 29, 58, 130, 144,
    182
    and forgetting, 103
    and German colonialism, 121
    and the Law, 100
    Lithuanian, 173
    and multiculturalism, 120
    at Oxford, 30
    and postmodernity, 191–200
    Rabbi Singer's, 87
    theater, 20
    and translation, 89, 95, 97,
        102, 105
    and transnationalism, 120–22
Yiddishism, 192
yortsayt, 73
Yom Kippur, 12, 13, 24, 26, 28

Zephaniah, 149
Zionism, 125, 155, 169n, 176
zodiac, 21
Zohar, 142
Zukier, Henri, 119